£15

GLASS
A CONTEMPORARY ART

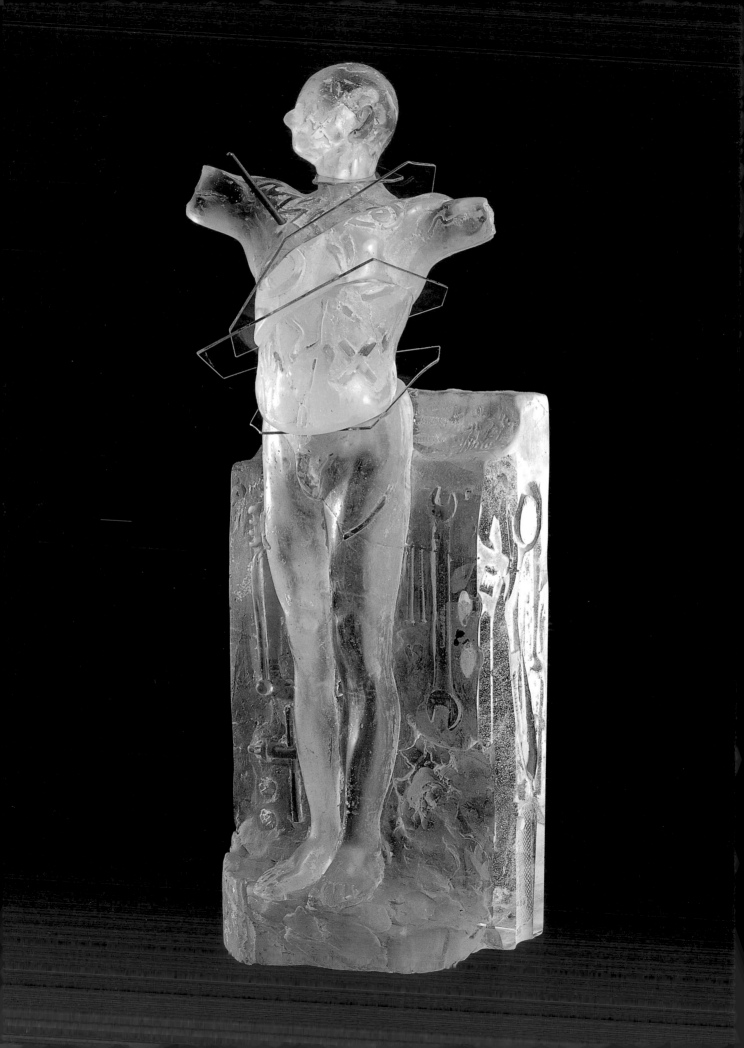

GLASS
A CONTEMPORARY ART

Dan Klein

COLLINS

My very special thanks to Irena Goldscheider
for her help during all stages of preparing and writing
this book. Her calm support and limitless enthusiasm greatly
enhanced the task in hand.

First published in 1989 by
William Collins Sons & Co., Ltd
London · Glasgow · Sydney
Auckland · Toronto · Johannesburg

© Dan Klein 1989

Art Editor: Caroline Hill

British Library Cataloguing in Publication Data
Klein, Dan
Glass: a contemporary art
1. Glassware
I. Title
748.2

ISBN 0 00 412228 3

Set in Goudy
by Ace Filmsetting Ltd, Frome, Somerset
Originated, printed and bound in Singapore
by C. S. Graphics Pte, Ltd

PAGE 1: **Etienne Leperlier**,
'Passage Protégé', 1988, *pâte de
verre*. 26 x 12 x 37 cm (10¼ x
4¾ x 14½ in)

FRONTISPIECE: **Clifford Rainey**,
'Standing Figure', cast glass
sculpture. H. 58.5 cm (23 in)

CONTENTS

PREFACE 6

1. INTRODUCTION 8

2. NORTH AMERICA 30

3. CZECHOSLOVAKIA AND EASTERN EUROPE 84

4. WEST GERMANY, AUSTRIA,
   SWITZERLAND AND SCANDINAVIA 118

5. BRITAIN, HOLLAND, FRANCE, BELGIUM
   AND ITALY 144

6. CANADA, AUSTRALIA, NEW ZEALAND
   AND JAPAN 190

MUSEUM COLLECTIONS AND GALLERIES 216

NOTES 218

SELECTED BIBLIOGRAPHY 220

INDEX 222

PREFACE

This book is about the amazing developments that have taken place in glass since the Toledo workshop of 1962 when a group of American academics, artists and glass technicians began investigating whether glass could be worked by an artist in the intimacy of his studio. What was intended as little more than a simple experiment has ended up causing a major revolution in the glass world. Developments since 1962 have resulted in a change of status for glass, elevating it from its long-established traditional role as an industrial material to the new place it now also occupies in the world of contemporary art. It is perhaps the most significant change in its history since the chance discovery of glass over two thousand years ago. It has affected glass-makers all over the world and every area of glass-making, from modest vessel forms to monumental sculptures and glass elements in architecture. The scope of this book is limited to vessel forms and sculpture conceived as works of art. It has not been possible to do more than touch on the subject of artistic flat glass or stained glass, which are now made in such large quantities as to merit an account of their own. There are so many artists worldwide working in glass that it has been impossible to include all of them, but an attempt has been made to record major influences that have contributed to making the art what it is today.

The last twenty-five years of glass history have been one long voyage of discovery, which began with a period of random experimentation mainly in hot glass. This was followed by long years of more reasoned artistry and technology during the 1970s and early 1980s, during which the art of contemporary glass became fully established. It was a period of great historical significance, though we are probably still too close in time to be able to see it in perspective. With something as new as the art of contemporary glass hindsight will play a very important role. Only when we have seen what happens over the next decades will it be possible to look back and evaluate more fully the work of those who have laid the foundations. At present, after so many years of glass celebration a sort of 'glass fatigue' has set in. A younger generation of artists does not want to go over what has rapidly become old ground. A previous generation proved time and again what visual delights glass could offer when skilfully worked. Now that a basic glass syntax exists for the new generation to work with, the time has come to be

more adventurous in artistic terms. It is no longer enough to let the material speak for itself. The artist must explore its powers of expression more fully if the art is to survive and flourish. The real test of whether glass is a lasting contemporary art form lies in the years ahead.

Dan Dailey, 'Fern-O', 1982, Vitrolite and plate glass, gold and chrome-plated brass, aluminium chassis. L. 153 cm (60 in)

I would like to thank all those whose co-operation has made it possible for this book to be written. Artists from all over the world generously responded to requests for information by sending biographical details, articles about their work, and transparencies. A number of glass gallery owners greatly reduced the labour of tracking down vital material, in particular Doug Heller of Heller Gallery, New York; Ferdinand Hampson of Habatat Galleries, Detroit; and Ruth Summers of Kurland Summers Gallery, Los Angeles. Alena Adlerová was kind enough to read the section on Czechoslovakia, and assisted greatly in obtaining pictorial material relating to Czech artists. Judy LeLievre of Wagga Wagga Art Gallery in Australia helped considerably with the Australian section. Laura Donefer, the current president of The Canadian Glass Art Association, as well as Canadian glass artist Max Leser made the Canadian section possible with the material provided by them.

I. INTRODUCTION

It is now nearly thirty years since that momentous seminar of 1962 at the University of Wisconsin, during which a way was found of melting glass in a furnace small enough to be used away from the confines of industry. 'The workshop of 1962 was probably as significant a moment in the history of glass as the time when glass was first blown.'[1] For a decade after this event there was a frenzy of activity at art schools and on university campuses as new glass programmes were set up. By the mid 1970s over one hundred glass programmes were operating in America alone. Indeed, the glass renaissance was essentially an American affair, and it is in America that it has taken root most firmly since the 1960s. But it very soon became an international phenomenon and from the outset American ties with Europe have been close. Over the years glass styles have changed, and a piece from the early 1960s looks dated today. Such a lot has happened, and so fast, that it has been difficult (recently in particular) to keep abreast of new trends. By now a sophisticated technical language has evolved; the birth pangs of the 1960s have been forgotten; and there is even a tendency to be blasé and dismissive of origins.

Harvey Littleton, University of Wisconsin, 'Vase – Sculpture with Expanded Prunts', 1965, free-blown glass coloured with oxides. 16 x 19 x 11.5 cm (6¼ x 7½ x 4½ in). (Victoria & Albert Museum, London)

OPPOSITE: **Erwin Eisch**, 'Littleton's Headache', 1976, one of a series, mould-blown glass. H. 41.5 cm (16¼ in). (The Corning Museum of Glass, Corning, New York)

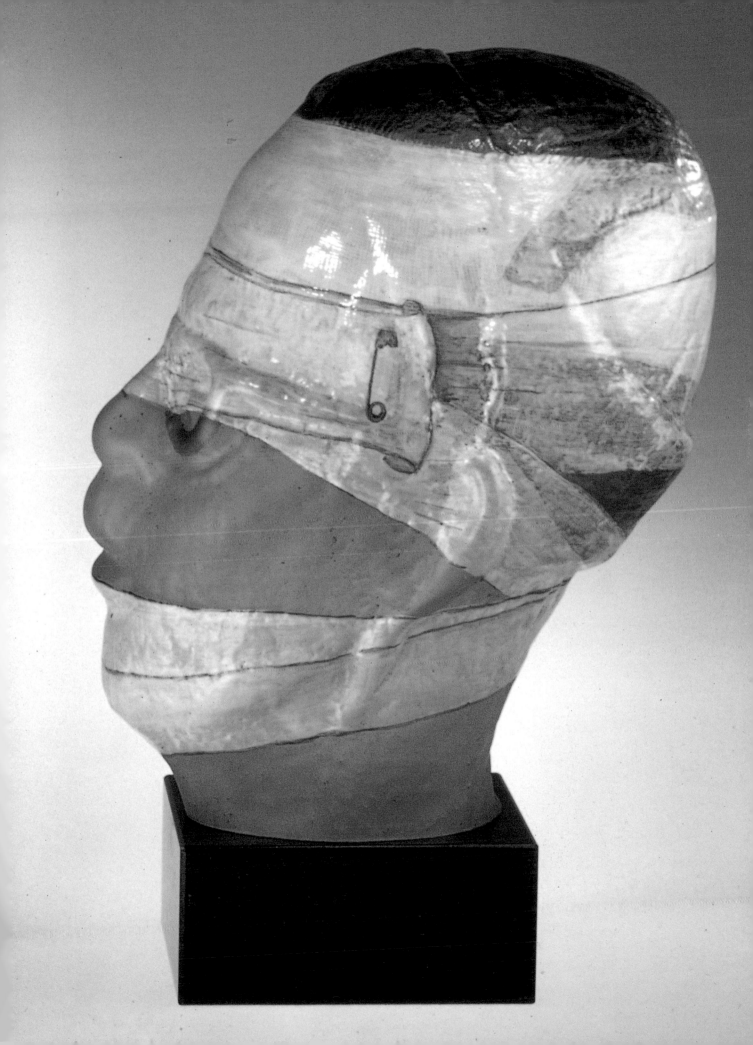

Dale Chihuly, 'Star Bayeta', 1976, blown glass with marvered lampwork decoration and iridescent surface. H. 30.5 cm (12 in)

THE 1960s

Of the various reasons why glass was so popular in America during the 1960s, one of the most important was a general preoccupation with self-expression. There was a growing dissatisfaction with the Establishment and, after the war in Vietnam, a deep distrust of it. 'In the '60s many talented young men and women, and some not so talented, turned away from the traditional paths of fulfillment in a money-oriented society to the ideal of shaping their lives by shaping objects with their hands.'² Experimenting with a material that offered so much unexplored artistic territory was particularly appealing. The great craft revival was closely related to this desire to create from within oneself without reliance on others; to make with one's own hands, or, in the case of glass, 'to make a form with human breath'.³

During its early history the glass movement was about exploration; those involved in it felt free to twist, tweak and pull glass in all directions, until the basic bubble survived only as a ghost. Both the spirit of the times and the fact that the experiments were being done away from a critical public, in the liberated atmosphere of the university campus, encouraged artistic licence. There was little interest in commercial gain. Dale Chihuly remarked, 'For the first ten years that I blew glass I never sold any work; it just wasn't a consideration at the time.'[4] There was tremendous excitement about the new game of blowing bubbles of whatever colour and shape seemed interesting or appealing. How far could one go? What was one to do with these misshapen lumps? With the enthusiasm of adventurers charting unknown territory, glass-makers were carried along by their own curiosity, generating an impetus which lasted well into the following decade.

Most of the work, unlike today, was in hot glass. The impulsiveness of glass-blowing suited the impatient enthusiasm of pioneering discoverers. At about this time Harvey Littleton wrote the first manual for the contemporary glass-blower, and his words capture the prevailing mood: '[In hot glass] artistic creation must occur in crisis, it cannot be planned or divided up; a blistered, mottled, collapsed, unidentifiable handblown glass object may be more valuable than a crystal swan.'[5] It was a period of innocence; teachers learnt as they taught and were surprised by their own findings; there were no critics around to dampen their ardour, and had there been, the loose experimental style of the 1960s would never have been allowed to develop. It had the charm, the irresponsibility and the carefree abandon of something in its infancy. It did not feel the threat of challenge from outside its own confines, because hardly any outsiders thought developments in the glass world worthy of note. Only in retrospect has the historical importance of those years become apparent, and all critical comment must make allowances for that. The 'wobbly bubbles' and 'lumpy globby shapes'[6] of the 1960s were the seeds of much that is in full flower today.

THE 1970s

In the early 1970s Harvey Littleton made the famous quip 'Technique is cheap',[7] thereby implying that one should not be inhibited by traditional methods, that the only thing left to do with the existing rules was to break them. Erwin Eisch, who had met Littleton in 1962 and felt he had found a kindred spirit, echoed these sentiments, proclaiming, 'technology does not

Erwin Eisch, 'Telephone', 1971, mould-blown glass. H. 15 cm (6 in). (The Corning Museum of Glass, Corning, New York)

Marvin Lipofsky, piece from
'Small California Loop' series,
1978, glass and mixed media.
H. 21.5 cm (8½ in),
L. 45.5 cm (18 in).
(Photo: M. Lee Fatherree)

Mary Shaffer, untitled
sculpture, 1975, stacked and
fused sheet glass and metal chain.
10 x 30.5 x 23 cm
(4 x 12 x 9 in)

interest me – it merely serves my artistic aims'.[8] But ironically, all that these artists were doing by breaking old rules was making new ones.

Those attracted to glass during the 1970s sought to unlock the 'voice of the material'.[9] A new vein of invention had been struck and there was a need for extended technical frontiers. Because the blowpipe on its own was considered too primitive an instrument, many warm and cold glass techniques were explored, sometimes as a substitute and sometimes to add embellishment to blown forms. Glass technology saw developments on a scale that is unlikely to be repeated ever again. Blowing, slumping, laminating, casting, optical cutting and sand-blasting all benefited from great intellectual and artistic input; the technique became the art form. There was a great deal of enjoyment and excitement at this time and it was not until the 1980s were well under way that the glass world became disenchanted with technical discovery. The fact of doubting brought the period of 'technical thrills' to a close. But until this happened it was one of the most productive in glass the twentieth century has known, in retrospect a sort of golden age, when the art was in full bloom. The sheer number of individual artists worldwide working in glass was astonishing, and most of them had something to say, owing to the sudden realization that so much had previously been left unsaid.

THE 1980s

More recently, glass artists have grown suspicious of the face-value beauty of glass and have voiced concern at the way in which the artist has allowed glass to speak for itself, working simply to reveal the natural beauty and expressiveness of the material. The feeling is that, by letting this happen, the artist has somehow become a slave to his material. It is a predictable reaction to the priorities of a previous generation of artists who had considered technical invention to be an art in itself. But in the 1980s the mood is different: it is no longer possible just to go forth and invent, because priorities have changed. Artists now feel they must use the knowledge available to them to construct something that has meaning and relevance beyond what has already been said. Much of the sense of fun has gone, giving way to serious new issues. 'Glass worship' is definitely a thing of the past. 'When the success of a piece is reliant on the material alone, it will forever remain suspect on a conceptual level.'[10] Such sentiments have resulted in work that makes for less comfortable viewing.

Many collectors who were active in the 1970s can no longer accept what is happening because they, along with the artists whose work they collected, were primarily glass lovers. There is a mixed reaction to current trends. Some feel that the new generation is being unfaithful to glass and is trying to negate the discoveries made by their predecessors. But among the artists themselves there is an attempt to equate glass with other materials, such as paint, wood, marble or bronze. In the 1987 edition of *Glass Review* there are many examples of this. Stanislav Libenský, who was a member of the jury responsible for the choice of work, observed in his jury statement, 'Glass seems to be employed more for contrast or for its harmonious relationship with other media, and less as an art form in its own right.'[11] These developments are especially noticeable among some of the younger artists included in the review; in a piece by Lee Harvey, for instance, fuse-cast glass

and stone look remarkably similar. Lisa Gherardi's 'Box With Daggers'
combines sand-cast glass and wood in a piece with considerable emotional
force. Her use of glass is particularly interesting, because while denying
many of its conventional qualities, she uses it to maximum effect. The glass
content of this piece is only hinted at where it shines through in places with
more poignancy than in many pieces made entirely of glass.

A number of artists whose involvement in glass has been of longer dura-
tion also feel drawn towards a combination of materials. Ann Wolff (Ann
Wärff), whilst losing none of the skills and talents she developed as a glass-
maker, has felt a need to bring her glass imagery into contact with metal and

Lisa Gherardi, 'Figure', 1985,
sand-cast glass

Ann Wolff, 'Nut's Daughter', 1986, glass and metal sculpture, the glass acid-etched, sand-blasted, and painted with black enamel. H. 105 cm (41½ in). (Photo: Anders Qwarnström)

stone in order to make a more valid artistic statement. Diana Hobson, who during the 1970s was busily occupied with *pâte de verre* techniques, now incorporates stone, wire mesh or crushed sea-shells into her work, thereby enriching her vocabulary of materials and giving her work an opulence that has lifted it onto a new plane. She has worked with glass for more than a decade and it is interesting to hear how she feels about her work in the future: 'I want to carve stone and combine it with glass; the image I have is of something that is very light and translucent resting inside the stone.'[12]

Whilst the 1970s seem in retrospect to have been one long glass celebration, recent developments make the 'revelries' of that past decade seem too craft-orientated, and artistically naive. The time has definitely come to reconsider the role of glass in the art world.

CRAFT OR ART?

The one question that has obsessed glass artists since the 1960s is whether their work should be categorized as craft or as art. There is no answer except to say that there is plenty of scope for artistry in glass, just as there is in music, writing, architecture and painting. The last quarter of a century has seen such great technical and creative leaps that it has understandably led to an identity crisis for those who found themselves working as independent artists in a material limited for centuries by a more restricted craft tradition. They felt the need to be called artists and were suffering from what the American painter and art historian Darby Bannard has referred to as 'art envy'.[13] At times it reached a surprising degree of paranoia. At the beginning of the 1980s the Dutch glass artist Bert van Loo talked of the necessity to break through the isolation of the 'crafts-field' and move into the fine arts. 'If this does not happen,' he said, 'there is a real danger that the Glass Movement will die.'[14] At the Glass Art Society conference in 1985 the young American glass artist Suzanne Muchnic felt she was speaking for the movement when she said:

> My colleagues and I are participants in a continuing effort to elevate glass into the arena of high art. In short, to help liberate it from its craft-conscious technique-laden ghetto. The bottom line, of course, is that we can't do that. We do not have the power to turn the products of any medium into art. Only artists can do that. Among the so-called craft media, glass has a special problem. It's the pretty girl of the art world, and as such, it has to try harder to prove itself serious.[15]

Every branch of the arts, including what is called 'fine art', has its own boundaries. Important conceptual changes in glass have led to a degree of confusion about scope. It was difficult to know where to slot contemporary glass into the hierarchy, where to exhibit it in museums, what sort of commercial galleries to use for shows. There was a basic anxiety that because it was glass it would be viewed and judged in the same light as a utilitarian object, that it would not be accorded the status it deserved. Gradually, however, these fears have subsided. Glass cannot and should not be compared with other art materials. Given the fact that it is a legitimate material for the artist to use in his quest for communication, there is no point in any such comparison, it is as pointless as comparing, say, watercolours with oil, or bronze with wood.

Diana Hobson, 'New Texture Series No. 5', 1988, *pâte de verre* and pebbles. H. 20 cm (7¾ in)

It is wrong to say that glass has not had any impact on the history of art, though perhaps right to say that as yet too little notice has been taken of it outside the ghetto. The impact of contemporary glass has been enormous, adding a whole new dimension to the art world. But in evaluating glass and work involving glass, one has to apply special criteria. Each branch of the arts has its idiosyncrasies, involving the intrinsic disciplines, skills and 'soul' of the material which has to be worked. Paint is there for the artist to squeeze out of a tube, but glass has first to be made with sweat, toil and consummate skill. Despite this hurdle, and sometimes because of it, great artists have been drawn to glass. There has been nothing short of a cultural revolution in the glass world since the 1960s, based on the simple discovery that the alchemy of fusing sand and silica can provide a substance with as much potential for expression in the hands of an artist as canvas and paint. It is a development that has increased the flow of artistic energy to the glass world and has opened new doors. There is no cause for paranoia or alarm. 'The history of glass is on the verge of transcending its historic connotation as a craft material.'[16]

THE TOLEDO SEMINARS AND THEIR INFLUENCE

Undoubtedly there is one single event which marks the new dawn in American glass history, and that is the workshop in glass-blowing organized by the Toledo Museum of Art in 1962. Referring to this, Paul Hollister wrote, 'And Littleton created the world in six days in Toledo in '62, and Littleton said, "Let there be glass!" And Labino went and made the glass, and Littleton saw that it was good.'[17] Historically speaking, this was no isolated event, but rather the result of a growing curiosity about whether or not glass could be formed by the independent artist working alone in his studio. The work of Gallé, Daum, Marinot and Lalique had already broadened artistic horizons in glass, and in 1959 at the American Craft Council conference at Lake George, Colorado, the question was raised once more as to whether glass, especially blown glass, was a suitable medium for the artist. This was also the year of 'Glass 1959, A Special Exhibition of International Contemporary Glass' at the Corning Museum of Glass. Harvey Littleton, who attended the American Craft Council conference, took it upon himself to investigate the matter and to try to 'develop the techniques necessary for a person to work alone as an artist in glass'.[18] Littleton, like so many of his contemporaries who took up glass-making, had until that time basically been a potter who had experimented briefly with glass. At the next American Craft Council conference in 1961 he was able to report some progress, and the following year to interest both the University of Wisconsin Research Committee and the Toledo Museum of Art in the project.

In the summer of 1962 two seminars on the subject were organized at the University of Wisconsin. At the first of these in March Littleton, together with Norman Schulman, the instructor in ceramics, adapted a pot furnace and tried to use it for melting glass, but they were unsuccessful. They had already consulted Dominick Labino about an easy-to-melt glass formula and he had provided them with one, but they were unable to handle it properly. They consulted Labino again, who told them to forget the pot furnace, put a liner in it and convert it to a tank furnace. Labino had already had thirty years of glass experience in the industry, working with what he describes as 'the chemistry and physics of glass. My glass fiber developments and silica fiber used in the Mercury, Gemini and Apollo Space Missions, and later to make tiles on the outside of the Space Shuttle, Columbia, were far removed from Glass as a Medium of Art.'[19] He decided to attend the conference, bringing with him some of his No. 475 marbles (used for making glass fibre), which were easy to handle and would melt quickly. The marbles caused a sensation and the workshop took off. Those who saw the results described them as pitiful attempts at glass-blowing; but there was such enthusiasm about the possibilities that the museum decided to hold another workshop in a garage later on in the year. It lasted for two weeks, during which a retired Toledo glass-blower, Harvey Leafgreen, advised and helped the group of struggling potters and assorted craftsmen with their 'garage art'. The implications of what was achieved during those two weeks of fun is beyond dispute, and are nicely contained in a statement made more than a decade later by Joel Philip Myers, who wrote in the introduction to an exhibition catalogue in 1976, 'Had I not been aware of the Toledo Glass Seminars I wonder if I would have seen the dual possibilities of producing glass for myself whilst designing for the factory.'[20]

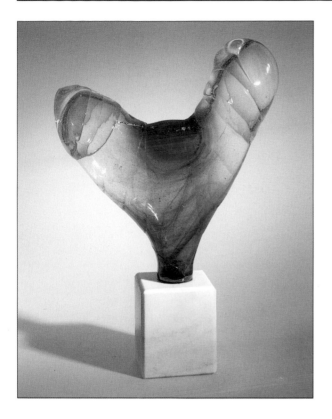

The Toledo seminars were historically rather than artistically important and resulted in Labino managing to secure a grant from the Johns Manville's Corporation (where he was employed as a research scientist). This enabled Harvey Littleton to set up a glass programme at the University of Wisconsin, and there was the added bonus of a generous gift of Johns Manville's No. 475 marbles for melting. Labino continued his own attempts at building a portable furnace and annealing oven, working on his farm near Grand Rapids, Minnesota, and by 1964 Littleton was able to take portable equipment developed by Labino to demonstrate at the World Crafts Council at Columbia University in New York.

Labino's invention and the Wisconsin programme proved immensely popular and served as a model for the many glass programmes that opened up right across America. The news of what had happened at Wisconsin spread like wildfire, and many universities decided to start glass programmes. In academic terms the attraction was considerable, combining the possibility for technical research with the challenge of creating new formulas by questioning and probing past standards. Many of Littleton's early students went on to create their own glass programmes at other American universities and have since become established artists, teachers, or a combination of the two. As well as the many programmes in glass at universities throughout America, there are also summer schools, including the oldest at Haystack Mountain School in Maine and the world-famous Pilchuck School, which started modestly in 1971 as a summer workshop led by Dale Chihuly. 'American studio glass exploded across the world like a volcano. The sonic boom and tidal wave of studio glass have reached the shores of Japan and Australia and dashed up the marble steps along the Grand Canal; no place today is immune to its influence.'[21]

ABOVE LEFT: **Harvey Littleton**, 'Y Form Sculpture', 1965, from the 'Prunted, Imploded and Exploded Form' series, blown glass coloured with cobalt oxides on a marble base. H. 32 cm (12½ in)

ABOVE: **Joel Philip Myers**, 'Blue Field on White', 1976, vase, blown glass with applied decoration. H. 25.5 cm (10 in)

Stanislav Libenský and
Jaroslava Brychtová, 'Evening,
Red Sky, Table', 1988, cast glass
sculpture. 30 x 39 x 33 cm
(11¾ x 15⅜ x 13 in)

THE INTERNATIONAL GLASS MOVEMENT

Whilst there are definitely certain national characteristics, the glass movement is an international one, marked by the frequent exchange of information and ideas at the numerous gatherings that have taken place over the
years in various parts of the world, and by the international flavour of journals partly or wholly concerned with glass which are published in a number
of countries. There have also been several important exhibitions, making it
possible for artists and critics to survey and evaluate the changing trends.
The formation of glass associations has been a mixed blessing. On the one
hand it has provided the glass world with an arena in which to air its concerns, and has proved the ideal way of achieving some sort of focus within a
field remarkable for its disparity. It has, however, also resulted in something
of a ghetto situation, with glass-makers concerning themselves too much
with one another and not enough with the world to which they should be
relating. Although there was a real need for the various groups and associations that were formed, most were not established until the 1970s. All of
them began with just a few members and expanded rapidly, and most strive
to have an international membership and international conferences.

   As the movement has grown, so has the range of topics dealt with. Conferences are now no longer simply a way of exchanging technical information. All aspects of the art and craft of glass are discussed, and recently there
have been serious attempts to broaden the scope of the meetings by inviting
painters and architects to attend and speak. In countries which for political
or geographical reasons are isolated, these meetings have played a particularly important role: the various symposia in Czechoslovakia, Australia and
Japan come to mind as examples of this. However, the important meetings
are not always organized by these associations; in Czechoslovakia, for
example, the symposia at Nový Bor have been organized by the glass industry (Crystalex) in conjunction with Art Centrum, the central agency for art
sales. In Britain the Royal College of Art has been responsible for two major
conferences, one on hot glass in 1976 and one on glass in architecture in
1986. In America, Australia, Japan and West Germany, museums have
hosted similar important events.

GLASS JOURNALS

Apart from the importance of the events in themselves, the publications connected either with a particular association or with a special event are of great documentary value. No glass historian will ever feel the lack of written commentary on what happened in the glass world between 1962 and the present time, but over the years one has relied on a handful of serious commentators for a realistic assessment of the developing situation. The first journal to appear devoted entirely to new glass was called *Glass Art* (later renamed *Glass*), which was published in America in 1972 and appeared monthly. The bimonthly American publication *New Work*, published by the New York Experimental Glass Workshop, has been appearing since 1979 and is currently one of the best glass journals available.

One of the longest-surviving magazines is the bilingual (German/English) German quarterly magazine *Neues Glas*, edited since it began in 1980 by Helmut Ricke, the director of applied arts at the Kunstmuseum, Düsseldorf. For half a decade it was the only international magazine devoted to glass, and it is certainly the most important historical source for the first half of the 1980s. Before that time there were sporadic articles in the American magazine *Craft Horizons* (which was later renamed *American Craft*) and in the British *Crafts* magazine, which first appeared in January 1976. The bimonthly Czech periodical *Glass Review* is a magazine of long standing and appears in a number of foreign editions, including English (although it must be said that the English translation very often reads like a foreign language). More recently there has been French commentary in *La Revue de la Céramique et du Verre*, and two Australian journals, *Craft Australia* and *Craft Arts*, have had excellent articles on both Australian glass and glass worldwide.

Apart from these journals there have also been important exhibition catalogues, and those for major shows like the Corning Museum exhibitions of 1959 and 1979 or the Coburg Glass Prize exhibitions of 1977 and 1985 are already collectors' items. Corning Museum has also provided an invaluable yearly publication called *New Glass Review*, a survey of objects designed and made in the year of publication. (This began in 1976 as *Contemporary Glass* and was published for three years in microfiche form.) It is intended as a review of significant new works in glass, as well as a record of change and adaptation in contemporary glass. The work is chosen by a panel of judges from a selection of slides submitted by the artists. Each review is limited to one hundred slides. In 1976 the images were chosen from slides submitted by 397 glass-makers in eighteen countries. In *New Glass Review* 8 (1987) the task was far more daunting, with 2300 slides submitted by 800 artists and designers.

DEVELOPMENTS IN AMERICA AND EUROPE

The 1959 Corning exhibition served both to mark the end of one era and as a catalyst for the new dawn. Nearly all the work chosen for exhibition on that occasion was submitted by manufacturers. With hardly any exceptions the exhibits were functional vessels of one kind or another as the exhibition was limited to 'table glass made since 1955, every type, from the mass-produced machine-made product to the unique handmade one-of-a-kind piece'.[22] Artistic though some of it was, glass was still being treated in these exhibits as a staple commodity which formed part of everyday life. The exhibition was in the spirit of the great industrial shows, the world fairs, or the Milan Triennale exhibitions for which the Great Exhibition of 1851 had more or less been the template.

Long after its famous seminars Toledo Museum of Art continued to take an interest in the glass world, and in 1966 mounted the first of a series of 'Glass National' shows, which were held biennially and were basically surveys of what was happening in glass around the country. They were important because they provided an overall view by gathering work together in one place, and also because they heightened the awareness of the general public, as well as that of other museums, a number of which had already begun collections in the 1960s. In 1974 there was another World Crafts Council glass workshop at Oaxtepec in New Mexico, attended by the most comprehensive international group ever assembled. Conferences and exhibitions took place with greater frequency in America; glass programmes were being instituted; Pilchuck School was founded in 1971; the first art galleries devoted to glass were opened – among them Habatat Galleries in Michigan and the Heller Gallery in New York. In 1971 Harvey Littleton's *Glass Blowing – A Search for Form* was published, a sort of manifesto for the new generation of artists in glass, and in 1975 the first comprehensive book on contemporary art glass was written by Ray and Lee Grover.

It took just over a decade for the new world of glass to become fully established and operational. There are no really discernible breaks to mark when one period ended and a new one began, but Paul Hollister, in his essay 'The Studio Glass Movement' in the exhibition catalogue for 'New American Glass: Focus 2 West Virginia', made a division in 1976, writing of the earlier period, 'Knowledge of glassworking developed through teachers and their students learning together. The basic bubble was blown and pulled, tweaked and twisted, sagged and flailed, imploded, smashed, refused, and embellished with the trappings of a circus act. Some very beautiful pieces were created, and a great quantity showing incompetence and frivolity.'[23]

While the American glass movement was establishing itself in this way, there were parallel developments in Europe. In 1962 Harvey Littleton and Erwin Eisch had met in Frauenau, West Germany. Erwin Eisch, who at the time of their meeting was thirty years old, came from an old Bavarian family of glass engravers. The strength of his work lies in the unorthodox approach he had towards working the material. During the 1960s his work includes a series of grotesque portrait heads of Harvey Littleton, finger sculptures, beer mugs with breasts, and soft telephones. 'Along with other pop artists Eisch was poking fun at the world, and trying to turn everything on its head. Because he chose to do it in glass, he was something of an innovator, and in the glass world such personal statements were far ahead of their time.'[24] It was some time before Eisch was taken seriously in West Germany, but his ideas were well suited to the mood in America, and it was there that his influence was greatest.

Until the late 1970s the rest of Western Europe lagged far behind Eisch. Most European glass still adhered to an industrial studio glass environment, although individuals like Bertil Vallien in Sweden, Per Lutken in Denmark and Benny Motzfeld in Norway very soon began responding to the news

OPPOSITE: **Bertil Vallien**, designed for Kosta Boda, Sweden, 'Captivity No. Unik 3476', 1978, bowl, blown and sand-blasted glass with iridescent surface. H. 20.5 cm (8 in)

Per Lutken, designed for Holmegaard, Denmark, 'Glass Egg', 1970, blown glass with applied decoration

from America within that environment. In Britain a young group of artists
recently graduated from the Royal College of Art gathered round their
teacher, Sam Herman, to form a co-operative in London called The
Glasshouse. Some European museums also took note of what was happening and there were a few important exhibitions. One of the first was at the
Museum Boymans van Beuningen in Rotterdam; it was a joint exhibition of
studio glass from Europe and America, and included the work of Erwin
Eisch, Sam Herman, Harvey Littleton and Marvin Lipofsky. An exhibition
at the Museum Bellerive in Zürich in 1972 added considerable respectabil-
ity to the status of contemporary glass. There were also a number of other
important events between 1970 and 1976, including the opening of the
glass museum at Frauenau (Erwin Eisch's home town) and the 'Hot Glass
Symposium' at the Royal College of Art in London in 1976. By 1977
enough was happening in Europe to make a very distinguished showing of
glass at the first Coburg Glass Prize exhibition, where there were over five
hundred exhibits on show.

Many of the exhibits at Coburg came from Czechoslovakia, which has
played an important role in the international studio glass movement.

Although there has been a relatively free exchange of ideas between artists from Czechoslovakia and the rest of the world, Czech studio glass from this period has an individuality that sets it apart from glass elsewhere. Historically, Czechoslovakia has one of the longest traditions of glass-making and, against all the odds, the period since the communist regime came to power in the 1940s has been one of the most creative of all time. This has a lot to do with the dynamic personality of Stanislav Libenský, whose teaching at the Prague Academy of Applied Arts and whose work as an artist have virtually shaped the history of Czech studio glass over more than thirty years. During the 1940s the glass industry went through difficult times in Czechoslovakia. There were many trained glass-makers, but in an atmosphere of depression the industry could not always provide outlets for their talent. Libenský and his contemporaries worked in comparative isolation. The following decade was a period of great artistic invention in Czechoslovakia, and regardless of its difficulties the glass industry was keen to maintain its reputation. Economically, there was no possibility of establishing individual studios at this time, and in the main, artistic ideas were carried out within the industry. Despite major changes since then, this has essentially

Stanislav Libenský and **Jaroslava Brychtová**, sculptural bowl, 1954, cast glass. L. 29 cm (11 ½ in)

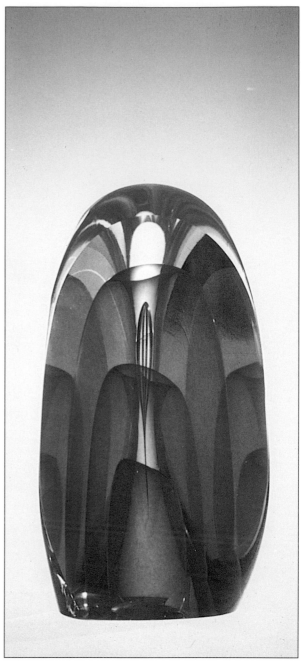

remained a feature of Czech studio glass, where the creative artist still relies mainly on industrial skills for the execution of his ideas.

Just as the 1959 Corning exhibition had marked the end of one era and the beginning of the next, so it was with the 1979 show. It contained both the work of those who had by now become the 'elder statesmen' of the art and exciting new ideas by up-and-coming artists. A beautiful 'Immersion Series' piece by Dominick Labino, entitled 'Triangular Fountain', using hot-glass techniques exclusively, harked back to the beginning of the movement, whilst 'Banded Bronze' by Thomas Patti, in laminated and blown coloured and colourless glass (the piece chosen for the front cover of the catalogue), looked to a new degree of technical finish and the sort of

ABOVE LEFT: **Karel Vaňura**, vase, 1958, blown glass with abstract decoration in transparent paints.
H. 43 cm (17 in)

ABOVE: **Dominick Labino**, 'Triangular Fountain', 1978, overlaid with coloured inclusions.
H. 19 cm (7½ in)

evolved visual statement that has been characteristic of more recent times. An important aspect of this major exhibition was that for three years after its opening at Corning Museum of Glass in 1979, it travelled across America and then on to Paris and London. Since then glass has extended its horizons so far that it can never be possible to do this sort of worldwide survey again.

In the years following the Corning exhibition there have been a number of more specific and smaller-scale surveys, such as 'Americans in Glass' at the Leigh Yawkey Woodson Art Museum at Wausau, Wisconsin (1981); various European, American and Japanese surveys staged in Japan, including the yearly series of 'American Glass Now' exhibitions; and two exhibitions devoted to contemporary glass at the National Museum of Modern Art in Kyoto, the first in 1980 showing European and Japanese glass, and the second in the following year with Australian, Canadian, American and more Japanese glass. A significant exhibition for Australia was the first survey held there in 1982, which was organized by the Art Gallery of Western Australia and toured the country. The most important European event of the 1980s was the second Coburg Glass Prize exhibition in 1985, which made it clear how far the art had advanced in Europe since the first exhibition in 1977. Another development was that surveys of Czech contemporary glass were held in Czechoslovakia (the first in 1984); before then Czech contemporary glass had had only moderate exposure on home ground and had principally been shown at exhibitions abroad.

There was a general frenzy of activity in the wake of the Corning shows; more symposia and meetings were organized from one end of the world to another and commercial galleries devoted to glass began to open wherever there was an interest. Generally there was a far greater awareness that glass formed a part of the art world and many museums hosted either group shows or one-man exhibitions. As general surveys became unmanageable there was a move towards the specific, both in the commercial galleries and in museums. In 1983, for instance, the Tucson Museum of Art staged an invitational sculptural glass show. As artists have felt technically more secure there has been greater technical refinement and also a tendency to think on a larger scale. Those involved in making glass have become increasingly fascinated by the opportunities for glass in architecture, and architects have at last begun to respond to the achievements of glass artists. Glass has travelled in light years rather than calendar years since those tentative opening moves in 1962.

SUMMARY
Throughout the period since 1962 glass artists everywhere have adapted technology to meet their own artistic needs. If American glass technology as applied to the decorative arts was in its infancy at the beginning of the 1960s, that was certainly not the case ten years later. The realization that all glass-making techniques could enjoy the same measure of conceptual freedom as blowing came quite soon, and a number of artists either abandoned glass-blowing completely for 'warm' or 'cold' techniques (slumping or cutting, for instance), or tried combining the two. Obviously the wider the technical base could be, the broader the range of expression. Every aspect of glass-making was explored and the sheer technical wizardry of the period

since the early 1970s has been astounding. There was a voracious appetite for technical discovery and the artistic possibilities related to it. Hot glass, which (for reasons already explained) had enjoyed what seems in retrospect a disproportionate degree of popularity during the 1960s, lost ground to other techniques, until it was felt during the 1980s that it had been almost completely phased out. One reason for this is perhaps the virtuoso skills demanded by the technique. Only very few can master the art, and an even smaller number are lucky enough to combine such virtuosity with any sort of artistic vision. Ironically, the very technique which led to a revolution in glass is the one where artistic results are most difficult to achieve, particularly for an artist working on his own. And yet it is probably a glass-blower who dominated the American glass scene for ten years from the mid 1970s: Dale Chihuly, one of Littleton's first and most talented pupils, was very much on the scene as a young man in the 1960s. Due to an unfortunate accident in which he lost the sight in one eye, it has been difficult for this remarkable artist to execute his ideas in blown glass by himself. Nonetheless, his work has shown the world what artistry can be achieved with blown-glass forms.

The surprise factor, what the American glass artist Henry Halem once referred to as the 'Oooooooo' factor or the 'Wow!' factor, has had a lot to do with the success of contemporary glass over the last decade.[25] Enjoyable as it is, however, the element of surprise fades fast, and the important issue is what remains. If a surprising new idea can be developed into a workable art form, it will survive and flourish. The recent art of contemporary glass has been very bound up with technical invention, but the successes have been when the inventor has also proved himself to be an artist. There has been such a proliferation of ideas over the last decade that the effect has been somewhat overwhelming, and it is perhaps a little early to be able to sort out the good from the bad. One can, however, see how much an artist has been able to do with a particular technique, and perhaps this is one of the important criteria for judging contemporary glass. As far as American glass is concerned, there is no doubt that Howard Ben Tré has given a new meaning to the art (rather than the technique) of glass-casting, that Dale Chihuly has done the same for glass-blowing, Paul Stankard for the paper-weight technique, Michael Glancy for electro-plating, and Dan Dailey for the many techniques that he combines. If there is a national characteristic that distinguishes American glass, it is sheer bravado.

Glass from other countries is far more identifiable, mainly, of course, because in terms of volume nowhere is comparable with America. The art is more contained elsewhere, the influences less diffuse, and the end result more of a piece. European borders still matter, so glass from Czechoslovakia, East Germany, West Germany, Hungary, Scandinavia, Holland, France and Britain have their own characteristics. The most obvious example of a national identity is the case of East German glass, because of the strong lampworking tradition and the fact that most artists who live there work in that technique. In other countries identity has to do with a combination of factors, including glass education, studio facilities, glass heritage, or the landscape. In Czechoslovakia there is no doubt that Stanislav Libenský in Prague and Václav Cigler in Bratislava have deeply influenced two generations of glass art. Another decisive factor in that country has been the

Howard Ben Tré, 'Burial Box: Type II – Rose', 1978, cast glass. H. 10 cm (4 in)

opportunities for glass in architecture. Wherever there have been fine artists, like Libenský in Czechoslovakia, Ann Wolff and Bertil Vallien in Sweden, and Richard Meitner in Holland, they have had an influence on the state of the art in their own countries. Paradoxically, however, the international flavour of contemporary glass is equally strong and as a result its chief characteristic is that it is a worldwide movement.

In the Pacific, first Japan and then Australia and New Zealand were affected by the 'sonic boom'. The interest in Japan has been great, but developments have been slow. Either the Japanese have been too bound by their own strong traditions in the applied arts, or they have copied the American art too closely. Kyohei Fujita, who over the years has emerged as the leading glass artist in Japan, is one of the only examples of a Japanese artist who has evolved a strong personal identity. But there are signs of change on the way. In New Zealand, and particularly in Australia, the situation is very different. The Australians have only recently been affected. When in 1973 and 1974 the Australia Council conducted a survey of the country's crafts and sent out a questionnaire, only thirteen of the 1165 artisans who responded said they were interested in glass; at that time not a single institution offered courses in glass-blowing. Today, however, with young artists such as Warren Langley and Brian Hirst, and teachers such as Klaus Moje at Canberra, the future looks bright.

At present the situation in general looks about to change again. A new generation of art students starting out on a career in glass are in some ways spoilt, but in other ways not as fortunate as their predecessors. The excitement of discovery is no longer possible in the way that it was. So much has been invented and so much said in glass that it is now much more of a problem to be either inventive or original. Artistically the demands on the young are greater than they ever were, but with the technology available, the benefit of hindsight, and a tradition to build on, one can only hope that the art will reach new levels of maturity.

2. NORTH AMERICA

TWENTIETH-CENTURY BACKGROUND HISTORY

Glass art since 1962 has added a whole new dimension to American culture. Before this, most Americans working with glass were either designers for industry or industrial technicians. They had few artistic pretensions and their main aim was to make good consumer products. But whereas the industrial designer has a customer and his needs to consider when working on a product, the artist needs to impose no such restraints on himself. At the beginning of the twentieth century Louis Comfort Tiffany had combined great entrepreneurial talent with extraordinary taste and provided America with a range of glass that has come to be considered historically important. Frederic Carder, after designing for Stevens and Williams from 1881 to 1902, came to America and founded the Steuben glassworks in Corning in 1903. Tiffany died in 1933 and Carder thirty years later, but both their companies are still flourishing today, though only the name of Steuben is now associated with glass. During the 1920s and 1930s the company was more or less solely responsible for an American glass tradition with a range of crystal, the best of which was a superb series of beautifully engraved pieces.

Since the Second World War Steuben has continued to be in the forefront of American artistic glass production. Their Corning location has been largely responsible for close ties with the contemporary studio glass movement and a concern about the 'marriage of artistic vision and glass-making technology'.[1] The full-lead crystal produced at Steuben is 'a most wondrous substance'[2] and in recent years has inspired Peter Aldridge, David Dowler and Eric Hilton 'with the full technical support of Steuben to create a remarkable collection of sculptures that are the most complex, personally expressive and beautiful works ever rendered in crystal'.[3]

There have also been a few individuals with production companies of their own who are in a sense the real forerunners of the American glass movement. But the break in 1962 was so radical that they are not usually considered in the same light as the new wave of glass artists in America since that time. However, their very individual way of working could well have been a contributing factor to the questions that were raised at the end of the 1950s about the artistic possibilities of glass.

OPPOSITE: **Peter Aldridge**, Steuben Glass, 'Metronome', 1988, cut lead crystal. H. 63.5 cm (25 in)

Heaton, Higgins and Eckhardt are the three names that come to mind when thinking about American glass during the 1940s and 1950s. Maurice Heaton came from a British family whose associations with glass, and particularly stained glass, were well known. His family moved to New York and executed some important glass commissions, including a large window for the Rockefeller Center in 1932 entitled 'The Flight of Amelia Erhardt Across the Atlantic' (since destroyed). The techniques which Heaton developed for himself have a lot in common with the inventiveness so characteristic of American glass in later years:

> He cuts and grinds the glass to shape and then attaches the glass to a plate glass turntable. He makes his design directly on the shaped glass by tapping powdered enamels through graded sieves and over curved and angled templates to create overlapping shadows. The completed design is fixed with an adhesive spray, placed in a sheet iron mold into which it is slumped in the kiln while the enameled design is fired on. Heaton himself makes the molds and all his tools.[4]

Michael and Frances Higgins showed the same sort of technical ingenuity in their work, which involved a process of fusing enamelled glass and producing it in all forms and sizes from earrings to screens and church windows. They evolved a process of using silk-screen stencils to apply enamels to sheets of glass. Edris Eckhardt considered herself to be a sculptor: 'I'm only happy when I am working with three-dimensional forms. I work in glass from an artist's viewpoint, not a craftsman's.'[5] Before 1952 she had been a widely exhibited potter, but in that year she began making her own coloured glass from scratch. A year later she discovered for herself the ancient method of laminating gold or silver foil between two or more layers of glass. She also invented her own primitive tools (the rolling pin played an important part in her working processes).

Maurice Heaton, two rectangular dishes, fused glass with enamelled decoration

Michael and **Frances Higgins**, bowl, c. 1960, fused glass with multi-layered colours. Diam. 43 cm (17 in). (By kind permission of Kells & Meshell Jesse)

There are various remarkable similarities between these artists and the ones who came after them in the following decades. In their own way Maurice Heaton, the Higgins and Edris Eckhardt were as original as could be. The important difference between their work and that of the next generation was that from the 1960s onwards glass-makers felt free to enjoy total artistic emancipation, and the credit for this 'freedom from slavery' must go entirely to the Americans.

TECHNICAL AND ARTISTIC DEVELOPMENTS SINCE 1962

For almost two decades there was an obsession with gaining artistic credibility. The primary aim of American glass-makers during the 1960s and 1970s was to make art, and to fight the accusation that what they had achieved had only minimal value as an artistic medium. There is no doubt that today's glass artists are accepted as being able to make valid artistic statements, but on the flight to freedom there have been many bumpy moments when one really did wonder whether the early pioneers could ever achieve any sort of worthwhile artistic status. The lack of inhibition shown by the first generation of post-1962 American glass artists was remarkable, and made an impact on the few that saw and appreciated it at the time. The power in those first pieces of glass was derived from their complete originality. For the first time in its history the blowpipe was used to express gut feeling. Previously, for two centuries, as soon as the initial bubble of glass had been formed its imperfections had been ironed out in a process of technical refinement. Suddenly, starting in 1962, a group of American artists thought about the inherent power of the moment of conception and decided to build on it. This basic approach has a directness about it that is essentially American. But it was no chance discovery; it was born out of a desire to be 'American' in glass, to escape from the shackles of tradition, and discover the 'simple gifts' which Americans value so highly.

As soon as American glass-makers found out how expressive glass could be there was no holding them back. The American tendency to be bigger, bolder and freer gave the glass bubble a new lease of life. Harvey Littleton, Dominick Labino, Robert Fritz and Marvin Lipofsky were among the first to make expressionist shapes in hot glass, in which colour and form were allowed free rein. Their primary aim was to make art and to express themselves freely in an art form which until then had been one hundred per cent vessel-orientated. Vessel form became the subject of intense philosophical debate, and there was an attempt either to redefine it or to depart from it altogether. In trying to do the latter, many artists have merely ended up by highlighting its power as a basic concept in glass. The arguments surrounding vessel form persist to this day. At first there was a tendency to experiment with vessel shapes and see how the vessel reacted to liberation. Most attempts at sculpture during the 1960s and early 1970s were vessel-related; indeed, there is very little that can be done in hot glass about breaking away from the vessel. Even so, most of the first generation of artists worked the bubble and enjoyed the new sculptural possibilities which they found inherent in it. There was, however, a growing compulsion to do without the bubble, and for this there was ultimately no alternative but to move away from hot glass towards other techniques of glass-making in which the bubble is not a basic requirement. Slumping and casting were obvious alternatives and during the 1970s they became increasingly popular as basic techniques which could be worked upon and embellished with a whole variety of cold processes.

The greatest American contribution to the art of contemporary glass has been a new casual approach. Since the craft element in glass has ceased to occupy centre stage, glass has become much more light-hearted. The American glass artist feels completely free to be himself, to make the material cry or laugh with him, to make it express his sorrows and his joys. Humour is an important part of any cultural heritage, but until recently there has been very little evidence of it in glass. Until Dan Dailey, Richard Marquis and Rick Bernstein, for example, came along glass never really raised a laugh. Dan Dailey's wall reliefs in Vitrolite, glass and metal are epigrammatic masterpieces with titles such as 'The Principles of Decor' or 'Nude on the Phone'. In the first an appalling design-conscious young couple who have misunderstood all the principles of fashion are poring over a book from which the piece derives its title. The man is sitting in a chair which combines all the worst aspects of modern design. The piece is to the point and extremely funny. Rick Bernstein has used similar techniques in a series of 'floating fables' where he expresses his own brand of humour with great skill and a nice feeling for paradox, parody and the absurdity of chaos.

GLASS EDUCATION IN AMERICA

The new American way of working in glass is taught in glass programmes from coast to coast, most of them attached to a university. The first of these programmes was set up by Harvey Littleton at the University of Wisconsin, Madison, during his tenure there as Professor of Ceramics in the early 1960s. Littleton is now considered the grand old man of American glass; in his case, what he did for glass is just as important as what he did with it. By

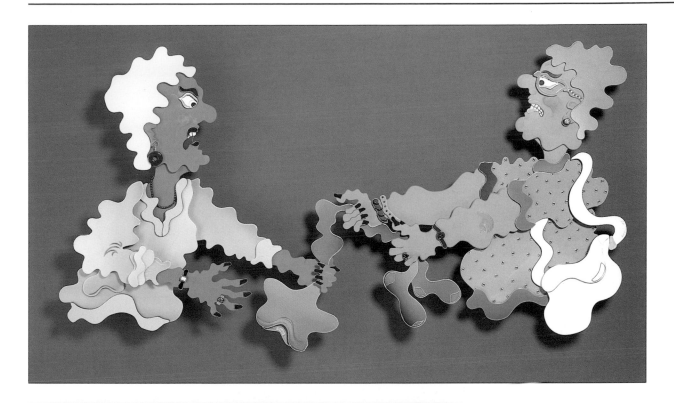

ABOVE: **Rick Bernstein**, 'Basement Daze', 1988, wall piece in multi-coloured Vitrolite. 106.5 x 213 x 23 cm (42 x 84 x 9 in)

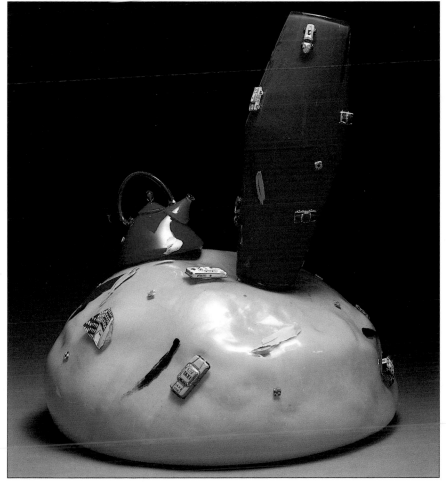

Richard Marquis, teapot, 1988, blown glass and other materials

Harvey Littleton, 'Four Seasons', 1977, blown barium/ potash glass with various colouring oxides. 14 × 35 × 30.5 cm (5½ × 13¾ × 12 in). (Photo: John Littleton)

introducing it to the university campus, he provided glass with the sort of intellectual credibility that it had never had previously. 'All I need is a garage,' he said modestly, in seeking funding to initiate a glass programme.[6] Otto Wittmann, the director of Toledo Museum of Art, offered him the use of the building in which the museum's lawn-mowers were kept for a workshop seminar. This garage, as we have seen, assumes extraordinary importance in the history of contemporary American glass.

What Littleton did during the 1960s, both as an artist and as a teacher, has set the pattern for America's newest art form. During the course of a long career he has experimented with colour, form and light. In the 1960s he made simple statements with blown tubes, rods, columns and 'eye' forms (a series in which different-coloured hemispherical shapes rested inside one another). He also 'sliced hollow cylinders at both ends to concentrate light in the curves and reflect it back off the edges'.[7] Littleton explains: 'For me the turning point, the change from the still functional container forms to "broken open" forms came in 1963. These smashed, re-melted, "double-bubble" shapes were my first obvious denial of function.'[8] During the 1970s he was occupied for almost a whole decade with a series of folded forms and loops, 'tubes bent onto themselves when still hot on the blowpipe, which fell according to gravity's pull, creating graceful curves'.[9] More recently he has 'explored color relationships with a series of geometric pieces concentric circles of color encased in crystal which appear to be suspended in light'.[10]

Marvin Lipofsky, piece from 'Otaru' series, 1987–8, made with help from Mitsunobu Sagawa, blown glass, cut, ground, hand-finished, sand-blasted and acid-polished. H. 21.5 cm (8½ in), L. 35 cm (13¾ in). (Photo: M. Lee Fatherree)

Many of Littleton's pupils were fired with his pioneering spirit, and a surprising number of them feature among America's leading artists. Many of them have also been involved in glass education in America. In 1964 Marvin Lipofsky founded the second glass programme in America at the University of California, Berkeley, and this was in operation until funding cutbacks caused it to close down in 1972. He then moved to California College of Arts and Crafts where he took over and expanded the glass programme; he remained head of this for fifteen years. Dale Chihuly, another of Littleton's students at Wisconsin, has also played a major role in American glass education, first at the Rhode Island School of Design where he established a glass programme in 1967, and then at Pilchuck near Seattle, a summer school with a worldwide reputation and an international flavour that is unique.

Pilchuck began in the summer of 1971 as the Pilchuck Glass Center; in the beginning it was set up as a summer camp with the simplest of amenities. Its early history is described by Thomas Bosworth, the architect responsible for the first buildings there: 'The making of art merged with the rest of life – cooking and eating, building living shelters and work facilities.'[11] The land on which this first summer camp was held belonged to John Hauberg, a collector and benefactor of the arts. The site consists of 'forty acres of high rolling meadowland interspersed with stands of western hemlock, cedar and Douglas fir; it overlooks the fertile Skagit river delta, and beyond the Olympic Mountains, the straits of San Juan de Fuca and the San Juan

Paul Marioni, 'Frida and Diego', 1984, fused glass. 51 x 51 cm (20 x 20 in)

islands'.[12] Hauberg has since that time become very involved with the American glass movement, and thanks to his generosity the magical site has become a glass centre with permanent buildings that have been purpose-built. The hot shop was designed in the autumn of 1972 and completed the following summer. It is a remarkable building, 'shaped to fit the movements of the glass-blowing process and to accommodate equipment, including six large glass-melting furnaces . . . really an open-air pavilion, not unlike the tent shelter it replaced'.[13] The flat shop was designed and built during 1976, and since then dormitories, lecture halls and other campus buildings have gone up, giving more and more an air of permanence. Every summer teach-ers and students from all over the world congregate there to further the art in a series of workshops lasting two to three weeks and covering all aspects of glass-making. Many American artists have decided to make their homes nearby (Charles Parriott, Paul Marioni, Billy Morris, Flora Mace and Joey Kirkpatrick among others), so that Seattle has become an American glass centre with numerous galleries, workshops and production studios.

At least three other Wisconsin graduates started glass programmes during the 1960s: Kent Ipsen conducted programmes throughout the mid-West and taught at the Chicago Art Institute in the late 1960s; Fritz Dreisbach taught at Penland School of Crafts in North Carolina; and Tom McGlauchlin ran courses at Toledo Museum of Art. The first non-Wiscon-sin graduate to set up a glass programme was Joel Philip Myers, who, after designing for the industry from 1961 to 1970 at Blenko Glass, West Vir-ginia, established a programme at the University of Illinois in 1971.

MUSEUM INTEREST

As glass has come to play a more important role on the American art scene, more space has been devoted to it in museums throughout the country. Nothing can compare with the major role played by Corning Museum of Glass, which has sponsored important exhibitions and prizes, and has the most comprehensive permanent museum collection of contemporary glass anywhere in the world. Partly because of Corning's close involvement with Steuben, curators and museum directors there have been deeply concerned with the contemporary glass scene. They have been building a collection since the American studio glass movement was in its infancy, with the sort of perception possible only through intimate involvement with a developing art form. Several other museums and art associations throughout America have also given great assistance with sponsorship and shown a genuine interest in the art. The American Craft Council, for example, has helped with exhibitions at the American Craft Museum in New York and gave Harvey Littleton his first one-man show in 1964.

Museum interest has been a decisive factor in the enthusiastic way Americans have responded to developments in contemporary glass, either by means of special exhibitions or with permanent museum collections. The Toledo Museum of Art held a series of biennial 'Glass National' exhibitions, the first of which was in 1966 and all of which had printed catalogues that documented significant trends and innovations. These exhibitions were of major importance because they offered the first opportunity to survey what was happening across America by bringing it all together and making sense of it. The catalogues provided the first intelligent comment with their jurors' statements and introductions. Many other museums followed Toledo's example of invitational exhibitions, providing incentive for the artists and generating much interest from the museum-going public. Among the most important of these exhibitions were the two entitled 'New American Glass: Focus West Virginia', Part I held in 1976 and Part II in 1986, at Huntington Galleries, Huntington, West Virginia. The Leigh Yawkey Woodson Art Museum at Wausau, Wisconsin, has also organized a series of exhibitions, entitled 'Americans in Glass'. These exhibitions have served not only to show what is new, but also what has had staying power. A large percentage of American artists who started in the 1960s are still making significant work today. Ten years separated the Focus I and II exhibitions in West Virginia, but twenty-eight per cent of those who exhibited in the second exhibition had also been represented by work in the first.

GLASS CO-OPERATIVES

Because so many glass programmes were initiated during the 1960s, most people involved in glass were in some way connected with a campus somewhere. A number of artists set up on their own when they left, whilst others joined forces and established partnerships which have often been lasting and successful – for example, Mace and Kirkpatrick, Jervis and Krasnican, or Magdanz and Shapiro. Partnerships such as these have had the dual benefit of shared expenses and a marriage of complementary talents. Glass lends itself particularly well to a partnership situation, because so many different disciplines are involved in the craft as a whole. There is nearly always room for more than one pair of hands and one type of skill.

Glass-making is an expensive process and, unlike the individual potter or woodworker, the individual glass-maker can find himself needing equipment which demands the sort of heavy financial outlay that once again converts it into an industry. The balance between remaining an artist and having access to sophisticated technical equipment is a delicate one. A successful compromise has been found, however, by forming a kind of artists' co-operative where time and money are shared, and where there is also sometimes a sort of 'bread and butter' industrial designer production line which earns artists the freedom to experiment with their own work. The Glass Eye in Seattle was started in 1978 by two glass artists, Rob Adamson and Charles Parriott, with a 65 sq m (700 sq ft) space. From modest beginnings it has developed into a 1858 sq m (20,000 sq ft) space with forty makers, twenty-five of whom are on the permanent payroll. Despite the joke notice at the entrance announcing 'No Art Beyond This Point', some of the glass produced there is very much in the new spirit.

The idealism of Littleton and the early pioneers has had to undergo a process of modification in order to provide the ideal environment for the modern artist in glass. The hippy dream of a converted garden shed has severe limitations. Those who set up the New York Experimental Glass Workshop in 1977 conceived it as a place where 'artists could share their technical and aesthetic concerns in working with glass as an aesthetic medium, with facilities in glass-blowing, scientific glass-blowing, flame working, engraving, cutting, metalizing, casting, painting, slumping, fusing, neon and glass staining'.[14] It is a formula that makes sense and has provided many artists with the sort of facilities they need for large commissions as well as an environment for more intimate work. As the name suggests, it provides an artist with the possibility to experiment in a sympathetic environment. Outside university this is very difficult to do in America. In the glass industry expenses have become such that artistic experiment is too costly a luxury to allow, and yet after all the artistic development of the last quarter of a century, this is precisely what the contemporary glass artist needs most. He can no longer content himself with the simple tools of the trade that sufficed for the first two thousand years of glass history. So many artistic possibilities have been discovered in the recent past, crafted with the most modern technical skills, that today's American glass artist has to demand access to them if he is to succeed. The modern-day artist's greatest problem is where to work, and how to remain an artist in control of his material, whilst availing himself of the sort of modern technology that goes into the art as it is now.

GLASS GALLERIES AND GLASS COLLECTING

It is of course essential to his survival that an artist be able to sell his work. In the 1960s artistic glass was sold and collected casually at craft fairs and craft galleries throughout America where it was on display along with all manner of other merchandise ranging from home-made jam to driftwood sculpture. Comparatively few people at that time were ready to think of themselves as independent artists in glass. It was only when the idea of a glass movement gathered momentum and it became obvious that there was a new art form in the making, that glass began to attract a group of collectors whose commitment was financially and emotionally more serious. Both art

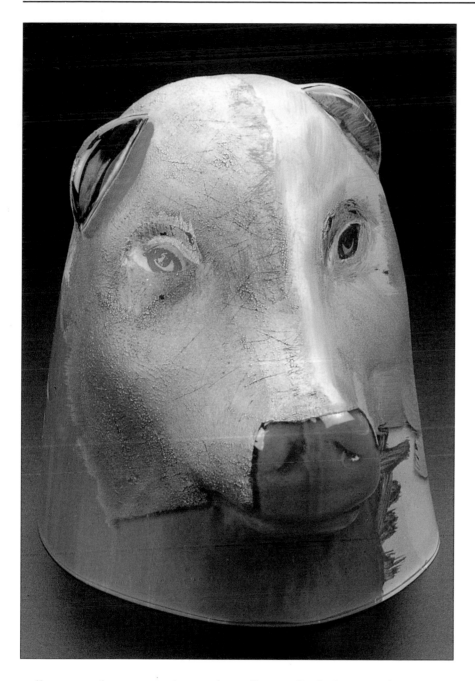

Charles Parriott, 'Teddy Bear', 1987, blown and enamelled glass sculpture. H. 30.5 cm (12 in)

collectors and artists need specialist galleries. Craft shops or department stores in America cannot provide a suitable showcase for the work of the new generation of glass artists: craft shops (now largely a thing of the past) stood for a tradition of earthiness, and department stores suggested luxurious ornamental gifts, neither of which established the right environment.

The first two American galleries devoted to glass were Habatat (in Michigan), founded in 1971 by Ferdinand Hampson and Linda Boone, and the Heller Gallery (in New York), now run by the Heller brothers, which started in 1972 as The Contemporary Art Glass Group. Both galleries have expanded their premises and their activities enormously since then, and between them have been mainly responsible for the large and enthusiastic nucleus of American glass collectors who make it possible for the art to flourish in the way it does today. Heller and Habatat both began at a time when there could have been very little real prospect of building up a successful commercial enterprise. Their idealism was a gamble that has paid off, but in more than business terms. Realizing the significance of artistic developments in glass early on, they passed on their enthusiasm through a series of one-man and group shows. Since 1972 Habatat has held 'Annual National Glass Invitational Exhibitions', which, as Hampson himself wrote, 'for more years than any other glass exhibition . . . made a significant statement about the "State of the Art" '.[15]

With more than two thousand glass artists working in America today, other galleries have opened (and some closed) since the early 1970s. The West Coast is well served by the Kurland Summers Gallery, which opened in Los Angeles in 1981; Maureen Littleton, the artist's daughter, has worked successfully from a gallery in Washington for several years; and a number of other galleries throughout the country are also beginning to make their mark. Galleries have been instrumental not only in building up private collections, but also in selling glass to museums all over the world and generally creating the sort of interest that only a successful selling exhibition can. Interestingly a number of art galleries not specializing in glass have branched out in this direction. Charles Cowles in New York and Betsy Rosenfeld in Chicago include glass-makers among their artists.

American collectors, themselves pioneers of a sort in that they were prepared to back their own hunches in a highly speculative field, have often been closely involved with universities, museums and other organizations which support the glass movement. A number of private collections have recently had museum showings, such as the Saxe Collection of Contemporary American and European Glass, which was exhibited at the Oakland Museum in California and the American Craft Museum in New York. The collection of Jean and Hilbert Sosin was shown at the University of Dearborn in Michigan. There is a certain element of competition among American collectors for exposure of this kind; American museums have largely been funded by private endowment and there is a degree of exhibitionism about American art collecting which at best must rank as a part of the Great American Dream. The American way of collecting is certainly very special and open to a degree of criticism and scepticism, but one must consider very seriously the role American collectors have played in giving their country the national art collections it has. In this respect, the American tradition of glass collecting has contributed greatly to the establishment of the lively American glass scene that exists today.

THE COMBINING OF DIFFERENT TECHNICAL SKILLS

American glass is so varied that it almost defies categorization. Historically speaking, there are clear divisions, which have already been referred to and which apply internationally. If there is anything that stands out about the American history of glass in the last quarter of a century, it is its range of inventiveness and the influence that developments in America have had on the rest of the world. In the beginning Harvey Littleton and his followers were mainly concerned with the artistic possibilities of hot glass, but these were soon exhausted and the problem was where to go without sacrificing the new-found freedom of the artist working alone in his studio. The

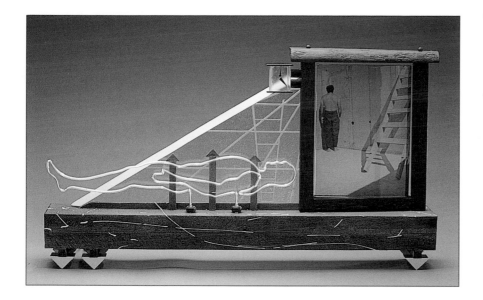

Mary van Cline, 'The Unbearable Lightness of Being', 1985, photo-sensitive plate glass and other materials. 122 x 63.5 x 20.5 cm (48 x 25 x 8 in)

misshapen bubble of the 1960s was so important because the American glass-makers who experimented with it totally flouted convention, thereby setting a precedent which could be applied to other areas of glass-making. The next logical move was to explore every aspect of glass-making, and in the decade between the late 1960s and the late 1970s slumping, casting, sand-blasting, enamelling, fusing, lampwork and *pâte de verre* techniques were all developed beyond recognition by those artists who used them. Part of the process of technical exploration was to see which techniques could be combined. During the late 1960s and the 1970s technical experimentation in glass justifiably became the means to an artistic end.

One of the most interesting developments was the extent to which hot and cold techniques were combined. Artists like José Chardiet, Mary van Cline or William Le Quier use a variety of different processes in one piece.

William Le Quier, 'Sentinel Series', blown glass and plate glass, sand-blasted, slumped, cut, polished, acid-etched, assembled and glued. (Photo: D. Schaible)

This poses problems as each different technique requires a specific skill. Some artists prefer to master all the skills they need, whilst others are content to entrust the work to specialist technicians if necessary. Even when they do so, the atmosphere in which the work is created bears little resemblance to the inhibiting confines of industry. Marvin Lipofsky has availed himself of the skills of master glass-blowers like Gianni Toso in Italy or Petr Novotny in Czechoslovakia; Dan Dailey gets invaluable help from the metal-working skills of his wife Linda MacNeil, a distinguished glass artist in her own right; and of course the art of Dale Chihuly is largely dependent upon choosing the right team of workers to execute his ideas. In none of these instances does there have to be any sort of artistic compromise. On the contrary, this marriage of skills seems to work particularly well in glass. The trend has been to choose one technique, like casting or fusing, and then to find ways of refining or embellishing which will add textural content, colour or form. A number of artists whose blowing techniques involve gathering many layers of glass have experimented by slicing into them when the glass is cold to reveal a busy inner life. Josh Simpson, Jon Kuhn and William Carlson (in his earlier pieces) have produced complex imagery using variations of this idea.

As the language of glass has evolved over the last two decades, with its technical vocabulary dramatically increased, more and more choices have become available to those starting out on a career in glass. The problem of young artists in glass today is not that they are limited by their chosen material, but that there is an overwhelming choice of how to work. College leavers are now able to launch themselves from an altogether different

BELOW LEFT: **Jon Kuhn**, 'Petroglyphic Sculpture' series, fused glass

BELOW: **William Carlson**, scent bottle, 1981, blown, cut and polished glass. H. 15 cm (6 in). (Photo: Stephen S. Myers)

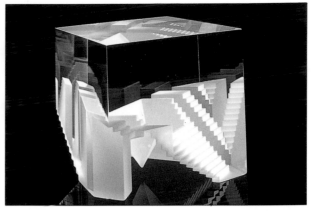

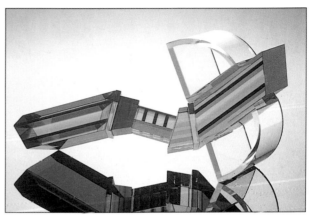

plane, with a sophisticated panorama of recent technical discoveries at their disposal. They have the remarkable spirit of invention of a previous generation of artists to thank for this. When Kreg Kallenberger or Steven Weinberg, for instance, have finished blowing or casting a piece, they set about cutting and polishing, adding to a basic sculptural form with complicated optical effects. Optical cutting and polishing have been used in the making of scientific instruments for a long time, but only recently have artists begun experimenting with them. Kallenberger sometimes also uses lampworking techniques and applied glass in his work. Like so many of their contemporaries, both these artists are using a combination of traditional techniques which have been refined for artistic use.

ABOVE LEFT: **Kreg Kallenberger**, 'Interlock System Series No. 287', 1986, blown, cut and polished glass. 20.5 x 20.5 x 20.5 cm (8 x 8 x 8 in)

ABOVE TOP: **Steven Weinberg**, piece from 'Cubes' series, 1987, cast, cut and polished glass

ABOVE: **Michael Taylor**, 'Photogenerator Series 6', 1986, laminated, cast and cut glass. L. 58.5 cm (23 in)

GLASS-BLOWING

The primary technique in glass, or at any rate the oldest one, is glass-blowing, and new-wave American glass artists of the 1960s were essentially glass-blowers. Glass-blowing was the most noticeable area where there was innovation during this period. Littleton and Lipofsky, and a little later Chihuly, dominated the scene and all of them are still actively involved in making glass twenty-five years on. Some other artists, like Kent Ipsen, John Lewis and Mark Peiser, who were blowing glass during the 1960s, have preferred to move on to other techniques, whilst still other glass-blowers from this period (most of whom were early pupils of either Lipofsky or Littleton, such as Michael Boylen, Donald Carlson, Boris Dudchenko or Frank Kulasiewicz) have either given up or disappeared from view.

American ideas in glass-blowing were related to what was happening in Europe. Littleton's chance meeting with Erwin Eisch in August 1962 at Frauenau had an important influence on the American artist, and in turn on many of his pupils. Littleton reported on Eisch's activities in *Craft Horizons* in 1963. Eisch then came to the first World Crafts Council meeting in 1964 and taught a class with Littleton at the University of Wisconsin that year and again in 1967. News had also reached America about the original blown work of artists like Pavel Hlava and René Roubíček in Czechoslovakia. But by the end of the decade the misshapen bubbles of the 1960s were somewhat played out and attitudes to blowing changed. Today Lipofsky is one of the few American artists whose style remains rooted in the aesthetics of that time. The misshapen bubble relied heavily on chance or accident and certainly there were blown pieces with a great deal of character, but the random approach to glass-blowing obviously has its limitations.

The one glass-blower who has influenced not only this particular technique but the whole spectrum of American glass is Dale Chihuly. 'In his progression from "Indian Blanket" to "Basket" to "Sea" forms to the new series "Macchia", his freedom in working with brilliant and fresh color juxtapositions and his play with diaphanous clarities of glass show him updating art history through an unexplored medium.'[16] Chihuly is, among other things, a consummate showman and has understood the way to win over an American public. In winning glamour for himself he has won it for the art as a whole, and he has allowed many other American artists to be caught up in his success. He displays his sense of showmanship in everything he does. The illustrations in the catalogues he produces are exquisite, setting new standards of excellence for glass photography. The glass-blowing sessions

OPPOSITE: **Dale Chihuly**, pair from 'Macchia' series, 1982, blown glass, threaded and marvered. W. 33 cm (13 in). (Photo: Dick Busher)

BELOW LEFT: **Dale Chihuly**, cylinder, 1984, blown glass with marvered decoration. H. 30.5 cm (12 in). (Photo: Dick Busher)

BELOW: **Dale Chihuly**, 'Sea Form' series, 1984, blown glass. W. 25.5 cm (10 in). (Photo: Dick Busher)

are theatrical events, with artists flown in from around the country, specially chosen music and delicious food.

Chihuly's method of working is to direct a team; he recognizes and acknowledges talent freely, and many of those involved in helping him with his work over the years have become successful artists in their own right. Jamie Carpenter was the first of Chihuly's collaborators to have since achieved renown himself. Flora Mace was instrumental in perfecting the drawing techniques which made Chihuly's Navajo blanket cylinders possible. William Morris was discovered by Chihuly when as a twenty-five-year-old in 1978 he was driving a truck at Pilchuck, and within six years he had developed into an accomplished glass-blower. Today Morris is a virtuoso artist and technician, having learnt much that he now knows in the course of helping Chihuly with his work. 'Chihuly, with his team of skilled artists, has made a permanent mark on the American glass movement. Both the glass and Chihuly's way of working have had an impact on what glass is and how it is made in the US.'[17]

A number of other American glass-blowers have created wonderful 'organic' shapes that make science fiction look more luscious than nature, such as Stephen Dee Edwards with his colourful organic imagery and Flo Perkins with her eccentric plant forms inspired by the desert landscape of her native New Mexico. Both artists finish off their work with a variety of cold processes, but the magic lies in the lifelike quality of the strange inanimate objects they create. Two other artists, Flora Mace and Joey Kirkpatrick, one of the most productive partnerships in the history of contemporary American glass, have used blown shapes to create a menagerie of strange doll-like figures with a character all their own.

ABOVE: **William Morris**, two 'Stone Vessels', 1985, blown glass with applied glass decoration. 42 x 25 cm (16½ x 9¾ in)

OPPOSITE TOP LEFT: **Flo Perkins**, 'Desert Plankton', 1987, blown glass and steel. H. 90–130 cm (35½–51 in)

OPPOSITE BELOW LEFT: **Flora Mace** and **Joey Kirkpatrick**, 'Wishing Will', 1984, blown glass with wire drawings embedded while hot. H. 33 cm (13 in)

OPPOSITE TOP RIGHT: **Flora Mace** and **Joey Kirkpatrick**, 'White Chord', 1986, blown glass and slate. 73.5 x 25.5 x 10 cm (29 x 10 x 4 in)

OPPOSITE BELOW RIGHT: **Stephen Dee Edwards**, 'Pink Tripod', 1982, blown glass, sand-blasted and acid-etched. H. 30.5 cm (12 in)

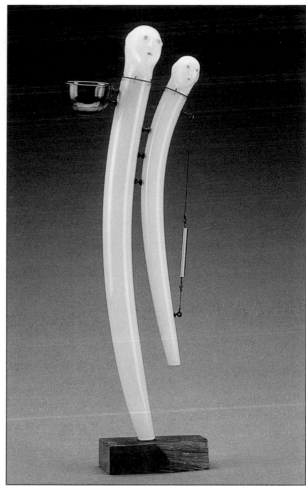

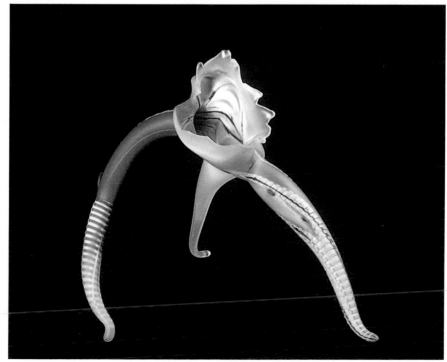

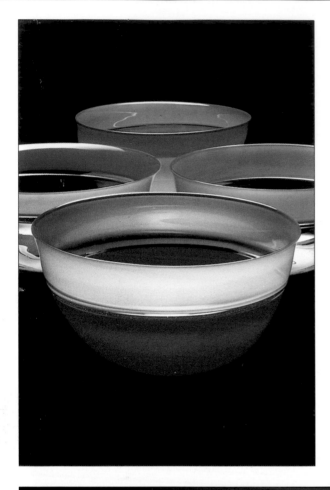

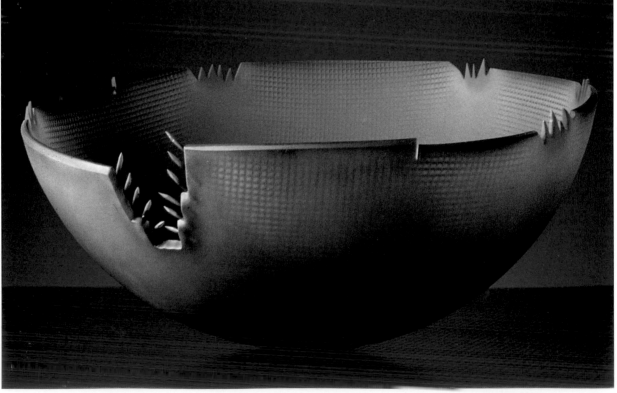

Other glass-blowers are more vessel-orientated. The most traditional American vessel maker is perhaps Sonia Blomdahl, but her blown bowls in brightly contrasting primary colours are more than simply functional vessels. She sees them as symbols of wholeness and balance, and has turned the process of combining two coloured bubbles of glass into an art form. She puts heart and soul into making her work, and her efforts to create a perfect balance of colour and form go beyond anything for which there might be time in an industrial situation.

There is great variety in the way American glass-blowers coaxed the basic bubble away from symmetry. The generation of glass artists who followed the first Wisconsin alumni realized that distortion was not the only way of turning the bubble into art. Thomas Patti's basic bubbles are beautifully controlled and often provide a focal point of balance within his complex abstract imagery. Form is an essential factor in the work of Joel Philip Myers and Jay Musler, who use their glass-blowing skills to create the forms which they later embellish in a variety of ways. James Harmon and Robert Levin also rely on their blowing skills, both of them assembling an assortment of blown shapes in their work, but with completely different results. William Bernstein has developed a technique using hot cane to 'draw' colourful portraits on glass. The recurring imagery in his work includes self-portraits, his balding father, and a nude female with a snapping dog or lizard. His impressionist portraiture is expressive and remarkably relaxed considering the complexity of the skills involved. So although glass-blowing has perhaps been less to the fore in more recent work, it remains an essential glass-making skill, and one which can be used in an infinite variety of ways to expand the art form.

OPPOSITE TOP LEFT: **Sonia Blomdahl**, bowls, 1982, blown glass. 15 x 30.5 cm (6 x 12 in) each

OPPOSITE BELOW: **Jay Musler**, 'Overrule', 1981, oil paint on pyrex. 43 x 18 cm (17 x 7 in)

OPPOSITE TOP RIGHT: **James Harmon**, wall piece, 1987, blown glass and neon

William Bernstein, goblets, 1983, blown glass with coloured cane portrait drawings. H. 16 cm (6¼ in)

ABOVE: **Joel Philip Myers**, untitled sculpture – vase, 1985, blown glass with applied elements. 38 x 33 x 7.5 cm (15 x 13 x 3 in)

LEFT: **Joel Philip Myers**, untitled sculpture – vase, 1980, blown glass with applied decoration. H. 23 cm (9 in)

WARM TECHNIQUES

There are very few hot glass-making techniques apart from blowing, although several additive processes, like casing or marquetry, are carried out while the glass is hot and tend only to be used in conjunction with glass-blowing. Joel Philip Myers must be the first abstract artist to use marquetry with the skill of a painter. In his 'Contiguous Fragment' series the vessels are

free-blown and then decorated using a glass marquetry technique (in which glass elements are inlaid onto a body of glass). This technique has been painstakingly developed by Myers over the years. The elements he uses are made by blowing large thin-walled bubbles of opaque coloured glass, which are then cooled and cut into fragments with a hot wire. Using a hand torch, Myers then fuses these elements onto the surface of the glass. He uses hot,

Joel Philip Myers,
'CFGREEBKSG 19883', 1988,
blown glass with applied
elements. H. 38 cm (15 in),
W. 42.5 cm (16¾ in)

Paul Stankard, 'Cactus with Spirits', cloistered botanical, 1986, encased lampwork (cut and laminated by Jim Shaw). 14.5 x 7 cm (5¾ x 2¾ in). (Photo: Heller Gallery, New York)

cold, and what might be referred to as 'warm' techniques. This term was coined fairly recently and is described by the artist Valerie Arber, in relation to her own work, as 'a term that covers all the glass processes done primarily in a kiln such as fusing, slumping and enamelling'.[18] Basically this means any techniques which do not require the sort of extreme heat necessary for glass-blowing.

One can include lampwork in this category, a technique that was developed mainly in East Germany. It is used either as a way of making paperweights or to bend and shape thin rods of glass at will. In America Paul Stankard has been making paperweights since 1969; his art is so individual that it is in a class of its own, and yet in spirit he is very much one of the new-wave American glass artists. He abandoned a career as a scientific

ABOVE LEFT: **Valerie S. Arber**, 'Static Bend', 1981, kiln-formed and sand-blasted glass. Diam. 18 cm (7 in)

ABOVE: **Mark Peiser**, 'Palms and Moon', 1980, clear glass encasing lampwork decoration, blown. H. 35.5 cm (14 in)

Mark Peiser, 'Burning Bridges', 1986, cast, cut and polished glass sculpture. 20 × 23.5 × 12.5 cm (7¾ × 9¼ × 5 in)

instrument maker when he discovered the artistic possibilities of glass during the 1960s. His primary goal has been to 'create botanical realism with glass'.[19] In some ways his art is timeless and his work has much in common with that of the great paperweight makers of the past; but because he works on his own account and need not make economics his prime consideration, he has been able to develop the art far beyond its existing limits. The detailed poetry of his work lies in meticulously accurate observation of nature, combined with a willingness to spend the time and energy re-creating every detail. Mark Peiser also used what is basically a paperweight technique from 1975 to 1981, but after this time he felt he had come to the end of what he could express in that way and he abandoned the technique. During that period, however, he created 'Idylls of quiet beauty that

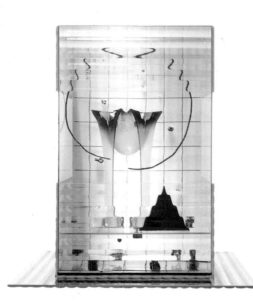

FAR LEFT: **Ginny Ruffner**, 'The Goddess of the Neon Tetras shows off her new oven mitts', 1987, lampwork glass and oil pastels. 48 x 38 x 30.5 cm (19 x 15 x 12 in)

LEFT: **Sydney D. Cash**, untitled sculpture, 1983, slumped glass and other materials. 56 x 40.5 x 28 cm (22 x 16 x 11 in). (Arlene & Raymond Zimmerman)

belied the intractable materials of lampworked glass'.[20] Ginny Ruffner has used the lampworking technique to create very different effects. In her hands lampworked glass looks like a three-dimensional coloured drawing; the fragility of the glass is emphasized by her use of other techniques, including sand-blasting, and colouring with acrylic paint and pastel.

One can see why slumping techniques (letting sheet glass sag slowly but systematically in the heat of the kiln) appealed to the first generation of new American glass artists. One of the earliest to experiment with it at that time was Sydney Cash, who has remained faithful to the technique for a long time and still continues to make artistic discoveries slumping glass over wire. His story is typical of what has made contemporary American glass so special. 'One year I sent up balloons. I thought I wanted to be an aeronautical engineer. I entered college in metallurgical engineering and ended up going through physics and finally wound up getting a degree in mathematics.'[21] He then worked at Bloomingdales and afterwards opened a trendy shop in SoHo, New York, selling a variety of items including mirrors. It was these that led him to glass. His own words reveal something about how artists of his generation made technical choices:

> I was a kind of hippie and my sense of spirituality was a little bit theatrical, like the times were. I had this feeling that glass and I were part of the drama that was going on in my life. It was a very romantic time. I discovered things by observation, by experimentation. . . . I take a sheet of glass and turn it into something with three dimensions, something that I've never seen before. That's exciting. A lot of the forms are discoveries. I have an idea what will occur, but there's a great sense of discovery when I come in the next day and pull the work out of the kiln.[22]

The same combined issues of risk and control led Mary Shaffer to experiment with slumped glass. Unlike Cash she uses stacks of sheet glass; those at the top are exposed to higher temperatures and slump more readily, providing a dramatic contrast with the glass in the lower half of the stack which

OPPOSITE: **Mary Shaffer**, sculpture, 1985, bronze and slumped glass. H. 210 cm (82½ in). (Photo: George Erml)

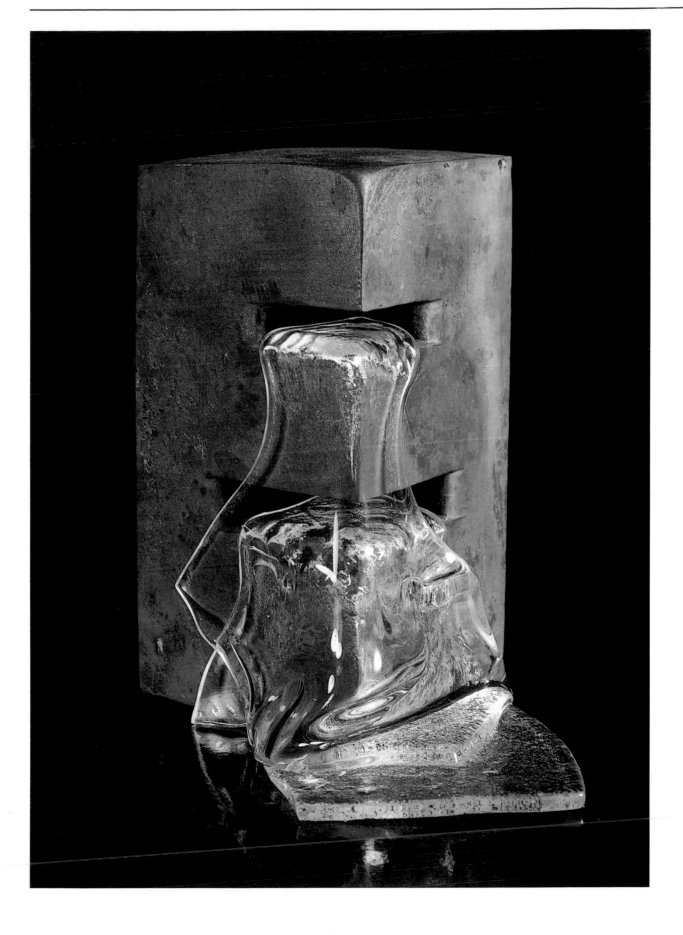

bends and sags less. The framework over and into which the glass stretches as it heats plays an important role. In the beginning Mary Shaffer used heavy chains, but later she used thin baling wire. Generally she works on a larger scale than Cash, and whilst the two share some of the same concerns, the contrast in their work serves to illustrate what varied results different artists can achieve using similar methods. Richard Lalonde and Ruth Brockmann also use similar slumping techniques (combined with fusing), but their work relies much more on bright colouring. Once again the two artists use closely related techniques, but whereas Lalonde is primarily a vessel maker, Brockmann is not (she is a caricaturist who makes vivid masks using this technique), and the technical similarity is in no way disturbing.

Most warm techniques involve the use of a kiln either for fusing or casting. In the hands of artists such as Howard Ben Tré, Steven Weinberg and Stephen Dale Edwards different casting techniques have resulted in some amazing sculptural imagery over the past two decades. All of these artists, and many more besides who cast in glass, are sculptors who, had they not been living and working in the latter part of the twentieth century would never have dreamt of working in glass. In the recent past, however, American artists have left us in no doubt that glass is as viable and varied a material for sculpture as others that have been tested and tried for much longer. It is, above all, the only material which lets light pass through it, illuminating the piece from within as well as from outside; and because light can also be blocked out from specific areas, whilst being allowed to travel through others, glass-casting allows the artist who knows how to work in this way greater flexibility than is possible with any other cast material. As Howard Ben Tré has shown in his more recent work it is just as suitable for monumental work as it is for the smallest sculptures. To any sculptor in the making, Ben Tré's work must suggest that glass is one of the most inviting materials available for sculpture today. To those who criticize the medium for being too complicated technically to allow an artist complete freedom, one must reply that the technical skills are comparable to those required by any sculptor using one of the many metal-working techniques available, which, like glass techniques, are based on industrial processes.

Those artists who are technically minded find themselves at a considerable advantage in this computer age. The great difference in glass technology for artists is that until recently it could not be taught in art schools; it had to be invented first, and for artists like Ben Tré who have been responsible for much that can now be taken for granted, the process has been a combination of technical invention and self-discovery. Ben Tré says, 'In learning how to put myself in my work, I learn about myself, which is what interested me in art in the first place.'[23]

It is the range of Ben Tré's imagination as a sculptor that is so impressive. Whatever the scale of his work, which over a period of ten years has gone from table size to monumental, one is as much struck by the sheer skill of his pieces as by their rich visual imagery and commanding presence. They are cast in a factory in Brooklyn, using the sand-casting method, and finished in his Providence, Rhode Island studio with a texture evocative of buried treasure or decaying ruins. During this period there have been three phases in his work: from 1977 to 1978 his smaller ritualistic pieces were inspired by early Chinese bronzes and also by medieval church floor plans;

Richard Lalonde, 'Long Amazonia', 1986, fused and slumped glass. 30.5 x 48 x 53.5 cm (12 x 19 x 21 in)

Ruth Brockmann, 'Crocodile Man', 1985, fused and slumped glass. 43 x 40 x 14 cm (17 x 15¾ x 5½ in)

in the two following years his pieces resembled machinery parts; and most recently his pieces suggest architectural fragments.

Steven Weinberg does not use colour. He uses the transparency of the glass to create elaborate imagery in which there are intricate frozen patterns of geometric design and veiled effects which seem to play visual games as one moves around the piece. Stephen Dale Edwards is one of the few artists who is skilled as a glass-blower and also makes cast pieces. He has travelled widely to New Guinea, Thailand, Egypt and other parts of Africa, and has been influenced by the folk art of these countries.

A great many Americans have experimented with casting, all of them developing personal skills to suit their artistic needs. Some use cast elements as part of a larger piece, such as Richard Posner with his collages made up of numerous 'bits and pieces', or Mary van Cline, whose sculptural pieces include cast elements. In the case of other artists, including Stephen Nelson and Susan Shapiro, casting plays a more fundamental role. For the

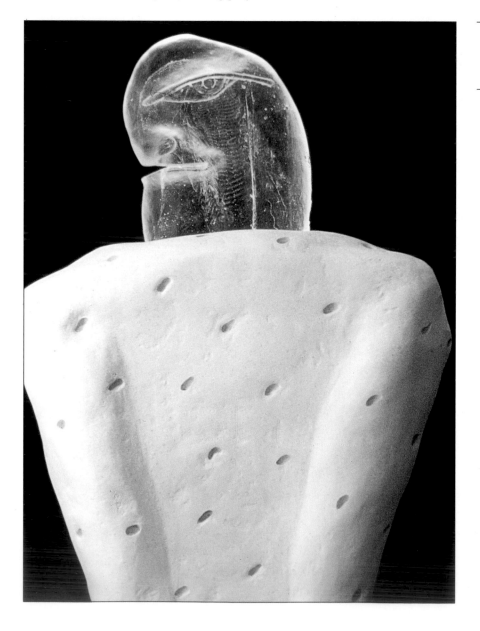

Stephen Dale Edwards, 'Man', cast glass and concrete (light inside body). 135 × 90 × 30 cm (53 × 35½ × 11¾ in)

glass artist wishing to work alone in his studio, casting has the advantage of demanding comparatively manageable machinery, unless, as with Ben Tré, the cast elements grow to monumental proportions, necessitating industrial-sized kilns.

Pâte de verre also involves casting skills and has proved very popular recently, treacherous though it can be as a working method. It is a process in which crushed or broken glass is placed in a mould and then fuses to form an opaque substance when fired in a kiln. After a long period in oblivion, the technique was revived and developed by a number of French artists (Henri Cros, Georges Despret, Gabriel Argy-Rousseau and Almeric Walter) in the first thirty years of this century. Several Americans have chosen this technique to work in, with astonishing and varied results. Doug Anderson has followed closely in the footsteps of his French predecessors, Almeric Walter in particular, with a series of pieces which bear an uncanny resemblance to reality. His imagery is usually taken directly from nature, but sometimes he plays with unusual juxtapositions using unrelated subjects – a pair of pliers, an envelope, or a toy motorcar – in conjunction with flora and fauna. It is realism that borders on the surreal. Karla Trinkley, on the other hand, is less concerned with imitation; she has developed a dis-

ABOVE LEFT: **Doug Anderson**, 'Flower Patch', 1988, *pâte de verre* and lost-wax casting. 2 x 20.5 x 35.5 cm (¾ x 8 x 14 in)

ABOVE: **Karla Trinkley**, 'Perriwinkle', 1985, *pâte de verre*. H. 14 cm (5½ in)

Mary van Cline, 'Directional Time Flow', 1986, flat glass and other materials. 51 x 66 x 51 cm (20 x 26 x 20 in)

tinctive style with ritualistic vessels that look like fossilized micro-architectural forms with revealed constructional detail.

Both these artists are making increasingly large pieces as they feel surer of the technique. Anderson created 'Finders Creepers', a 77 cm (30½ in) slice of woodland floor complete with ivy, pine cones, vines and a snake, which won him a major prize from Corning Museum of Glass. One of Karla Trinkley's most recent pieces (which combines *pâte de verre*, concrete, glass, plaster and paint) measures 113 × 38 × 13 cm (44½ × 15 × 5 in). Another artist, Tina Marie Aufiero, works in the same medium but is more concerned with figural representation, with 'the figure and its placement in the landscape. The landscape is a metaphor of form. It is where the figure lies, nestled, wrapped and dreaming.'[24]

The process of fusing glass is by no means limited to *pâte de verre*. Many American artists have been interested in the artistic possibilities of laminating, fusing or bonding sheets of glass which can then be worked on in a variety of ways. The glass can be colourless, tinted or opaque, and American artists in particular have found the soft look and the wide colour range of Vitrolite very tempting to work with. David Huchthausen, in a series called 'Leitungs Scherben' made of laminated Vitrolite which has been polished and cut, has worked round a central theme, infinitely varied by colour and form. He refers to his work as 'enigmatic artefacts, fragments ripped away from a larger structure, alluding to some previous existence or purpose'.[25] The hard-edged, sophisticated, brightly coloured pieces are crisp and clean-cut. Without any hint of plagiarism, the work of a number of American artists has ended up with a similar look. William Carlson, whose sculptural pieces combine clear glass and Vitrolite, feels that the process came as naturally to him as blowing did when he first started working in glass. Both for

ABOVE LEFT: **Tina Marie Aufiero**, 'King Q', cast glass. 30.5 x 25.5 x 10 cm (12 x 10 x 4 in)

ABOVE: **David Huchthausen**, piece from 'Leitungs Scherben' series, 1984, fused, cut and laminated glass. (Photo: Roy Adams)

OPPOSITE: **William Carlson**, 'Contrapunctual' series, 1984, cast, laminated, cut, ground and polished optical glass and granite. H. 43 cm (17 in)

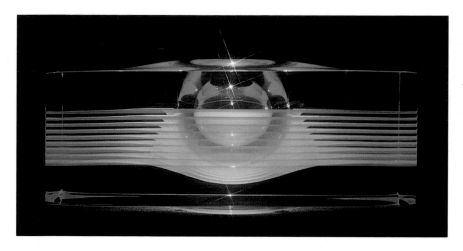

Tom Patti, 'Compacted Solarized Band', 1987, stacked, fused, blown and polished glass. L. 15 cm (6 in)

him and others working in similar techniques, part of the attraction lies in the twofold nature of the work involved. 'Up to a certain point all the work, the casting, the laminations, is additive. Then all of a sudden I have begun to reduce it by cutting and grinding.'[26] It is a method that allows a wide range of visual effects. Michael Taylor's glass constructions also use laminating techniques combined with cutting and polishing.

Two artists who use variations of the technique, but rely less on colour, are Thomas Patti and Sidney Hutter, though their work is in no way comparable. Thomas Patti's work makes one feel that he is perfectly in tune with his time and his own comments might explain why: 'It is integral in my work to force the relationship of art and technology.'[27] He feels that the artist owes it to his material to give it artistic credibility. 'If the material can justify its presence in the object and you can see its beauty, then you've given it a right to exist.'[28] The work is technically very complex, though it gives the appearance of being simplicity itself, and Patti works very slowly. When writing about him in 1983 Paul Hollister counted that he had produced only about eighty pieces in eight years. Despite his limited output, however, he is considered to be one of America's leading artists in glass. Sidney Hutter has chosen a less complex working method but has managed to create an immediately recognizable style with a series of laminated plate-

Tom Patti, 'Survey Slider', 1985, water, glass. 1.2 x 8 x 7 m (4 x 26 x 23 ft)

OPPOSITE: **Sidney R. Hutter**, 'Quasi Modern No. 3 and Vase', 1988, cut, ground, laminated and polished plate glass. 67 x 42 x 42 cm (26½ x 16½ x 16½ in) and 60 x 40 x 40 cm (23½ x 15¾ x 15¾ in). (Photo: Charles Mayer)

glass vessel forms, which have occupied him for nearly ten years. In contrast with Patti he is immensely productive and is content to play around endlessly with variations of the same formula.

COLD PROCESSES

Hot and warm techniques are nearly always embellished or finished off with one of the innumerable cold methods of working, many of which are less awesome and labour-intensive to use. One can cut, polish, engrave, grind or sand-blast with comparatively simple equipment, but, depending on individual skills, to great effect. There are also numerous options for adding colour using oil paint, acrylic or enamel paint. Choosing the right method to achieve a desired effect is part of the skill involved in being a glass artist. Sand-blasting seems to have been one of the most popular ways of treating a glass surface among American artists. The abrasive effect of sand propelled under pressure onto the surface of glass can shape an object or change its surface from shiny to matt. It is one of the most effective ways of altering texture in glass and allows for subtle graduations, producing softer and subtler results than cutting or polishing. In many instances it prepares the surface of the glass better and provides a more welcoming ground for colouring agents. It can also be used after the colour has been applied in order to reveal areas of the glass surface, allowing light into the piece in varying degrees that can be subtly controlled. Margie Jervis and Susie Krasnican produce work in which an almost silken surface texture is achieved by sandblasting. James Watkins and Howard Ben Tré has each developed a very personal way of sand-blasting to create painterly effects. It is not however the technicalities of sand-blasting in their work that strike you in the first

BELOW LEFT: **Margie Jervis** and **Susie Krasnican**, 'Folded Silhouette' (Blue Pitcher and Glasses), 1984, fused plate glass, sand-blasted and enamelled. 29 x 15 x 7.5 cm (11½ x 6 x 3 in)

BELOW: **Margie Jervis** and **Susie Krasnican**, 'Double Folded Silhouette', 1984, fused plate glass, sand-blasted and enamelled. 34.5 x 20.5 x 9 cm (13½ x 8 x 3½ in)

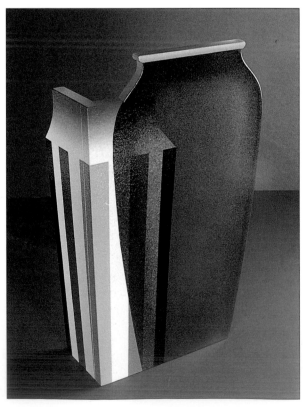

James Watkin, 'Head and Book', 1988, glass, oil paint, epoxy resin and wood. 28 x 45.5 x 7.5 cm (11 x 18 x 3 in). (Photo: Barnaby Evans)

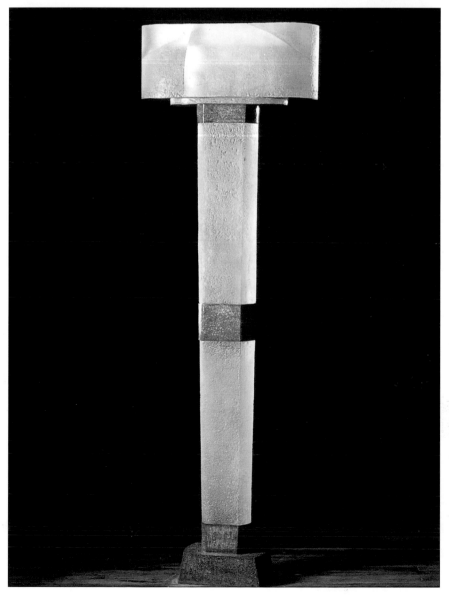

Howard Ben Tré, 'Column 39', 1987, cast glass and copper. H. 236 cm (93 in). (Los Angeles County Museum of Art, California)

David Schwarz, untitled glass sculpture, 1987, blown, overlaid, sand-blasted, ground and polished glass. 30.5 x 28 x 45.5 cm (12 x 11 x 18 in). (Photo: Joe Feldsman)

Keke Cribbs, 'Hurricane Jezzabell', 1985, blown, overlaid, sand-blasted glass. 30 x 17 cm (11¾ x 6¾ in).

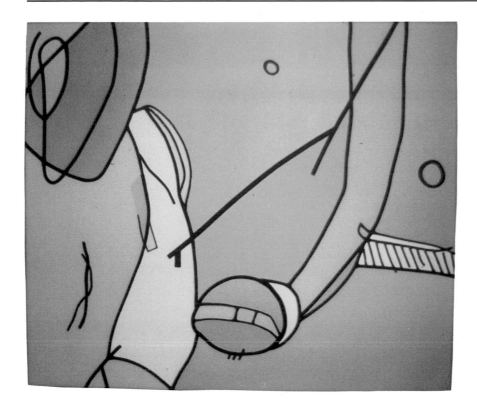

Robert Kehlmann,
'Composition XXXIX', 1977,
glass, lead, appliquéd glass form.
80 x 92 cm (31 ½ x 36 in). (Leigh
Yawkey Woodson Art Museum)

instance, but rather the sensuous overall effect of the work, which then leads you to wonder how it is done. David Schwarz uses sand-blasting and cutting on his blown forms to move, bend and distort space and reality; the facets he creates provide optical windows which lead the viewer towards the interiors of his pieces. He draws directly onto his cased glass vessel forms with tape, laying boundaries which are then cut, polished or sandblasted to achieve the desired effect. Keke Cribbs also uses sand-blasting in mixed-media work which, apart from the glass she uses, can incorporate wood, papier mâché, beads, shells and paint. Her work is both humorous and decorative and often inspired by American Indian art (particularly that of the prehistoric Mimbres Indian tribe). Joel Philip Myers, Jay Musler,

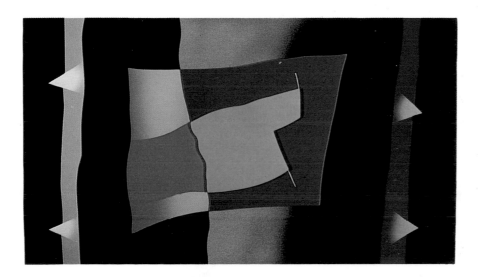

Henry Halem, untitled piece,
1983, multi-coloured Vitrolite,
cut, sand-blasted, polished and
assembled. 61 x 104 cm
(24 x 41 in)

Robert Kehlmann and Henry Halem, all of whom use a lot of colour in their work, are some of the many other artists whose working methods include sand-blasting.

Cutting the glass deeper and creating sharper angles for the light to catch has always been a concern of glass-makers. The unique way in which light can travel through glass and the possibility offered of changing its trajectory by cutting into its surface allow for dramatic visual effects. Glass-cutting has become infinitely more sophisticated during the course of the twentieth century and there has been a good deal of experimentation with all methods, from diamond-point engraving to slicing with optical cutting. As with gemstones, the more a piece is cut the greater its brilliance from refracted light; the effects are most dramatic when the glass is crystal clear, as in the Steuben pieces already referred to. Among American artists who use this technique one thinks of Steven Weinberg, Kreg Kallenberger or Larry Bell, all of whom are concerned with exploiting the inherent beauty of glass. But Michael Cohn, in his series of 'Space Cups' and a more recent series

Michael Cohn, 'Space Cup', 1988, blown glass. 18 x 40 x 26 cm (7 x 15¾ x 10¼ in)

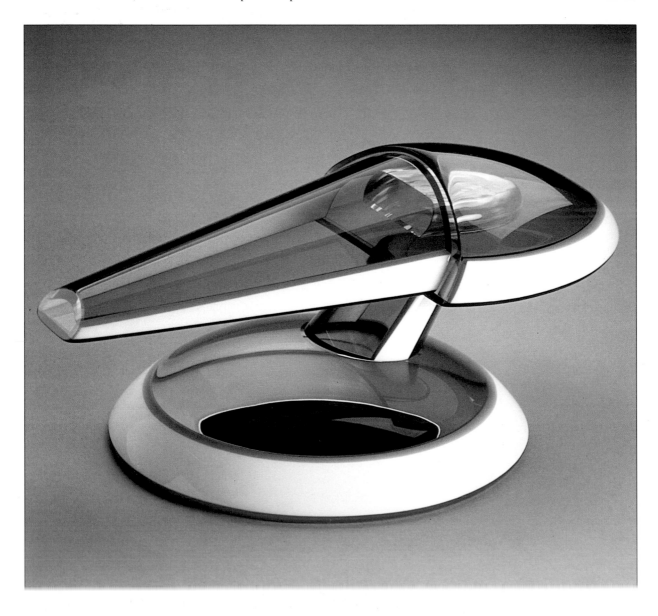

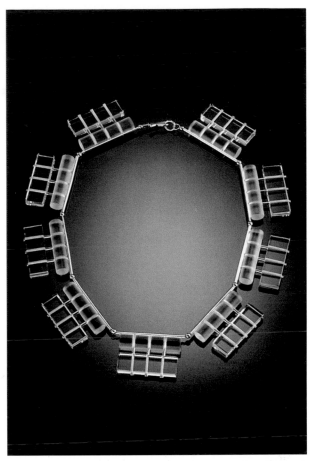

entitled 'Roll Over Mondrian and Tell Brancusi the News', uses cutting equally dramatically in coloured pieces, with the intention of 'focusing all visual effect on form and surface'.[29]

OBJETS DE VERTU IN GLASS

American glass artists have responded strongly to machine aesthetic from the smallest precision instrument to the heavy metal that goes into outer space. Some create jewel-like objects and there are a number of areas where the art of the jeweller, metalsmith and glass-maker overlap. Screws become ornamental details; intricately worked metal elements assume a vital artistic role. The work of Linda MacNeil comes to mind. Some of the things she makes using glass are intended to be wearable jewellery. She started out as a metal-worker and then began incorporating glass in her work. From necklaces, brooches and bracelets, she moved to a series of hand-mirrors, a crossbreed between jewellery and sculpture. Metal and glass are of equal importance in her work, and recently she has progressed to other materials, such as granite. For her the joy lies in the hands-on experience of making; she is a model builder who because she is also an artist can put her whole self into each object.

Linda MacNeil is married to Dan Dailey, whose wit, imagination and skill have been responsible for some of the most memorable work in American glass. One is convinced by it because of the complete satisfaction it gives. He is a brilliant raconteur who chose glass as his main vehicle for

ABOVE LEFT: **Linda MacNeil**, vase, 1984, plate glass, etched, with nickel-plated brass. 38 × 15 × 15 cm (15 × 6 × 6 in)

ABOVE: **Linda MacNeil**, neckpiece, 1984, etched and polished glass, and gold

Dan Dailey, 'Elvis-Caligula', 1986, blown glass, sand-blasted and acid-etched. H. 29 cm (11½ in)

BELOW: Dan Dailey, 'Sick as a Dog', 1984, Vitrolite, nickel-plated brass. 30.5 x 40.5 x 25.5 cm (12 x 16 x10 in)

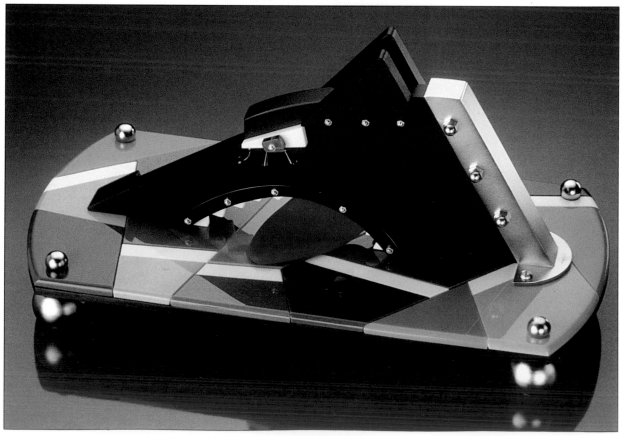

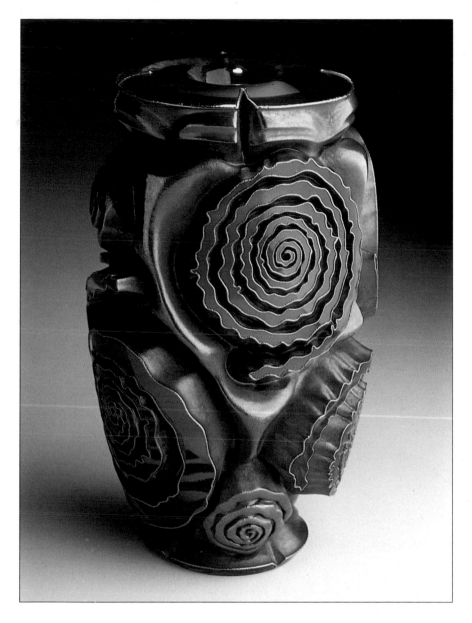

Michael Glancy, 'Iconistic Vortex', 1985, blown and sand-blasted glass. H. 25.5 cm (10 in)

expression. Whether he is working as a designer for Daum in Nancy or at his own studio near Boston, Massachusetts, the flow of epigrammatic humour seems unending. This, combined with a vivid technical imagination and a remarkable talent for choosing what materials to put together, gives his work seductive, instant charm as well as durability. They are period pieces, unmistakably of their time, but because they are the best of their kind they are destined to last well into the future. Is he a comedian, a glass artist, a skilled metal-worker or a clever technician? Perhaps he is all of these; but what counts is that Dailey has an individual talent which is self-evident however one chooses to describe it.

Michael Glancy is another artist whose skills as a metal-worker make one think of jewellery. Like a jeweller setting precious stones, he sets glass in metal, often giving it a gem-like quality. His work demands a specific kind of taste and receives mixed reactions in the glass world, but for those who appreciate 'objets de vertu', these are the ultimate objects of our time.

Howard Ben Tré, 'Blenko Project No. 2', 1982, glass and copper. H. 81 cm (32 in)

SPECIAL TECHNIQUES

In glass, as with all art forms, technique is the basic handwriting of an artist. But the true test of artistry is what can be said once the handwriting has been formed. Some glass artists in the 1970s were unable to go beyond the first stage, but a surprising number have had something worthwhile to say. Technique played an unusually important part; at times one got the impression that unless an artist was able to demonstrate some kind of new technical wizardry, there was no point in his work being shown in public. There was an obsession with 'making it new'. Some managed to do this very successfully, extending both technical and artistic barriers at the same time. Dale Chihuly did it with his blowing methods, Howard Ben Tré with his casting methods, and Thomas Patti with his laminated forms. There were also some particularly ingenious inventions, like the wire-drawing techniques of Flora Mace, first developed at Pilchuck. When she was working with Dale Chihuly on his Navajo blanket cylinders in the mid 1970s she said, 'I was still oriented towards sculpture and didn't think I'd ever work in glass, but welding brought me to glass through that flow of line.'[30]

Other techniques are less ingenious, but simple ideas like Concetta Mason's system of 'controlled breaking' can have considerable impact. She 'cracks blown glass with purposeful control'.[31] The broken pieces are then treated in a variety of ways (with painting or sand-blasting) and fired once more. The fragments are finally assembled into sculptural forms. In the beginning Paul Seide's idea of being an artist in neon was remarkable enough, but the way he has developed the art since he began working in that medium has given it a completely new lease of life, particularly since his recent highly successful experiments in which he uses it in combination with other glass techniques.

ABOVE: **Paul Seide**, 'Bio Morphic', 'Cloud' series, 1988, glass and neon sculpture. 45.5 x 20.5 x 30.5 cm (18 x 8 x 12 in)

BELOW: **Concetta Mason**, 'Cosmic Flare', 1987, blown glass, precision-broken, sand-blasted, enamelled and reassembled. 28 x 15 x 15 cm (11 x 6 x 6 in)

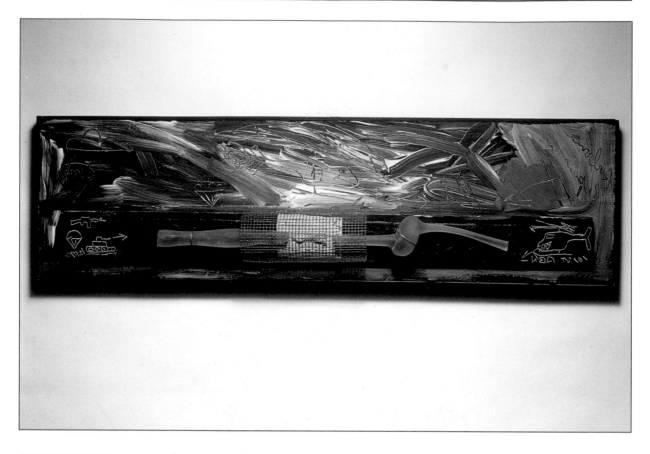

MIXED MEDIA

There has been such a wealth of technical invention among artists working in and around the glass world over the past quarter of a century that a reaction against it is inevitable. During the 1970s artists had no pangs of conscience about using technique for artistic effect in the way they did. The results show that, for a while at any rate, original techniques were considered a viable form of artistic inspiration in the glass world; that there was a place for heart and soul in technical invention. But like all sources of inspiration in the art world, this one began to run dry. Technical prowess came to be regarded with suspicion and artists began looking for a new kind of impetus to carry them forward.

One solution to this problem was a change of emphasis by combining glass with other materials. This was an obvious development as technical experimentation was partly to do with using glass in new contexts anyway. Michael Aschenbrenner was one of the first glass artists to attract attention with his unexpected juxtaposition of materials. He served in Vietnam and was wounded in the leg, an experience which inspired his 'Damaged Bone Series: Chronicle 1968', a mixed-media mural measuring 3×4.5 m (10×25 ft). 'What perceptive writers about war have said in words, Aschenbrenner appears to have said in glass, string and twigs.'[32] Another artist, Susan Stiensmuehlen, uses available commercial glass in her collages, freely adding paint, glitter and bits and pieces of other materials. Found objects definitely have a part to play in American glass, particularly among artists who use collage or those who assemble numerous elements to make sculptural icons describing some kind of 'secret world'. The debris that goes

Michael Aschenbrenner, 'Airborne Repair Kit', 1981, glass, paint on wood. 114 × 30.5 × 10 cm (45 × 12 × 4 in)

Susan Stiensmuehlen, 'Bobo the Harlequin', 1984, parts blown, hand-rolled glass, painted, with various metals. 90 x 55 cm (35½ x 21½ in)

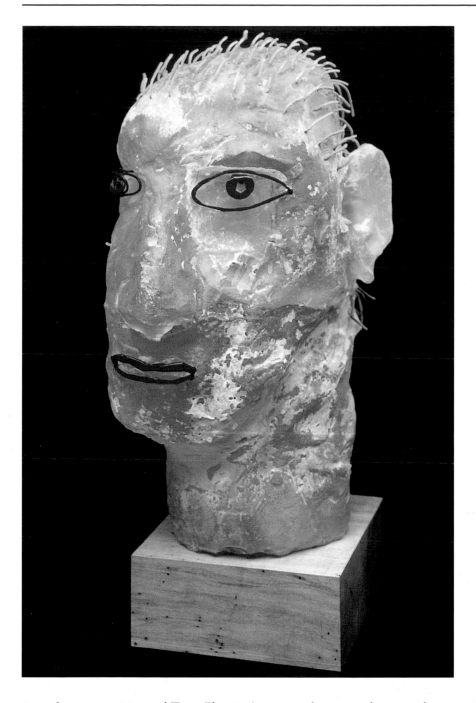

Hank Murta Adams, 'Noke', 1986, cast and blown glass, and copper

into the composition of Tom Fleming's pieces, for example, is made up mostly of broken glass fragments which take on an unexpected air of non-glassiness by the time he has finished with them. Hank Murta Adams makes sculpture full of wit and imagination, usually with a leaning towards the grotesque for which he has a highly developed sense. The glass elements in his work, just like the other materials he uses, seem perfectly cast in the various roles they are called on to play.

There is now a growing tendency among artists to find out what happens to glass if one can resist the temptation of being seduced by its natural beauty. Whilst one group of artists has been endlessly fascinated by working the material to its limits and making artistic statements that are primarily to

OPPOSITE: **Thomas M. Fleming**, 'Gaea's Travois', 1988, blown, slumped and found glass, broken or cut and assembled. 66 x 66 x 7.5 cm (26 x 26 x 3 in)

do with the intrinsic prettiness of glass, amongst other artists there has recently been less reverence. Glass is now often used more as a background and is surprisingly flexible in this role. Many whose talents might in the past have led them to a career in painting on canvas or sculpting in bronze are today attracted by the extra dimension that recent developments in glass have brought to the art world. Thermon Statom does not show much respect for glass. In a statement made about work included in the 1984 'Americans in Glass' exhibition at the Leigh Yawkey Woodson Art Museum in Wausau, Wisconsin, he wrote, 'These pieces are representative of the most recent type of work that I am doing that utilize glass. I would have preferred that they were made of ice; then they would melt, be cold and disappear. But they aren't and the glass has done adequately for now.'[33]

Thermon Statom, 'Chair', c. 1982, assembled sheet glass, painted. (Galerie Clara Scremini, Paris)

Italo Scanga, untitled piece, 1987, glass, china and enamel paint. H. 33 cm (13 in)

Statom is one of a number of artists whose work suggests a broader approach which will extricate those involved in glass from the ghetto in which they have become trapped. Those who love glass for its own sake do not necessarily love the work of Thermon Statom, but he has nevertheless been instrumental in encouraging important moves away from glassiness. James Watkins is another artist whose work has a feeling of general culture rather than glass culture about it, and yet one is very conscious of the glass content of his work. He has found the way to use all the advantages of the material without letting it dominate, and is painter, sculptor and glass artist all in one. Henry Halem and Robert Kehlmann have also managed to achieve a balance in which the glass serves their need rather than the other way around. Halem loves and respects the material but does not let it take over: 'I pay attention to the voice of the material and the poetry of my ideas.'[34] Kehlmann, in the attitudes he expresses as well as in the glass he makes, fights against categorization.

This elimination of barriers takes some getting used to. There is always a degree of reluctance in accepting new developments until one has established comfortable points of reference with the past, but the way forward demands a degree of intellectual courage from artist and viewer alike. No sooner have we grown accustomed to the idea of glass being an acceptable art form which can be admired for its own sake, than we are asked not to think this way. A new generation of artists, as well as some not so new, have for some time been pushing for a change. Italo Scanga has been involved

Narcissus Quagliata, stained and leaded glass piece

with glass for over a decade, but it would be too restricting to call him a glass artist. As he says of himself, 'I've been involved with glass though I'm basically a sculptor.'[35] Without being obsessed by it he uses glass with great sensitivity in his work and freely admits that for him part of the attraction lies in the mechanics of glass-making: 'The glass shop was like a battlefield, with explosions and all of those violent tools.'[36] Narcissus Quagliata should also be included in the history of contemporary glass, although glassiness is not necessarily his primary concern; but he is important because he uses glass without any hint of its being a craft material.

SUMMARY

Ultimately any attempt to put American glass into categories fails. The moment one has decided one way, one realizes that any number of other ways would have been equally satisfactory. Apart from the convenience of doing so, it is something of a pointless exercise to place all makers of cast glass in the same category or to try to force all glass-blowers to be considered together. In other areas of the arts there is talk of 'schools' or 'movements'. Apart from the glass movement itself, there has been nothing similar in the American world of glass. In the beginning the influence of Harvey Littleton was obvious, but after the seeds of a new art form had been sown by him, everybody went their own way. Obviously teachers like Chihuly, Lipofsky and Dailey have had an influence; the 'star system' is a part of the American way of life and exists just as much in the glass world. Americans react enthusiastically to stars, and to a certain extent the public demands them and the system (galleries, museum shows, literature) caters to this need.

In the best American tradition contemporary American glass has been about the freedom and glorification of the individual and the glass artist has been encouraged to do his own thing. In terms of sheer originality one could not ask for a more exciting or productive period than the last twenty-five years have been. If there is one thing that has united glass artists, it is their commitment to being taken seriously as artists. Doubts have been expressed about the viability of such an aim and from time to time there has been a note of despair. David Huchthausen wrote in 1981, 'The "Studio Movement" has re-written the history of glass in twenty short years but has had virtually no impact whatsoever on the history of art.'[37] But as glass recovers from a period of introspection it is more and more able to address itself to similar aesthetic concerns as mainstream visual arts. It makes no sense to try to aim for the same goals as artists working in other media; an artist's chosen material is bound to limit his possibilities. The important point about Americans in glass is that they have proved to themselves, to their public and, most important of all, to generations to come, that an artist can entrust his soul to glass.

3. CZECHOSLOVAKIA AND EASTERN EUROPE

CZECHOSLOVAKIA

Whilst in American glass history there is little worth recording that happened over a hundred years ago, European tradition goes back many centuries. One of the most important glass centres since the fourteenth century has been Bohemia, which of course embraces what is today called Czechoslovakia. An interchange of ideas already existed between America and Bohemia during the Art Nouveau period; in the last decade of the nineteenth century Bohemian glass-makers reacted eagerly to the ideas of Louis Comfort Tiffany, and from 1897 onwards Max Ritter von Spaun, the owner of the Loetz glassworks in Southern Bohemia, manufactured his own brand of iridescent glass. Loetz glass was awarded a gold medal at the World Exhibition in Paris in 1900, and the success of this company inspired other Bohemian glass factories, like Lenora, Harrach and Pallme-König, to produce coloured iridescent glass.

During the first half of the twentieth century Bohemian ideas in glass were in line with the major art movements of the day; the Vienna secessionist designers used Lobmeyr and other Bohemian glass companies to execute their designs. Between 1910 and 1920 the vocabulary of Czech Cubism was reflected in furniture, ceramics and glass by artists who in 1908 had formed a group called Artěl, and later, during the Art Deco period, this same group of artists changed its style along with changing fashions. With the birth of an independent Czechoslovakian state in 1918, the young nation was keen to establish a continuing glass tradition at home and to publicize it abroad as a symbol both of Czech culture and Czech industry. The education of glass artists was taken very seriously at the main centres where it was taught – the Academy of Applied Arts in Prague and two specialized glass-making schools in Železný Brod and Nový Bor. The schools maintained close contacts with the industrial companies which bought their designs. In the period between the wars there was also some important architectural work in glass in Czechoslovakia, notably the work of artists such as Jaroslav Horejc and Josef Kaplický. Then, for a decade from the mid 1930s to the mid 1940s, Czech life was severely disrupted, first by the Second World War and then by the political change to socialism.

OPPOSITE: **Vladimir Kopecký**, 'Suddenly', 1987, flat glass, metal and acrylic paint. 50 x 50 cm (19¾ x 19¾ in). (Photo: Gabriel Urbánek)

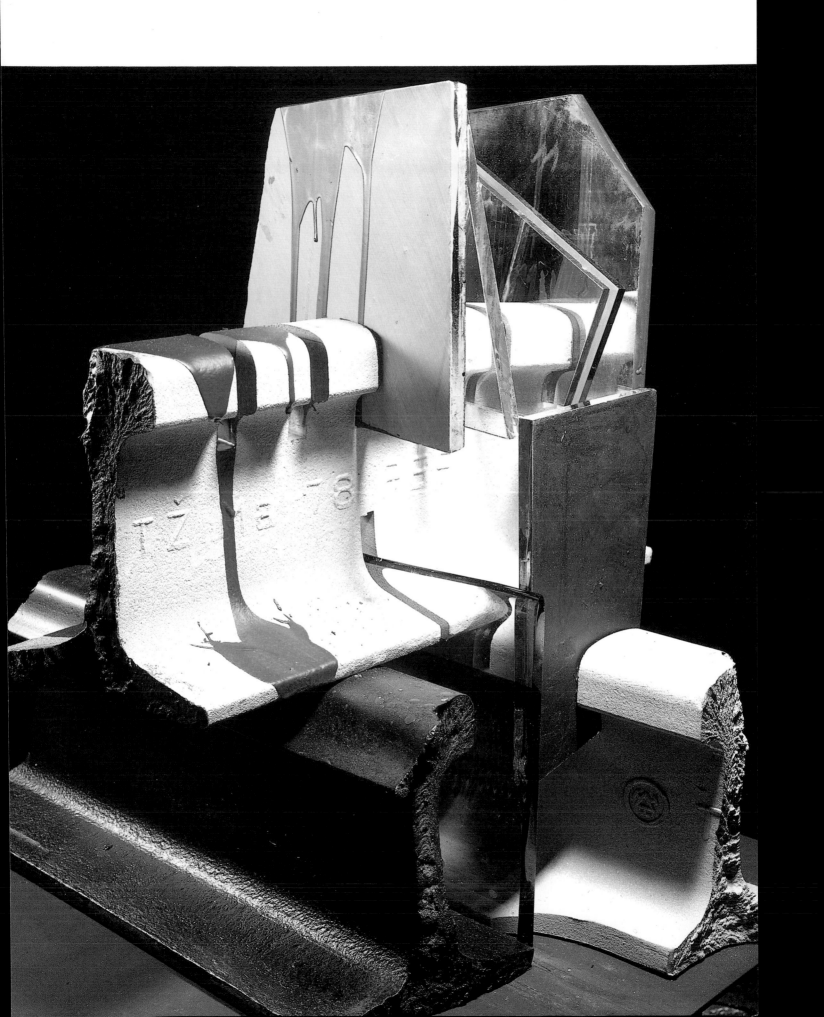

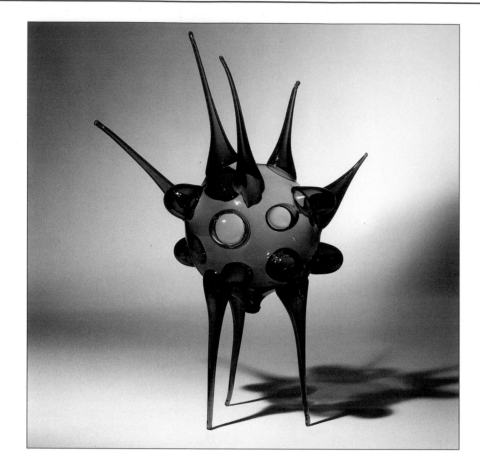

René Roubíček, free-blown glass form, 1960, engraved signature. H. 52 cm (20½ in)

Glass-making suffered along with everything else in Czechoslovakia and it took another decade at least for the glass industry to adjust to the effects of nationalization.

It is against this background that Czech glass-making has re-established itself in the years since the Second World War. There was no sudden year of rebirth like in America. It has been more a gradual process of picking up threads and building on an already magnificent industrial and artistic glass tradition. Since the war Czechs have looked on glass as one of their most exportable commodities. It was one of the more theatrical ways of attracting attention at major world fairs. At home there was no market for luxury goods, which of course include works of art; private art collecting does not accord with socialist principles. On the other hand, sculptural glass has been a very noticeable presence in the Czech environment, both in architecture and interior design. Most Czech glass artists have aspirations in this direction and have been trained for it during the course of their education. The making of large-scale sculptural commissions is less of a problem in Czechoslovakia than anywhere else in the world because the industry is geared towards it and takes its artistic involvement seriously; on the whole, many of those working full-time within the industry have received the same training as the artists with whom they are collaborating.

There can be no doubt that major commissions like René Roubíček's spatial glass collage, awarded the Grand Prix at Expo 58 in Brussels, had an important influence on the direction of glass in the West during the 1960s. Without any ceremony such as that which accompanied the major landmarks in American glass history, Roubíček was one of several Czech artists to use glass purely as an art material. He is an exceptionally modest person, whose importance has been somewhat overlooked despite the prizes he has won. He was born in 1922 and has spent a long life making glass of all sorts, ranging from tableware to lighting and architectural commissions, but some of his most important works were the blown pieces he made casually during the late 1950s, which were in a sense sketches for the Brussels Expo commission. There is a spontaneity about his humorous but lyrical free-blown shapes that was at the time completely original and the catalyst for an entirely new language in glass that was seized on by others.

Roubíček was one of a group of artists working towards the same ends at the time. It was a strange period in the history of Czech glass. The government invested in training a new generation of glass-makers, but at the end of their studies they found themselves facing a career in an industry that was experiencing one of the worst recessions it had ever known. Because of the closing of borders, Czech artists had very little contact with developments in the rest of the world. Alena Adlerová wrote of this situation:

> It soon became clear that there were far more artists than the glass industry needed. The few who found employment were only able to use a fraction of their talents. Among this generation of highly trained artists there was a lively exchange of ideas which were either related to one another or interpreted in totally different directions. This creative concentration served as the fertile ground for the development of the Czechoslovakian school of glass art.[1]

GLASS EDUCATION

The dominant figure in the glass world at the time was Stanislav Libenský, who, with his wife Jaroslava Brychtová, has continued to be at the forefront of developments in his country ever since. Apart from his career as an artist, Libenský was Professor at the Academy of Applied Arts in Prague for nearly twenty-five years (1963–86). He had begun his career in education in 1945, teaching painting on glass at the specialized school of glass-making at Nový Bor. In 1954 he was appointed head of the other specialized school nearby at Železný Brod where he remained for nine years. In a teaching career which spans over forty years his lively personality has influenced at least three generations of artists.

It was as a painter on glass that Libenský first made his mark as a glass artist in a series of vessels with elaborate etched designs coloured with a veil of polychrome transparent enamel paint. This is some of the most remarkable work of its time in any medium. Using a combination of traditional glass techniques, he achieved an astounding degree of originality, and above all found a way of expressing himself with complete freedom as an artist. The secret of this success was a combination of consummate technical skill in glass, outstanding talent both as a draughtsman and a colourist, and a rich visual imagination. Whilst a number of glass engravers in the past have displayed a similar degree of skill, none was ever able to express himself with the same artistic freedom.

Though glass has always fascinated Libenský, he says, 'My mental background was that of a painter.'[2] He very much likes the work of Ben Nicholson, Francis Bacon, Antonio Tapies, Caro and Tony Smith, as well as the artists of the early Renaissance. He mentions that Brancusi had an influence on him and that he admires the work of various architects – Lloyd Wright, Le Corbusier, Saarinen and Aalto. But, he says, 'I must admit that in the domain of glass I don't think anybody really influenced me.'[3]

In his early period Libenský showed himself to be a romantic interested in a variety of subjects ranging from religious or historical themes to detailed botanical drawings. He punctuated his stylized drawing with rhythmic geometric patterns reminiscent of Klimt. 'For the contour and inner composition of a painting he made exclusive use of an etched line, visible only in contrast with the surrounding colour and illuminated by the refraction of a ray.'[4] In 1955 he started to collaborate with Jaroslava Brychtová, his future wife and lifelong working partner. She was a sculptor and inherited an interest in glass from her father, who had been co-founder of the glass-making school at Železný Brod. It was a marriage of talents that proved extremely fruitful and the cast glasswork that resulted from it did much to establish a new tradition for sculptural glass in Czechoslovakia.

From almost the very beginning Libenský and Brychtová chose to work on a monumental scale. Their work struck a cultural vein which the Czech authorities recognized as being important and have made use of at major exhibitions throughout the world from the 1950s until the present day. Libenský and Brychtová worked on commissions as diverse as their first major piece – a glass wall measuring 3 × 2 m (10 × 6½ ft) for the Brussels Expo in 1958 – and a pair of stained-glass windows (1966–8) for St Wenceslaus Chapel at St Vitus Cathedral in the grounds of the Hradčany castle in Prague. Apart from major foreign commissions, like a 4 m (13 ft) high pyramid for Expo 67 in Montreal and the gigantic allegorical 'River of Life' sculpture (which measured 5 × 22 m/16½ × 72 ft) for Expo 70 in Osaka, there have also been numerous Czech commissions, including three reliefs in the Intercontinental Hotel in Prague and Libenský's most important commission to date, a complete glass frontage for the National Theatre in Prague. In addition, there has been a significant group of smaller sculptural pieces throughout their careers. Most of the cast work has been produced at the glassworks in Železný Brod.

Whilst on the one hand Libenský and Brychtová are beyond compare, Libenský in particular typifies the Czech glass artist and has served as a role model for all his pupils. As a student at the Prague Academy in the 1940s he had had the good fortune to be a pupil of the greatest teacher and designer of the time, Josef Kaplický. A period of basic technical training in all aspects of glass-making had been followed by a period of higher education to test creative potential. Trained in this way, Libenský has been able to spend a lifetime combining his career as a designer for industry with a parallel career as an artist in glass.

Glass training programmes in Czechoslovakia have a longer history than anywhere else in the world. The intention is that a graduate from one of these programmes should be proficient in all aspects of glass-making, and at the higher levels it is customary for those who choose a career in glass to diversify. There are two levels of glass education, starting with the basic programme at technical glass colleges from which a student can then graduate to university level at an art college that has a glass programme. The best-known technical colleges are probably the ones at Železný Brod, Nový Bor

Stanislav Libenský, '1001 Nights', 1945, vase, blown, engraved and enamelled. H. 24 cm (9½ in). (Victoria & Albert Museum, London)

and Kamenický Šenov, as well as the school specializing in laboratory glass-blowing techniques and glass jewellery at Jablonec. These central trade schools provide a thorough technical training and operate in connection with the glass factories in the vicinity; as a result, a school specializing in one sort of skill tends to be near a factory where similar skills are required. A variety of techniques are taught, ranging from glass-cutting, engraving and the technique of etching deeply onto sheet glass for use in architecture, to the delicate art of making lampworked figurines. There is also a tradition for experimentation in Czechoslovakia and it was at Železný Brod that

Stanislav Libenský and
Jaroslava Brychtová, 'Cylinder
in the Spheric Space', 1977,
cast and cut glass.
H. 30.5 cm (12 in)

Jaroslava Brychtová, assisted by her father, began her pioneering investigations into the possibilities of sculptural cast glass. The closeness of a glassworks nearby where such experiments could be worked on was a determining factor.

At university level there is a six-year study programme, which embraces further training for industry, architectural glass construction and, above all, the making of 'individual glass works made in different techniques and relating to aesthetic and emotional needs'.[5] Stanislav Libenský and Josef Kaplický have been responsible for the major revolution in modern Czech glass education since the 1940s because of their faith in the artistic possibilities of glass. They have endeavoured to provide a training programme at university level which combines mastering the wide range of modern technical possibilities with their application to art. Fifty years ago such techniques would have remained within the confines of industry, but Kaplický and Libenský believed fervently in the role of glass in the environment and the opportunities offered by glass in modern architecture. To their way of thinking the glass artist had an important new role to play in modern society and indeed this concept seems only natural in a country where glass has been such an integral part of cultural life since the Middle Ages. Over a period of three generations a training programme has been developed to turn that belief into reality.

Drawing and painting have also played an important part in glass education in Czechoslovakia as these skills were considered by both Libenský and Kaplický to be at the root of all artistic endeavour. Libenský has been interested in exploiting the light properties of glass, and his own sculpture has been largely concerned with exploring the optical properties both on the surface of glass and in its inner core. Cutting techniques have been of primary importance to Libenský and, influenced by him, a great many other Czech glass artists have used these techniques in their search for an individual style. If there is one particular quality that typifies contemporary Czech glass it is the way in which the optical properties of glass have been used for aesthetic ends. It has been done in a seemingly endless variety of ways. One of the great masters of this art over the past quarter of a century has been Václav Cigler, another pupil of Kaplický's, whose influence is clearly detectable in the work of the many artists who have been his pupils at Bratislava Academy of Creative Arts, where he headed the architectural glass programme from 1965 to 1979.

THE ROLE OF THE GLASS ARTIST IN CZECHOSLOVAKIA

The Czech glass artist has much more clearly defined career expectations than his counterpart anywhere else in the world. This is partly because the glass industry continues to play a traditionally important role within the Czech economy, and partly because more recently glass has assumed increasing importance both in architecture and in the environment. There is a demand for technicians and artists alike, and the sort of mutual respect and understanding between them does not exist elsewhere. Czech glass artists are most comfortable working with a team of technicians and have not felt the need for total responsibility by the individual. There has been the ideal atmosphere for producing the vast quantity of monumental glass that has found its way into the urban landscape of Czechoslovakia today in the form of windows, partitions, three-dimensional objects and lighting sculptures in banks, hotels, government buildings, theatres and underground railway stations. The Prague underground system, for example, has at least three 'glass' stations with work by leading artists; the best-known stations are Karlovo Náměstí, Národní Třída and Náměstí Republiky, where glass fulfils both functional and decorative needs. The entrance tunnels to the station platforms have glass facing tiles realized by Václav Cigler, Pavel Trnka and František Vízner.

The glass industry in Czechoslovakia is departmentalized and specialities have developed within the various glass collectives. Most large architectural commissions are carried out at the glassworks in Železný Brod or at the Crystalex Branch Corporation in Nový Bor (an amalgamation of various glassworks formed in 1953 as Borské Sklo and renamed in 1974). An artist has to belong to one of the numerous associations that exist for the purpose of organizing separate areas of glass-making. These associations serve as central gathering points for information, either to provide designs for industry, or to organize artists for architectural commissions and environmental sculpture. As already mentioned there is no home market for the smaller-scale artistic work, but at least two associations exist through which artists can send their work for exhibition abroad. Due to various pressures the Museum of Applied Arts in Prague has only recently been able to open a small part of its collection to the public, but over the years it has put together a good, representative collection of contemporary Czech glass.

EXHIBITIONS AND SYMPOSIA

At home Czechs have had great difficulty forming an overall impression of what contemporary Czech glass looks like. They see it here and there in the environment, but until recently there have been only a few exhibitions. It is ironical that Czech glass is better known abroad than at home. Not until the beginning of the 1980s was there any attempt to stage exhibitions on home ground, the first one being a glass sculpture exhibition held in Brno where more than one hundred works were exhibited by sixty artists. It was an important event which, apart from anything else, allowed the artists themselves to see their work in context for the first time. Those who saw the exhibition were overwhelmed by its scope yet at the same time aware of a certain narrowness. It was the first opportunity there had been to get a sense of some sort of overall identity for modern Czech glass. Alena Adlerová, the curator of glass at the Prague Museum of Applied Arts from 1962 to 1987, whose curatorial efforts as well as her role as historical commentator on modern Czech glass have been second to none, wrote in *Glass Review*, 'The optical character of glass plays the dominant role in Czech glass sculpture and the exhibition emphasized precisely this feature.'[6] If anything, this exhibition acted as a catalyst to bring about change in Czechoslovakia. Although there had been a few sporadic attempts at organizing glass exhibitions before, this was the first chance to see how one-sided glass aesthetic had become during the 1970s. Various events followed which have served to broaden horizons.

In 1982 the first international symposium of glass was organized in Czechoslovakia at Nový Bor with fifty artists participating from thirteen European countries. In the same year a group of artists got together to stage an exhibition called Prostor, intended as a protest. This was to be the first of a series of three, masterminded by the art critic Kristian Suda. The introduction to the catalogue states:

> It seemed to us that it was no longer possible continually to repeat shows and exhibitions which come under the problematic heading 'Glass Art'. The sealed showcases became a typical feature of these exhibitions just as did the sycophantic reaction of the mass media. We were looking to discover a space which would inspire humility, simultaneously encouraging the desire to fill it, to grasp it, to achieve it, a space which would encourage a different dimension of the object.[7]

In this and two subsequent exhibitions organized by the same group an attempt was made to break loose from current trends by allowing a given space – first a derelict interior and later an exterior setting – to dictate the nature of the sculptures. The aim was to 'make glass as a material disappear out of the centre of interest'.[8]

The changes that took place are in part simply a normal evolutionary process in which a new generation is trying to find a way forward. There has also been less isolation for Czech artists as they have been able to travel more and see what is going on in the rest of the world. When Libenský vacated his post as Professor at the Prague Academy in 1986 it was the end of an era. His term of office provided the sort of artistic homogeneity that will probably never be recaptured. His artistic leadership gave rise to a strong national style for a quarter of a century which may well turn out to be one of the most important periods in the history of Czech glass.

THE FIRST GENERATION OF 'NEW GLASS' ARTISTS
Historically, there have been two 'periods' in glass since Czechoslovakia became a socialist state in the 1940s. During the first, Kaplický's pupils

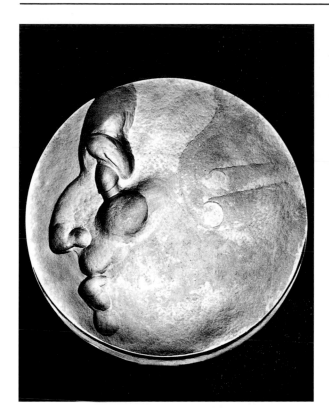 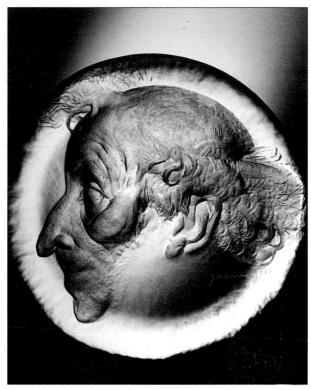

achieved maturity and provided the country with a formidable group of artists and teachers. Many of those who began working in the 1950s are still active today and much respected as 'elder statesmen' within the glass-making community. Even if they were not directly Kaplický's pupils, they began their careers at a time when his influence and that of his contemporary Karel Štipl, who also taught at the Academy in Prague, were the dominant ones in Czech glass. During the 1950s the work of most of these artists was vessel-orientated. Their style is best captured in a book entitled *Modern Bohemian Glass* (Artia, Prague, 1963), which illustrates more than three hundred pieces of glass from this period. But a tendency towards sculpture, which later became far more pronounced, was already clearly noticeable.

The most remarkable feature about the early work of this group of artists is its originality. Although working in traditional techniques, an entirely new spirit could be felt in what they were doing. Jiři Harcuba's achievements as a glass engraver put him in a league with the greatest engravers of all time, but perhaps more importantly, his refined sense of intaglio portraiture has elevated the art of engraving to a new plane. His engraved portrait medallions go straight to the soul of the sitter and have a kind of surrealism which comes partly from the unexpected expressive quality the artist has achieved in glass. Harcuba wrote:

Since 1971, I have been more and more involved with portraits. The issue is a testimony of man. My need to accept and pass on a message, as I understand it. Even with portraits I strive to apply the technique I developed in my previous work, that is, I create the portrait by means of the same articulate language of wheels. But here it is also a question of capturing and expressing the psyche.[9]

ABOVE LEFT: **Jiři Harcuba**, glass medallion with an engraved portrait of Joseph Haydn, 1982. Diam. 15 cm (6 in)

ABOVE: **Jiři Harcuba**, glass medallion with an engraved portrait of Marc Chagall, 1977. Diam. 12.5 cm (5 in)

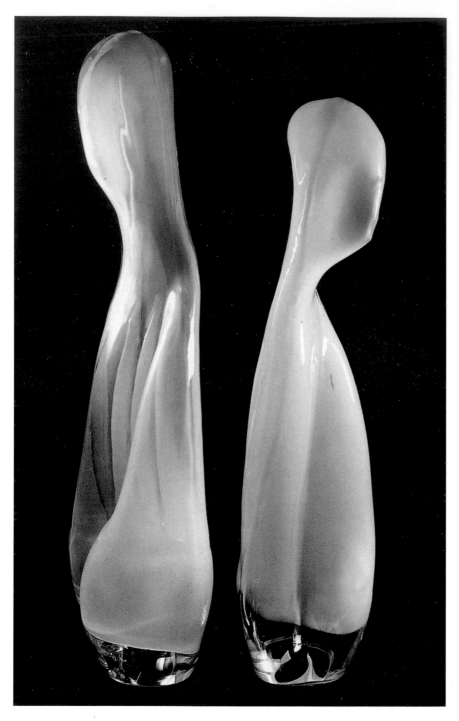

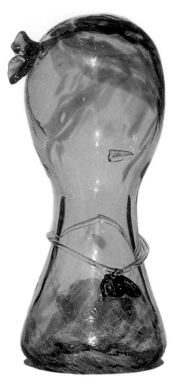

ABOVE: **Miluše Roubíčková**, 'Coloured Head with Flower', 1977, clear glass with applied coloured glass decoration, blown into a plaster mould. H. 40 cm (15¾ in), diam. of base 16.5 cm (6½ in)

René Roubíček, 'Two Heads', 1980, clear and white opaline glass, mould-blown and heat-shaped. H. 89 cm (35 in) and 82.5 cm (32½ in). (The Corning Museum of Glass, Corning, New York)

Reference has already been made to René Roubíček and his unconventional techniques of glass-blowing. Like practically every other artist of note of his generation, he has spent a good deal of his working life as a designer for industry; he was chief artist at Borské Sklo from 1952 to 1965. His wife, Miluše Roubíčková, is also a glass artist and has been responsible for a series of light-hearted blown-glass sculptures with titles like 'Lollipops', 'Ice Cream Cups' and 'Bouquets'. They are naive and have a certain charm. The two have also worked together as a team to produce a series of blown 'Heads', and recently René Roubíček has concentrated on sculpture in which he takes an anatomical detail which is then exaggerated and literally 'blown' to grotesque proportions. Sometimes it is a finger, sometimes a torso. He has a relaxed sense of humour which he translates into glass with a light hand. In talking about his work he says:

> The heads are without noses, eyes, lips, sometimes there is not even a fully blown-out shape. But each of them has its own expression, delicate, frightening, funny or dignified. Just like real people. In contrast, the expression of the figures is in their motion. Like my heads, they too are blown from a single mold, each a free deformation of liquid glass, sometimes accidental, sometimes even capricious.[10]

Pavel Hlava has also been an innovator in blown-glass techniques, though in the beginning he was mainly concerned with shallow relief engraving, a technique very popular in Czechoslovakia during the 1950s and used by a number of excellent artists, including Jiři Harcuba and Karel Wünsch. During the 1950s and 1960s Hlava developed a way of making indentations in glass vessels, providing his glass with an inner structure that suggests a skeleton visible inside the body of the glass. He has used these techniques with varying degrees of success in large-scale sculpture and has been most successful in the monumental lighting fixtures he has designed, notably the one in the new National Theatre in Prague.

Another technique characteristic of this so-called 'first period' was the use of transparent enamels on glass. Apart from Libenský's skills in using

Pavel Hlava, 'Civilization/Industry', 1983, coloured glass, blown and heat-shaped with punctures

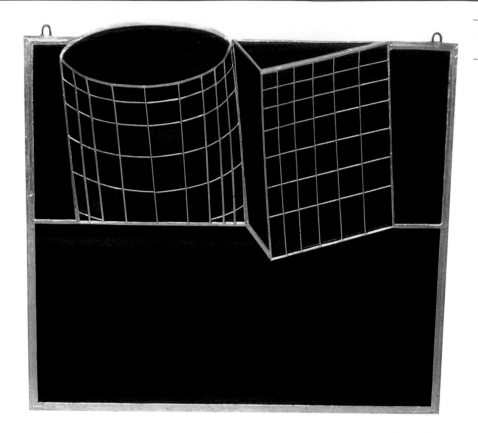

Karel Vaňura, wall piece,
1980s, leaded glass

Karel Vaňura, 'Portrait
Head', 1982, enamelled and
engraved flat glass

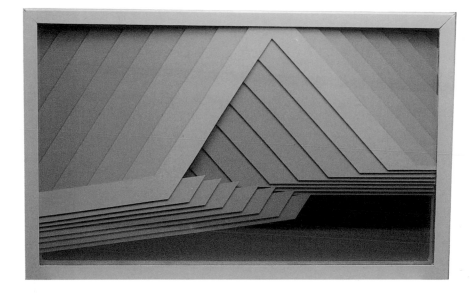

Vladimir Kopecký, untitled piece, layers of sheet glass, painted and sand-blasted, in metal frame

this technique, a number of other artists used it in a very personal way. In the 1950s Vladimir Kopecký and Karel Vaňura painted abstract designs in transparent enamels on clear glass vessel shapes, and František Tejml was another artist who worked in this technique, decorating his vases with stylized animal motifs. Both Kopecký and Vaňura continued to use colour painting and Kopecký in particular has used it to create perspective and space in his work. For a time he made sculpture in which glass sheets, each individually sand-blasted and coloured, were stacked together to make a three-dimensional painting. His palette of graded monochromatic tones or closely related colours was that of Op Art. More recently, the three-dimensional aspect has been more prominent and his work has become more sculptural.

Another artist of this period was Věra Lišková. In her artistic pieces she developed lampworking skills further than any artist had dared to in the

Věra Lišková, 'Winter Form', 1981, lampwork. H. 60 cm (23½ in), W. 45 cm (17¾ in)

Václav Cigler, 'Spatial Composition', optical glass, cut and polished

past, both in terms of scale and of sculptural concept. Her sculptures were either complete abstractions in glass, exciting because they took glass to the very limits of its fragility, or objects inspired by the animal and plant world. Václav Cigler also belongs to this generation of artists, most of whom were born in the late 1920s or early 1930s. With Libenský and Roubíček, Cigler was one whose ideas and skills created the necessary impulses for a new breed of glass artist. He had the most natural talent for sculpture among glass artists of his own generation, and has always managed to avoid the obvious in his work both as technician and artist. His interest in optical cutting stems from a commitment to the principles of kinetic art. He saw this technique as a way of creating the sort of imagery with reflections and optical illusions that would enable the viewer to enter the work, to have an effect on it, as it were. He was fascinated by the idea of a work changing as the viewer moved around it; by the idea of the viewer influencing a piece of work by his presence, the reflection of his image, his touch, and so on. There is a profound philosophical content to Cigler's work which always raises it above mere optical trickery. 'He is interested in the psychological idea of a person's reaction to a piece opening up a new process of thought and analysis.'[11] Cigler himself says, 'The properties of glass are an integral part of my vision. Glass has the ability to present its whole content to the viewer, not only the outer form, but the inner space as well. To work with a block of glass means therefore to work with its optical properties. The outer is influenced by the inner and vice versa, just as with man.'[12]

Jiřina Žertová and Dana Vachtová are both sculptors who work in hot glass. Žertová's free-blown sculptures show a remarkable colour sense, and colour is used in her work as an emotional force. Vachtová's main concern is with revealing the inner volume of a piece and the interplay that is possible between the inner and outer spaces of glass because of its transparency.

ABOVE: **Jiřina Žertová**, 'Oscillation', 1984, blown glass with wire inclusions on a metal base. 35 x 72 x 45 cm (13¾ x 28½ x 17¾ in)

Dana Vachtová, 'The Street', 1985, mould-blown glass and metal. 155 x 170 x 220 cm (61 x 67 x 86½ in)

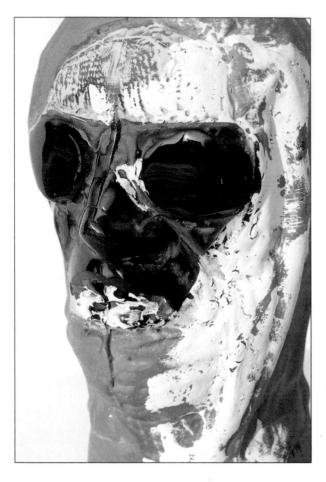

LIBENSKÝ'S PUPILS

The 'second period' in recent Czechoslovakian glass-making history coincides with the time during which Libenský was Professor at the Prague Academy of Applied Arts. Even those who had not studied with Libenský were affected by his width of approach and his liberal attitudes. His approach to glass created new horizons and appealed to a new sort of student whose main interests were far removed from industrial glass and who was attracted by the idea of artistic independence. Sculpture, of all sizes from table-size to monumental, was the focal point of interest at the Prague Academy, even though postgraduate students who went there continued their practical studies as studiously as before. In an attempt to summarize the wide spectrum covered by Czech glass artists during this period Alena Adlerová has divided them into two main categories. In the first, artists are concerned with 'the emotionally rich creation of objects formed of the hot glass mass', whilst the second group concentrates on 'abstract, geometrical shapes, cut out of the blocks of lead glass or optical crystal mass'.[13]

Blanka Adensamová's blown sculptures are usually stylized portrait heads incorporating symbolic flowers or trees. The blown forms are decorated by means of cutting, engraving, sand-blasting or painting. Jiří Šuhájek uses blown techniques as well, in combination with a number of decorative devices, including glass threads, enamels, gold, silver and mirror paint, to make humorous larger-than-life Junoesque figures which loll about or balance precariously: 'Renoir-like women, luscious and lascivious,'[14] Šuhájek

ABOVE LEFT: **Václav Machač**, 'Portrait of a Mountaineer', c. 1984, blown into a plaster mould, enamelled

ABOVE: **Dalibor Tichý**, 'Water Plant', 1984, coloured glass, cast and pulled. H. c. 18 cm (7 in)

Jiři Šuhájek, 'Sitting Figure',
1986, free-blown glass.
H. 130 cm (51 in).
(Photo: Jan Kříž)

is clever at suggesting implied movement. His concepts are worked out on paper, but there is a certain amount of improvisation at the furnace. He is a born showman who loves to 'perform' for the team of master craftsmen with whom he works.

Václav Machač makes figural sculptures inspired by the world of sport and has produced a series of human or animal heads. His main aim is to capture human feeling – pain, despair, excitement, aggression – and to make a statement about the closeness of life and death. In the very personal style he has developed, 'the surface finish of the glass permits only an extremely limited view into the core of the sculpture. The core of the glass block symbolically indicates the depths of spiritual life. In his work we encounter a combination of the classical methods of sculpture with the special technologies applied at a glassworks.'[15] Dalibor Tichý's hot-glass pieces are also expressive. His method of working was in itself original in that he devised a series of special instruments for stretching glass threads pulled

from the glass mass, which were then worked to suggest themes inspired by nature, such as flowers, grass, coral, birds' wings. During his short life (he died in 1985) he also painted and engraved on glass.

OPTICAL GLASS

The list of Czech artists in the second category, whose sculpture investigated the optical properties of glass, is the longest of all, and there is a feeling that after nearly two decades of experimentation in cutting glass the artistic possibilities of this technique have been thoroughly exhausted. If there is one geographic area where this type of work is done most it is Slovakia in Eastern Czechoslovakia, because of the teaching legacy in that part of the country. Askold Žačko, a pupil of Cigler, whom he succeeded as head of the art glass department at Bratislava Academy of Creative Arts in 1979, developed his optical cutting techniques in collaboration with Lubomir Artzt and Pavel Tomečko. There seem to be two basic approaches to optical cutting. In the first, the inner core of the glass is worked on, sometimes in conjunction with the outer surface and sometimes on its own. In this kind of sculpture a basic shape is worked on only as a means of creating some sort of special visual effect, but on the whole the artist's statement is contained within a fundamental shape like the cube or sphere. Jaromir Rybák is one artist who is very concerned with the inner structure of his pieces; with the inner world of the object. 'He wants to present his work not as an optical object, but rather as a sphere turned in on itself.'[16] Like that of so many Czech artists, Rybák's work has many sides to it. The gigantic

Jaromir Rybák, 'The Blue Project', 1987, cast, laminated and cut glass. 50 × 40 × 22 cm (19¾ × 15¾ × 8¾ in). (Photo: Gabriel Urbánek)

OPPOSITE: **Askold Žačko**, 'Baroque I', 1981, cut optical glass: 45.5 × 26.5 × 10 cm (18 × 10½ × 4 in)

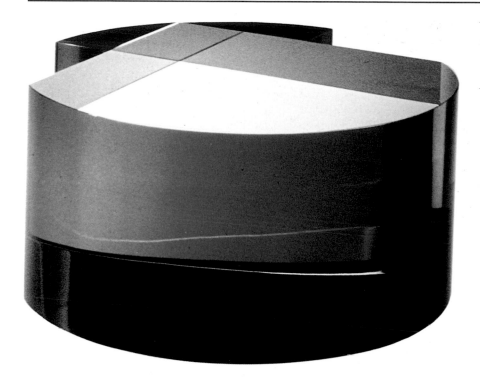

Pavel Trnka, two-part object, 1987, blue, red and clear glass, cut and polished. H. c. 10 cm (4 in)

'Figure of a Gentleman' that was made for the first Prostor show in 1982 could not be more contrasting in style. It is typical of the most talented of Libenský's pupils that they work convincingly in a number of techniques, though perhaps they often find that for practical reasons they end up concentrating on one or at most two basic methods.

Pavel Trnka, who studied with both Libenský and Cigler, is another sculptor who has created a strong individual style for himself by dividing up inner space with mathematical precision and experimenting with reflection and refraction. He often adds a touch of colour to his interior spaces for dramatic effect, with small areas of colour reflected in a larger area of crystal glass. Sometimes his work is composed of separate elements with two related shapes juxtaposed (a pentagonal and hexagonal prism, for example). His innate talent for arranging space makes him particularly suited for architectural work. Trnka also works in hot glass and since 1982 has been working on a series of 'non-vessels' with powerful imagery created by attacking the vessel in a most unconventional way:

A rebelling intervention rids the cylinder of its static and lethargic nature and liberates it from given conventionalities. Defiance of given laws creates excitement and a new beauty. In realising his artistic ideas, Pavel Trnka has perfected the cracking technology consisting of a process of dramatic cooling and repeated heating of the vessel. In the case of the new 'non-vessels' the artist removes a side wall or knocks out a corner perpendicular line. An agitated network of fissures spreads out on the sides of the artificial craters which originate in this way and lend the given work a romantic character. A piled up heap of glass splinters – often engulfing the space of the open object – becomes a part of the artistic object. The source of expressional tension of Pavel Trnka's glass objects appears in the contrast between the known and the new.[17]

OPPOSITE: **Jaromir Rybák**, 'The Tower of Babel', 1987, cast, laminated and cut glass. 38 × 21 cm (15 × 8¼ in). (Photo: Gabriel Urbánek)

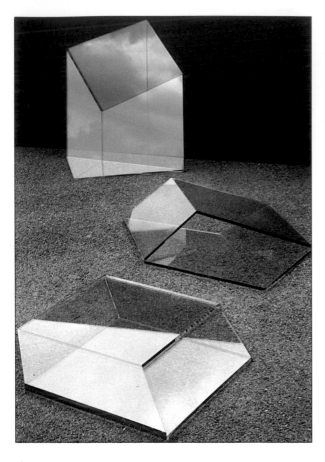

Marian Karel has also shown an individual talent for strong simple statements about the optical properties of glass. He has been particularly successful with his architectural pieces where he works with daring simplicity on a monumental scale, creating his effects with basic geometric shapes polished to perfection. His insistence on technical perfection for aesthetic ends embodies much of the spirit of new Czech glass sculpture of the 1970s. Oldrich Plíva is another artist interested in optical effects and has his own elegant way of dealing with cut and polished surfaces.

The other main artistic use of optical cutting is to provide contour, to 'carve' a shape out of a block of glass. Czech artists have been able to make the most of this technique because it is so well taught both at Bratislava and in Prague. One of the most exciting recent artistic discoveries about glass has been the way sculpture can be coaxed out of a lump of glass. Although it seems an obvious way of sculpting glass and is not unexpected technically after centuries of gemstone cutting (to which it is closely related), the technique has been a source of endless fascination to Czech artists. It is a logical progression from the art of glass engraving and not surprising therefore that it should have first been developed in a country renowned for that particular glass skill. Success in this kind of glass sculpture depends on technical imagination and powers of artistic invention. Until the 1960s no artistic use had been made of optical cutting so that it became something of an artistic goldmine for a whole generation of artists. Břetislav Novák has an innate feeling about what glass can do and his way of cutting reveals such qualities in glass that only an artist could discover. His main body of work consists of

ABOVE LEFT: **Marian Karel**, 'Illusive Cube', 1983, optical glass, composed of several parts, cut. H. 31 cm (12¼ in)

ABOVE: **Oldrich Plíva**, cone, 1980s, colourless glass, optical quality, cut and polished. H. c. 28 cm (11 in)

OPPOSITE: **Břetislav Novák**, 'Totem', 1980, smoky brown and blue flat glass, cut, with metal base. H. 220 cm (86½ in) (The Corning Museum of Glass, Corning, New York)

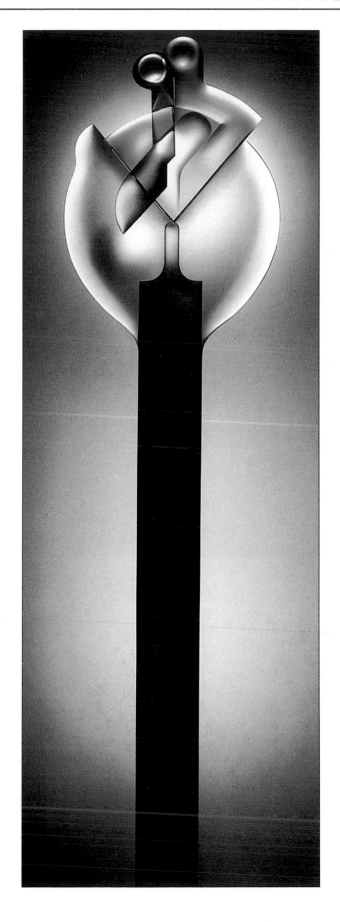

František Vízner, group of vases and bowls, 1972–80, cut, with sand-blasted matt surface

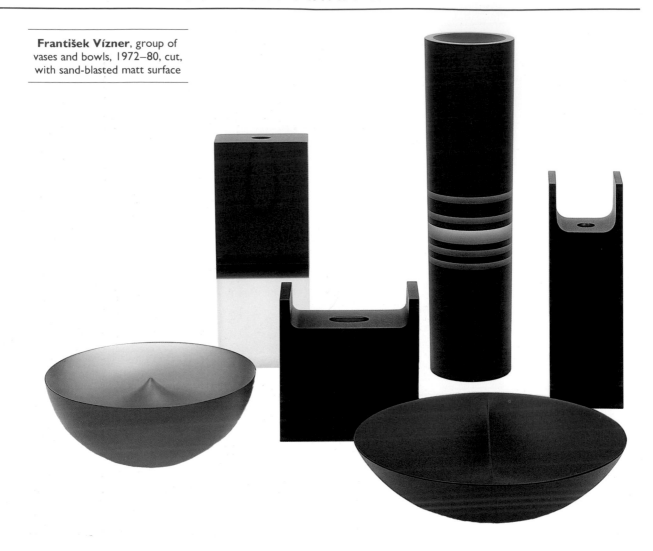

a series of visually compelling sculptures made up of interlocking parts which fit together with machine-like precision. Sometimes the glass is clear; sometimes there are tints of colour. In scale the pieces vary from small to monumental. 'Each piece is a resolution of harmonious form, proportion and colour, of the unique properties of glass to alter light.'[18]

František Vízner sees himself as a vessel maker, although his simple and deeply refined statements in glass are as expressive as any sculpture. In his artistic pieces the shape is modelled by cutting and given a matt surface by sand-blasting and etching. His own words, characteristically blunt, say a lot both about him and about the current state of the art in his country:

I come from a generation which was faced with a trend of many new young glass artists who considered themselves to be sculptors in glass. My ideas were shaken and I began to have doubts whether there would be sufficient serious themes for so many sculptors. The vase always was and still remains my positive destiny in glass. I feel that glass is deeply and irreversibly connected with the vase, the vessel, the bowl. I look upon the contemporary decline in interest in the functional value of glass and the preference for free creation as fashion and momentary demand. The shaping of glass is closely bound with

Dana Zámečníková, 'Family Portrait', c. 1987, layers of sheet glass with transparent paint and etched motifs, in a metal frame. 68.5 × 57 × 9 cm (27 × 22½ × 3½ in)

technology and pure craftsmanship which, for the artists, narrows the sphere of expression. What astonishes me most in this new glass art is a certain boundless use of glass. Artistic fantasy is given as an excuse for everything. The vase presents a frightening and at the same time beautiful limitation of functions. I like handcraft and I like beautiful objects. For our life they are as necessary as those things which I feel just and right.[19]

Whilst Vízner shows a taste for restraint in vessel form, Aleš Vašiček shows the same sort of restrained precision achieved through brilliant craftsmanship as a sculptor. He prefers to work on a massive scale with crystal blocks that he usually cuts into a precise composition to which he adds cut or engraved touches.

PAINTING ON GLASS

Painting on glass is another Czech speciality and one which also has historical roots. Dana Zámečníková is one of the internationally best-known Czech artists for her 'boxes' consisting of layers of clear plate glass onto each of which a fragment of an image is painted, sand-blasted, acid-etched or drawn with coloured pencil. When stacked together the fragments form a

Ivo Rozsypal, cased glass disc
with a cut and sand-blasted motif
of a bird, 1975, metal frame.
Diam. 42.5 cm (16¾ in)

Jan Exnar, 'Listener', 1988,
leaded glass. 118 x 118 cm
(46½ x 46½ in)

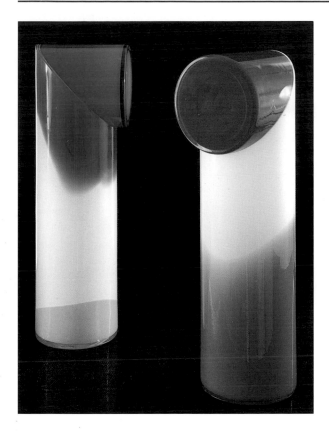

single image in which there is a feeling of space stretching to infinity because of the technique she uses. The images have a dream-like quality and are based on personal experiences. Zámečníková began her career as a stage designer at the Prague National Theatre and it is easy to see where her ideas about perspective come from. She was introduced to glass by her husband, Marian Karel, in the early 1970s and hit upon the idea of layers in 1977/8. Her very personal input into the sometimes too structured Czech glass scene has been like a breath of fresh air. Jan Exnar is another painterly artist whose techniques are basically those used in stained glass. He paints, sand-blasts and etches window glass set in lead, and the resulting pieces are sometimes conceived as windows for use in architecture or else are simply used as wall hangings. Although it is hardly his principal technique, Ivo Rozsypal has done some of his most successful work painting on glass. He is one of the most versatile of all Czech glass artists and has worked with equal success in industry, on architectural commissions and as a sculptor in glass.

There has recently been a strong revival of painting techniques among the youngest generation of Czech glass artists, with some remarkable work by graduates of the Prague Academy, including Gisela Šabóková, Martin Velíšek and Ivana Šolcová. The tendency generally among this generation is to diversify and move away from traditions set firm in the 1960s and 1970s. Artists like Vladimira Klumpařová, Stanislava Grebeničková and Milan Handl, all born in the 1950s, have been far freer in their use of bold colour, and there has been an attempt to bring painting and sculpture closer together in their work. But as yet there is no strong new national identity to compare with that of two previous generations.

ABOVE LEFT: **Milan Handl**, 'Tubes', 1981–2, blown coloured glass. H. 50 cm (19¾ in), diam. 14 cm (5½ in). (Photo: Jaroslav Bárta)

ABOVE: **Gisela Šabóková**, 'Portrait', 1985, painting on glass. 65 × 85 cm (25½ × 33½ in)

RUMANIA, POLAND AND HUNGARY

The international glass movement has had its effect in other Eastern European countries, too, none of which (with the exception of East Germany) has any strong glass tradition. In Poland and Rumania there are a few isolated glass artists, but they are not well known outside their own countries, although their work has been seen in the exhibitions that accompanied the two Coburg Glass Prizes. In Rumania a number of artists have studied glass at the Ion Andreescu Academy of Applied Art in Bucharest and earn their living working within the industry, although some of them, like Ovidio Buba, Dan Bancila, Silviu Dancea and Adriana Popescu, work independently. There is, however, a lack of technical facility and most of the artistic work is blown. The idea of glass as art has only recently been considered in Rumania. In Poland there is no one school known for glass but a few artists have felt the urge to express themselves in glass, among them Ingeborga Gladala Kizinska, Ireneusz Kizinski and Stefan Sadowski.

Dan Bancila, 'March-4', 1981, blown shapes from green glass, matt, with metal base. 55 x 20 x 18 cm (21½ x 7¾ x 7 in)

Silviu Dancea, anthropomorphic figures, 1984, free-shaped. H. 15–26.5 cm (6–10½ in)

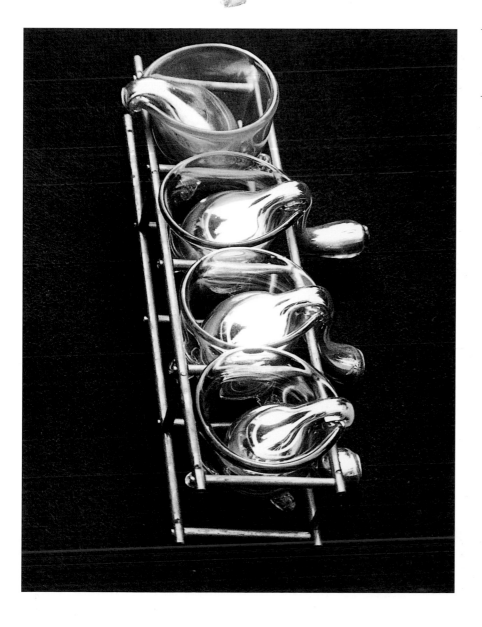

Valeriu Semenescu, 'The Charge I', 1979, blown glass and metal. 20 x 40 x 15 cm (7¾ x 15¾ x 6 in)

Zoltan Bohus, 'Space Spiral II',
1977, three separate elements of
green tinted glass, laminated, cut
and polished. H. 13.5 cm (5¼ in),
D. 31 cm (12¼ in)

In Hungary a faculty for glass design was set up at the College of Applied
Arts in Budapest under Gyorgy Gacs, and the first group of students graduated from there in 1970. Gacs was himself trained as a painter and muralist
and began using glass in combination with other materials in his architectural work. He was succeeded as head of the glass department by Zoltan
Bohus, one of his pupils, who has been working exclusively in glass since
1968. Bohus has earned himself a considerable reputation as a glass artist,
and a number of now established artists have emerged from the school
under his guidance. His own work shows the influence of Czech glass. He
has made a series of sculptures in which ordinary plate glass is anodized,
stacked and laminated, then cut and finally polished. 'The transparent
surfaces leave the topography of his sculptures exposed. His is the art of
missing edges and missing ends. Endlessness, the consideration of infinity is
elaborated in his sculptures on several levels. The internal planes repeat
like receding images in facing mirrors.'[20]

Bohus is married to Maria Lugossy, who has worked in glass since 1980.
Technically her work shows the influence of Bohus in that she too uses
stacked and laminated glass, but the imagery is all her own. She is interested
in two opposing aspects of nature – the hardness of crystal formations

Maria Lugossy, 'Primary
Rocks I', 1985, laminated sheet
glass, glued, sand-blasted and
polished. 40 x 16 x 7.5 cm
(15¾ x 6¼ x 3 in)

versus the softness of organic form. In her work the hardness of a clearly
defined outer form, either pyramids or disc shapes composed of giant
double convex lenses, encloses a busy cellular life cut or sand-blasted deep
into the basic shapes. There is a feeling of archaeological excavation about
the layered erosion of her inner structures. The works have evocative titles
such as 'Ocean of Silence'.

György Buczko is another pupil of Bohus and again his influence is
strong. He graduated in 1974 and has been both teacher and independent
artist since then. There are two sides to his work, one of which is seen in a
series of cold-worked laminated columns and cylinders, the other in his
hot-glass works, which are 'large irregular bowl forms with inner surfaces
pock-marked by hollows and mounds. These rugged pieces have the gritty
texture of a lunar landscape whose hills and valleys deny their functions as
vessels.'[21] Another artist, Maria Meszaros, works in a technique that has
attracted a number of women artists recently; she directly casts life-size figures by slumping on plaster body forms. At first the work was wholly figurative but it has become more abstract, 'fragmented, distorted, layered and
fused into re-arranged torsos . . . human imperfection and vulnerability is
rendered by the inanimate glass'.[22]

EAST GERMANY

Glass has been made in East Germany since the end of the sixteenth century, mainly in the Thüringen forest region and the village of Lauscha in particular. The forests have made it a natural place for glass production and there is a long tradition of making lampworked toys, beads, glass eyes for dolls, and Christmas tree decorations. In the past the work was done as a family enterprise with the men handling the lampwork whilst the women and children applied the painted decoration. Already at the turn of the century an East German artist, Karl Koepping, had achieved international renown for his exquisite lampworked flower-form goblets. In more recent times Albin Schaedel, who was born in 1905 and died recently aged over eighty years old, has been the patriarch of lampblown glass. He abandoned making glass animals in the 1950s and went on to make vessels ornamented with prunts and fine threads. He was awarded a special prize at the first Coburg Glass Prize in 1977 and was told, 'You laid the groundwork for a contemporary and innovative construction of lampblown vessels which has received the recognition of museums and collectors throughout the world.'[23]

Following Schaedel's lead a number of East German artists have produced fine lampblown work in recent years. It is an area of glass-making that stands apart and has its limitations, but within its narrow sphere artists have been able to create a very special magic, often due to the extreme fragility of the art. Otto Schindhelm's thin lampblown vessels are decorated with glass threads highlighted in gold and silver. Volkhardt Precht has had his own studio since 1963, and technically speaking is one of the most accomplished East German artists. Hubert Koch, who began a career in glass in the 1950s working on the production of glass eyes for humans, makes vessels decorated with polychrome threads and metallic oxides, and has developed one of the most identifiable personal styles.

A number of other East German glass-makers earn their living as artists and have produced work that is keenly sought by collectors and museum curators: Walter Baz-Dölle, Hartmut Bechmann, Albert Greiner-Mai, Günter Knye, Otto Schindhelm and Walter Schwarz have all contributed towards establishing one of the most charming glass traditions in the world today. The unpretentiousness of their work comes as a great relief and provides both a direct link with the past and a contemporary art form combining skill and artistry in line with the most recent artistic developments in glass.

ABOVE LEFT: **Hubert Koch**, bowl, 1980s, lampwork, applied enamel decoration. H. 15 cm (6 in)

ABOVE TOP: **Walter Baz-Dölle**, vase, 1980s, opaline glass, lampworked. H. c. 12.5 cm (5 in)

ABOVE: **Albert Greiner-Mai**, vase, 1980s, lampwork. H. 35 cm (13¾ in)

Günter Knye, vase, 1980s, lampworked with applied white threads. H. c. 12.5 cm (5 in)

4. WEST GERMANY, AUSTRIA, SWITZERLAND AND SCANDINAVIA

Although the first major exhibition devoted exclusively to European contemporary glass was not until the Coburg Glass Prize exhibition of 1977, glass-makers throughout Europe were certainly aware of earlier developments in America. The size of that first Coburg exhibition is proof enough, with over 1200 pieces submitted from nineteen different countries; this represented the work of over 265 artists. Tom Buechner, writing about the exhibition in *Craft Horizons* in December 1977, said:

> There is no question that our Harvey Littleton, Dominick Labino and their splendid progenies have been influential, but there is no question that radical change would have occurred in Europe without them. Eisch was bound to happen. . . . The Europeans are doing more different things than we are, both technically and aesthetically; there are fewer schools of work and more artists. Second, and this was unexpected, their work seems somewhat more inventive and innovative than ours.[1]

Buechner was of course referring to the whole of Europe, and Eastern European countries had been well represented at this exhibition, but in Western Europe there had also been a lively exchange of ideas since the mid 1960s. Erwin Eisch had already met Harvey Littleton; Sam Herman had come to Great Britain from America and set up a new glass programme at the Royal College of Art, inviting Czechs and Americans to learn and teach there. There was a well-established studio glass tradition in Scandinavian countries, too, Sweden in particular. The modern glass movement had rapidly gathered momentum in Western Europe, and the showing of glass at the second Coburg Glass Prize in 1985 left no doubts about glass having become an accepted art form.

WEST GERMANY

Although West Germany has been responsible for the two most comprehensive shows of contemporary European glass to date – and it is in Germany that the most widely read European glass journal, *Neues Glas*, has been published since 1980 – there is a basic problem about glass education

OPPOSITE: **Ann Wolff**, 'Frau Holle', 1986, bowl, acid-etched, sand-blasted on multi-coloured underlays. Diam. 35 cm (13¾ in)

Kurt Wallstab, group of vases,
1984, lampwork. H. 10–22 cm
(4–8¾ in)

there that has resulted in a somewhat random overall picture. Helmut
Ricke, writing in *New Glass in Germany*, published in 1983, said, 'If one
were to single out a certain method of treating glass that could be called
typical for Germany, then it would surely be that of glass blown at the
lamp.'[2] Indeed, some beautiful lampworked glass is produced in West Germany by Pavel Molnar, Gunther Kehr and particularly Kurt Wallstab, but it
is essentially an East German speciality. Two world wars have played havoc
with German culture in general and the resultant shifting of borders has
meant that much that was 'German' in glass during the nineteenth century
has ended up in other countries.

Glass education is mainly at technical schools where there is still little
concern for aesthetics. Klaus Moje, writing in *Neues Glas* about the German glass sculptor Willi Pistor, said:

*Willi Pistor has been teaching (at Hadamar) since 1963 in the grinding shop.
At the Fachschule all learning above and beyond what is needed for filling
orders for industry is met with resistance and closed mindedness by these
people; free artistic work must then appear particularly suspect to them.
Naturally this must restrict the hollow glass department in its development to
quite an extraordinary degree. Instead of encouraging unique individuals, trade
school education should, as they see it, produce a 'human apparatus' that can
grind out the 'witch's star design' a little more perfectly.*[3]

Erwin Eisch, mug (female),
1972, mould-blown clear glass
with platinum foil inside.
H. 15 cm (6 in)

The one notable exception is the Stuttgart Academy of Fine Arts, where an important glass programme was initiated by Hans Gottfried von Stockhausen, but it concentrates principally on flat or stained glass and therefore falls outside the scope of this book. As in all the arts the German approach is strictly determined by labelled categories, each of which tends to be clearly defined and somewhat limiting. There have been a few inspiring individual teachers at the technical schools, or 'Fachschulen', in Zwiesel and Haida, and Professor Gangkofner at the Munich Academy of Fine Arts has encouraged experiments with the optical properties of glass, but to this day glass education in West Germany for aspiring young artists who wish to work in this medium remains a problem.

It is against this background that Erwin Eisch embarked on a career in glass. From the beginning he set out to be something of a revolutionary, and his art has been one long protest against the Establishment. As an approach it is somewhat dated now, but in the early 1960s when Eisch first made his protests felt, he was a strong force and his impassioned statements both in glass and in prose had their effect. 'The vessel in craft is a gnawed-up bone that has no meat in it,' he wrote.[4] At the beginning of his career Eisch was concerned with destroying the validity of objects and subjecting them to sculptural change. He would use traditional shapes like the Bavarian beer mug, but add breasts or a penis to flout convention. He prefers to think of himself as an 'expressionist' more than a glass-maker.

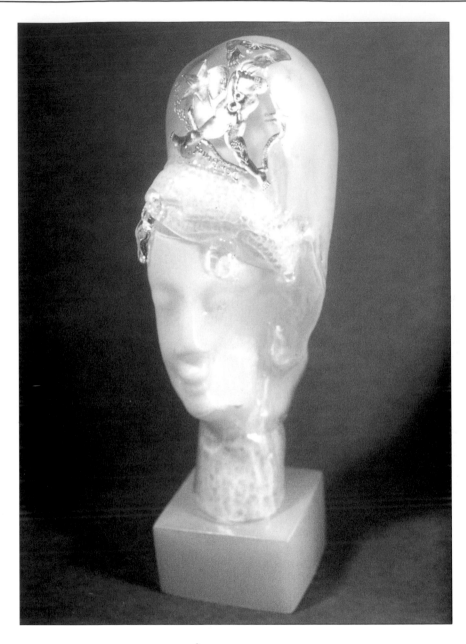

Erwin Eisch, 'Buddha's Head', 1982, mould-blown enamelled glass sculpture, engraved and gilded. H. 60 cm (23½ in)

Eisch was born in 1927 and began by studying glass engraving at his father's newly established glassworks in Frauenau. He continued his studies at the Fachschule at Zwiesel and from there went on to the Academy of Fine Arts in Munich to study glass design. He returned to Frauenau to found a glassworks with his brothers but then he went back to the Munich Academy to study painting and sculpture. His future wife Margarethe was also an art student there and together with Max Streck they formed an artists' group known as Radama. Margarethe and Erwin Eisch's first glass exhibition was in Stuttgart in 1962, the year of his famous meeting with Harvey Littleton. Although Eisch has exhibited extensively in Germany and was awarded first prize as the result of a controversial decision at the second Coburg Glass Prize in 1985, his work has met with greater understanding abroad, particularly in America, than at home. Unfortunately his healthy disrespect for the narrowness of the German craft tradition has had little effect in Germany, but it must also be said that he never really tried to be a part of any developments in glass outside his home town. Whilst he has taught at American academies, he has been loathe to do the same at home.

Eisch has always been against the inherent prettiness of glass, although he loves the material: 'I will work in glass in the future because it is a great medium. . . . Through the material I would like to show my way of living.'[5] At the same time, he has an ambivalent attitude towards glass technology, born of a suspicion that his work might be mistaken for craft:

> As one might expect from an 'expressionist' artist [Eisch's] forms are strictly personal. They are neither directly representational nor completely abstract. . . . To some people they are extremely ugly. In his quest to elevate glass to the level of an artistic medium, Erwin Eisch ignores the sophisticated attraction of the precisely shaped ornamental vessel and escapes that prettiness of chance suggested by much of the work that is being done in America.[6]

Some of Eisch's strongest and most original pieces are the funky sculptures from the 1960s – the series of Harvey Littleton heads, finger sculptures and melting telephones already mentioned. That body of work is imbued with a genuine crusading passion that has been difficult to sustain. At that period it was highly relevant to mock qualities of functionalism and glassiness. By introducing metallic veiling on the surface of the glass and by denying it transparency, Eisch felt he was giving glass an existence in its own right far removed from any suspicion of its traditional functionalism. His use of technique for sculptural ends, and those first heart-felt statements in glass, will always remain some of the most important pieces historically and artistically from that period and were the catalyst for major change in the world of glass. During the 1970s he worked on distorted vessel forms engraved and painted mainly with gold or silver lustre, with figurative symbols loosely rooted in 'expressionism'. Since 1982 he has worked on a series of mould-blown Buddha heads, continuing to use much the same engraving and painting techniques to decorate them. He has always liked to exhibit his oil or acrylic paintings alongside his work in glass.

WEST GERMAN LAMPWORKERS

Surprising as it is, Erwin Eisch has remained an outsider in his home country and there was no rush by other artists to follow his example. Apart from the many lampworkers, there are still comparatively few artists in glass working in West Germany. With the exception of three or four sculptors (and apart from all those working in flat glass), nearly all German glass is vessel-orientated. West German lampworked glass is distinguished by its wide colour palette. A number of artists have been influenced by the work of Kurt Wallstab, the longest-established lampworker (born in 1920), who, like many others, had studied techniques for making laboratory glass but changed course because of the lack of employment in that area. There are two basic types of lampworked decoration, both of which Wallstab has used. In the first, lightly iridescent glass is flecked and spotted with a range of colours; in most of these pieces the colours and shapes are pulled about whilst the glass is hot and the end result is a thin blown asymmetric vessel form. In the other type, vessels are more formally shaped and a brightly coloured marbled effect is achieved by the 'montage' technique, first developed by Wallstab and now used by a number of others, such as Walter Bahr, Kuno Hackl, Matthias Klering and Roderich Wohlgemuth, in which thin layers of colour are applied and often outlined in black to achieve a more dramatic colour separation. Pavel Molnar has proved a very popular colourist with his subtle range of coloured metal oxides. Lubomír Hora, who was born in Czechoslovakia in 1946 and emigrated to West Germany in 1968, discovered glass at a seminar for lamp-blowing laboratory instruments during his career as an atomic chemist, and established his own studio for artistic lampwork in 1975. Rosemarie Lierke and Gunther Kehr have both evolved a personal style of lampworking, Kehr with his cellular mosaic-like decoration and Lierke with a wide range of inventive techniques, including an effective *craquelé* effect.

HOT-GLASS ARTISTS

A number of West German artists also work in hot glass in a variety of styles, yet with the exception of Stanislaw Borowski, the reputation they have made for themselves is mainly restricted to their own country. Borowski is of Polish origin, as his name suggests, and he emigrated to Germany in 1982 at the age of thirty-eight. Since that time he has fast built an international reputation for himself with his highly personal demonic imagery on vessels, which combine technical wizardry with visionary imagination. The visions of horror he uses, reminiscent of Hieronymus Bosch, are cut through multiple layers of glass built up with thin layers of colour. Udo Edelmann is one of the few artists in West Germany who sculpts in hot glass, making free-blown organic shapes using mainly clear glass with touches of colour. Ursula Huth, who is a graduate from the Stuttgart Academy and also studied at the Rhode Island School of Design, has worked on architectural commissions, but she also makes small objects in free-blown glass, often with freely painted enamelled decoration. Theodor Sellner, and more recently Gerd Kruft, have both been using a variation of the Graal technique, originally invented in 1918 at Orrefors, Sweden, in which the decoration is engraved in between layers of glass which are then reheated gently, distorting the imagery in the process. Both these artists use either figurative or landscape decoration. The usual technique involves sand-blasting the decoration into the glass, but Sellner has incorporated a lampworking process into his Graal technique which allows for more flexibility. More recently he has been making three-dimensional figures composed of blown or lampworked elements, sometimes heads with mask-like faces, sometimes ritualistic objects inspired by tribal art. He is something of a satirist, with a penchant for 'magical objects whose ritual character stands somewhere between crypticism and the Devil'.[7] Reiner Modell, Gerhard Schechinger and Alois Wudy also all work in hot glass, each using an individual technique that gives the work its style.

GLASS ENGRAVERS

There are a number of talented West German glass engravers, but this technique, rather like lampworking, involves narrow disciplines which lie a little way apart from the less rigorous approach of most artists working in glass today. But Jiří Harcuba in Czechoslovakia and Ron Pennell in England have done a lot to change the somewhat separatist attitudes of glass

OPPOSITE TOP LEFT: **Stanislaw Borowski**, vase, 1981, blown glass, engraved and sand-blasted

OPPOSITE BELOW LEFT: **Ursula Huth**, 'Castle', 1984–5, free-blown glass. H. 25 cm (9¾ in)

OPPOSITE TOP RIGHT: **Gerhard Schechinger**, 'Fire and Water', 1983, free-blown glass with coloured decoration and iridescent surface. H. 23 cm (9 in)

OPPOSITE BELOW RIGHT: **Theodor Sellner**, 'Hilfe Glas', 1984, 'lamo' technique – a combination of lampwork and blown glass. H. 50 cm (19¾ in)

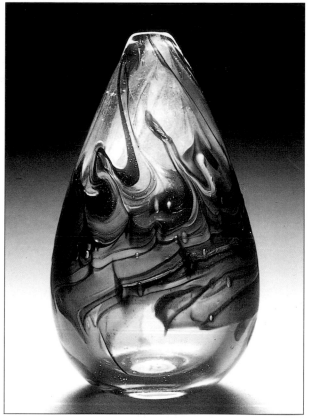

engravers. In West Germany two influential artists provided a basis upon which contemporary engravers could build. Wilhelm von Eiff (1890–1943) was the finest engraver of the earlier part of the century and taught cutting and engraving to a whole generation of glass-makers at the Stuttgart Academy from 1922 onwards. Hans Modell, who was a pupil of von Eiff at Stuttgart from 1929 to 1933, continued his master's tradition and has been a self-employed freelance artist in Stuttgart since 1933.

Among a younger generation of engravers the work of Kristian Klepsch, Helmut Köhler, Ernst Krebs, Karin Stöckle-Krumbein and Freia Schulze has been outstanding. Kristian Klepsch combines engraving with a number of other processes, including the Graal technique and casting. His imagery can be described as grotesque allegory, usually based on some literary quotation. It has something in common with that of Erwin Eisch and both of them were students at the Munich Academy of Fine Arts, though Eisch is younger by seventeen years. Klepsch has also used optical cut in a few sculptural pieces. Helmut Köhler was born in Czechoslovakia but emigrated to West Germany in 1977. Although his work is not really comparable to Klepsch's, he too engraves allegorical scenes on vessel forms, the surface of which is sometimes lightly iridescent. Ernst Krebs, who also studied at the Munich Academy of Fine Arts, is more of a stipple engraver and once again his imagery has a tendency to be allegorical, though it is more abstract than the work already mentioned. Karin Stöckle-Krumbein is another Munich Academy graduate, whilst Freia Schulze,

Karin Stöckle-Krumbein, engraved footed bowl, 1978

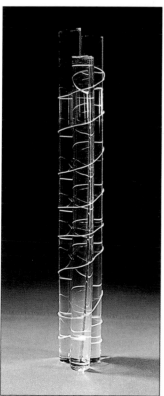

FAR LEFT: **Ernst Krebs**, 'Bundled Light II', 1984, three glass rods bound with wire. H. 53 cm (20¾ in)

LEFT: **Freia Schulze**, 'Glass Cylinder', 1984, sand-blasted glass, painted with enamels and engraved. H. 40 cm (15¾ in)

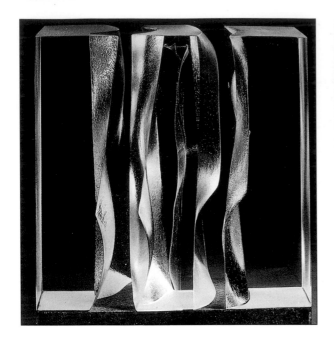

studied at Stourbridge in England and then spent eight months working in Erwin Eisch's studio at Frauenau. It is interesting to note how many of these engravers also studied painting either at the Munich Academy or elsewhere, and how all of them are to some degree a part of the German 'expressionist' movement.

ABOVE LEFT: **Willi Pistor**, untitled glass sculpture, 1982, cast optical glass, etched. 24 x 21 x 12.5 cm (9½ x 8¼ x 5 in)

ABOVE: **Karl Berg**, sculpture, 1985, clear optical glass, cut and polished, with aluminium base. H. 25.5 cm (10 in), W. 18 cm (7 in)

GLASS SCULPTURE

German glass sculptors have, like the Czechs, mostly used optical cutting in their work. Willi Pistor and Karl Berg are the best known. Willi Pistor, despite his thankless task teaching at the trade school in Hadamar since 1962, has produced an impressive body of work. His technique involves cutting blocks of optical glass which are then melted in fire-clay moulds; during the cooling process an exactly predetermined fine veil of bubbles appears inside his objects, which are then shaped and decorated with cutting. Karl Berg's fine optically cut and highly polished crystal objects are very much in the Czech tradition. Franz Xaver Hoeller, whose background includes studies both at the Fachschule in Zwiesel and the Academy of Fine Arts in Munich, shows both imagination and a feeling for colour in his sculptural work, which once again relies mainly on cutting and polishing for its artistic effect. Josef Welzel has taught at Hadamar along with Willi Pistor since 1963, and uses a combination of optical cutting and engraving in his work.

There is one sculptor working in Germany whose work is very different from the rest and who stands in a class on his own. Renato Santarossa was born in Italy in 1943 and worked as a construction engineer in Italy and Germany during the 1960s. He has been a freelance artist only since 1976 and now lives and works in Cologne, but he exhibits internationally. He works exclusively in window glass, carefully shaping it by cutting and then grouping it to form sculptural objects, which can be monumental in scale. The glass is cut with an ordinary glass cutter and there is no colour in his work apart from that provided by the refraction of light. The work is cool, clear and rational, and reflects the part of his life spent as an engineer.

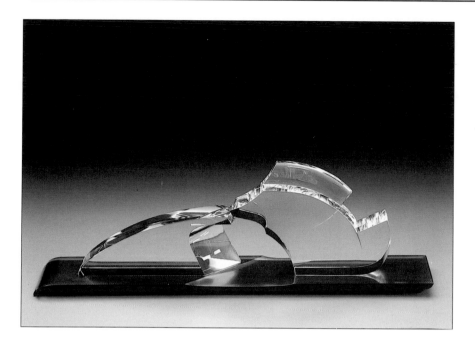

Franz Xaver Hoeller,
'Golden Bridge', 1981, optical cut
glass sculpture in three parts
(awarded Deutscher
Wirtschaftsjuniorenpreis 1981).
H. 25 cm (9¾ in), L. 70 cm
(27½ in)

Renato Santarossa, 'The
Princess's Fan', c. 1988, fused
glass blades with painted
decoration between the layers
of glass 3.4 × 2.1 m (11 × 7 ft)

PAINTED GLASS

Most of the painted glass in West Germany is to be found in architecture, with one notable exception. Isgard Moje-Wohlgemuth was born in 1941 and until the mid 1970s was married to one of the best-known and most individual of all German glass artists, Klaus Moje, who has been in Australia since 1982 and whose work will be discussed in Chapter 6. Klaus and Isgard Moje began decorating glass in the late 1960s, mostly lead glass blown to their specifications and decorated with metallic resinates painted in layers. Whilst Klaus Moje went on to work in another technique, Isgard Moje-Wohlgemuth has continued to work in the same way. She produces simple but very carefully thought out vessel forms; after a visit to Japan recently kimono shapes began to appear in her decoration. She has an unerring sense of colour and uses metal oxides with consummate artistry, always sensitive to effects that can be gained from varying degrees of transparency. The decoration is nearly always abstract and has a strong geometric feeling to it, with grid patterns and lattices in rich colours. Although Isgard Moje-Wohlgemuth has continued to use the same technique for a period of over twenty years, her work has always remained remarkably fresh in spirit and she has successfully maintained a developing style without repeating herself.

AUSTRIA AND SWITZERLAND

In Austria the firm of Lobmeyr has more or less single-handedly been responsible for any encouragement to young glass artists; the company has staged exhibitions at its showrooms in Vienna and invited artists from all over the world to use a special studio facility set up for them in Baden bei Wien. There are now a few independent glass artists working in Austria, the longest-established of whom, Jack Ink, an American by birth, has been working there since 1975, first as artist in residence at Lobmeyr and later in his own studio. He has worked principally in hot glass, translating a painterly feeling for impressionist landscapes into the language of glass. His main concern has been to feel as free when 'painting' in hot glass as he could if he were painting on paper or canvas. Helmut Werner Huntsdorfer also works in hot glass, making sculptural vessel forms that are inspired by nature.

There are only a few glass artists working in Switzerland, but since the early 1970s there has been some museum interest there; the exhibition entitled 'Glas Heute: Kunst oder Handwerk?' held at the Museum Bellerive in Zürich in 1972 included works by Erwin Eisch, Gian Paolo Martinuzzi, a number of American artists, and the Swiss artist Roberto Niederer. Roberto Niederer had his own glassworks and opened a contemporary glass gallery in Lucerne which was one of the first devoted exclusively to glass in Europe. Among the handful of other artists working in Switzerland, the best known are Monica Guggisberg and Philip Baldwin. The clear colours and pure lines in their work, particularly a series of large brightly coloured plates in cased glass with acid-etched or sand-blasted geometric designs, hark back to a two-year period when they both worked as assistants to Ann Wolff and Wilke Adolfsson at Transjö in Sweden.

OPPOSITE BELOW LEFT: **Roberto Niederer**, '4 Glass Panes for September', 1983, heat-shaped and cast glass. Diam. 26.5 cm (10½ in). (Photo: Emanuel Amon)

OPPOSITE BELOW RIGHT: **Monica Guggisberg** and **Philip Baldwin**, 'Checkered Wave', 1984, free-blown glass with colour overlay, sand-blasted. Diam. 38 cm (15 in)

Isgard Moje-Wohlgemuth,
two cylinders, 1972,
mould-blown glass, painted with
metal oxides in layers and fired
several times. H. 20 cm (7¾ in)
and 17 cm (6¾ in)

BELOW: **Jack Ink**, vase, c. 1986,
cased iridescent glass with
iridescent trailed colour

SWEDEN

There has been a lively Scandinavian studio glass tradition since the early part of the twentieth century, particularly in Sweden, where since the end of the First World War a special department has existed at Orrefors for the design of studio glass. It was here that the Graal technique was developed (starting in 1917) by Gustaf Bergqvist, the master blower at Orrefors, in conjunction with chief designers Edward Hald and Simon Gate. Gate and Hald remained in the forefront as designers for nearly half a century and the initiative at Orrefors inspired the glass industry throughout Scandinavia to follow suit with studio glass departments that by an unwritten law became almost obligatory in every glassworks. During the 1950s the Scandinavian studio glass tradition was at its peak and known worldwide. It was therefore something of a shock to the industry when artists began to think of becoming independent during the 1960s and started setting up their own studios. Many of them have been successful, but the studio tradition survives and is to some extent a positive influence because it serves as a constant reminder of quality. A respect for their material continues to be second nature to glass artists in Scandinavia today, many of whom began their careers in glass as designers for industry, and some of whom still devote a part of their time to this. It was in 1968 that Asa Brandt, who had just graduated from the Royal College of Art in London, introduced the new spirit of contemporary glass to Sweden. With Pauline Solven, another Royal College graduate who helped her for the first six months, she opened the first independent glass studio in Sweden in Torshälla. The two artists showed their work at an exhibition in Malmö shortly afterwards.

OPPOSITE: **Asa Brandt**, 'Kites', 1988, slumped, sand-blasted and painted glass

Ulla Forsell, 'Fragile Homes', 1988, assembled glass. H. c. 37 cm (14½ in)

WOMEN ARTISTS IN SWEDEN, AND BERTIL VALLIEN

Several Swedish artists followed Asa Brandt's lead, and a group comprised of her, Ulla Forsell, Eva Ullberg and Anders Wingard called themselves the 'free-blowers'. All of them work in hot glass. Asa Brandt says:

> I think it is impossible for anyone not living in Sweden, that famous glass country, to appreciate fully how revolutionary my idea about working with glass in a small studio was at that time. Swedish studio glass was born because I wanted to work with glass in the same way as I had worked with clay. For a period of eight years I was the only person in Sweden working this way. I had that dream about glass, the dream that glass belonged to the artist.[8]

She expresses herself in free-blown vessels and pastel colours. In Ulla Forsell's light-hearted fantasies small coloured glass elements, suspended away from the main body of the glass, sometimes with coloured thread, float like kites. She says, 'I don't care whether I blow the piece the "right" way or not, as long as I can bring light and poetry and humour into the glass and keep its magic.'[9] There is a charming naivety about these statements or Eva Ullberg's comment, 'I enjoy blowing goblets the whole day',[10] which is a key to this first departure from the conventional Swedish studio glass tradition.

Of the thirteen Swedish artists whose work was shown at the Coburg Glass Prize in 1985 nine were women, and in recent years feminism has played an important role in Swedish glass. Ann Wolff and Ulrica Hydman-Vallien, two of the leading artists in Sweden today, are both deeply concerned in their work with the role of women in the modern world. Each expresses herself with equal force but with totally different imagery. Both of them are or have been married to glass artists, and both have spent a good deal of their time as designers in the glass industry.

Ann Wolff (Ann Wärff) was born in West Germany, studied there, and came to Sweden to work in the glass industry right at the beginning of her career in 1960. From 1964 to 1978, during most of which time she was married to Goran Wärff, both of them worked as designers for Kosta Boda. As early as 1968 she was awarded the Lunning prize for her designs. During her period at Kosta she learnt diamond-engraving and sand-blasting techniques on double- and triple-overlay glass, and she has continued using these throughout her career. In 1977 she was awarded first prize at Coburg, and it was after this that she decided to become independent and opened her own studio with Wilke Adolfsson, Kosta's master glass-blower, at Transjö. They have since parted company and Adolfsson now has his own studio, but during their years of collaboration he blew the basic shapes under careful supervision from Ann Wolff; she then created her very personal imagery with the cold techniques that she had learnt at Kosta. She deals in her work with domestic tasks, marriage, divorce, childhood, motherhood, joy and sorrow, oppression and love of life. There is often a reel of cotton in her imagery, binding man and woman together, binding woman to a bird, to her child, to her furniture. Private symbols – scissors, tables, chairs, milk-urns, the trappings of a woman's everyday life, each of which is imbued with special significance – make repeated appearances. 'Ann Wärff shows us the path between reality and the soul; she shows us

BELOW: **Ann Wolff**, 'The Large
Game', 1984, sculpture – plate,
acid-etched, sand-blasted on
multi-coloured underlays.
Diam. 60 cm (23½ in)

BELOW: **Ann Wolff**,
'Cup and Saucer', 1980s,
blown cased glass,
sand-blasted and acid-etched.
H. c. 12.5 cm (5 in)

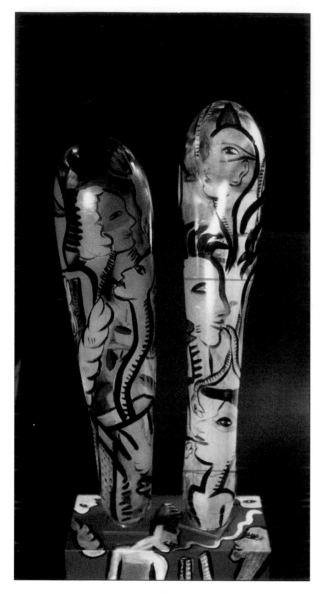

woman with her earth-bound body and her soul trying to escape heaven-wards. Her long hair is a sign of liberation, floating like a cloud, but threat-ened by the scissors of a child.'[11]

Since 1982 Ann Wolff has been interested in printing, at first with glass plates and then with copper ones. In recent years her work has changed. The symbols now form a background; in the foreground a haunting woman's face, a sort of fertility goddess, dominates the work. New colours have begun to appear. Since 1986 she has collaborated with Dirk Bimberg to present the work in a more sculptural context. 'A compact, short pulled glass stem supports the round disc; it assumes, so to speak, the function of the body.'[12] She has also begun to use supports other than glass. Her talents are outstanding; she has an innate feeling for glass, but this is combined with a very personal talent for both drawing and watercolour, all of which she has used with consummate skill and imagination in her work as a glass artist. She is living proof that if the artistic talent is there, all of it can be used in glass.

ABOVE LEFT: **Ulrica Hydman-Vallien**, 'Free Relations', 1985, free-blown, painted sculpture. H. 75 cm (29½ in), W. 37 cm (14½ in)

ABOVE: **Ulrica Hydman-Vallien**, 'Bird Nest', 1975, free-blown and painted glass. H. 52 cm (20½ in), W. 30.5 cm (12 in)

Feminism is the only link between Ann Wolff and Ulrica Hydman-Vallien, though Ulrica Vallien's view of it concentrates on a different aspect:

I don't very often paint men as they look because they are . . . kind of dull to look at. A woman is more interesting. They paint themselves up and there is something in their hair and they're so fun. Men are so boring to look at. I always make them in different shapes; if they are strong they are animals, very strong animals; when they are weak, they can be a birdman . . . . I don't know how to make a man, just an ordinary man.[13]

When Ulrica Vallien started working in glass, she began painting her dream-like fantasies directly onto it. Her painting is spontaneous, with a tendency towards the naive. Her background training was in ceramics, which she studied at the National College of Arts and Design in Stockholm from 1958 to 1961 and then in Mexico and America for a further two years, and she maintains this interest by designing ceramics for Rörstrand. It was not until 1972 that she began freelancing as a designer at Kosta Boda. As her glass skills improved she worked in a technique that is a combination of sand-blasting, etching and painting on an underlay and overlay of crystal glass in different colours.

Ulrica met her husband Bertil Vallien when they were both students at the same school in Stockholm where, among his many activities, Bertil Vallien taught from 1967 to 1982. He is one of the greatest all-rounders in the glass world today. His reputation as a teacher, designer and, above all, one of the most imaginative living artists in glass is worldwide. He is the ideal person to be working in glass, because the material suggests so much to him and he manipulates it with amazing dexterity. Certainly he is one of the most versatile artists in the world today, but impressive though it be, his technical skill is never intrusive. It is he who controls the glass and not the other way around. As an artist he has both a public and a private life. For six months of the year he designs blown-glass products for the commercial market at Kosta, where he has been since 1963. Apart from this he teaches and also designs in a number of materials other than glass, including ceramics, stainless steel and wood, sometimes executing large sculptural commissions in a combination of materials. He has his own studio at Afors where these are produced. But the most important part of his life remains his artistic work in glass for which he is responsible only to himself.

His earliest unique pieces were produced at Kosta Boda, where much of his artistic sand-cast work is still produced now. At the beginning of his career there was some similarity between his work and that of his wife, with dream-like imagery on bowls decorated with birds carrying human figures in top hats through a starry sky, and reindeer standing on crags below. 'It's a story about freedom and captivity all the time; a top-hatted man with his wings represents . . . me or someone who had the courage to try his abilities. In Sweden . . . you wear the top hat at occasions like a death or a marriage, when you are at the peak of your career, become a professor or something.'[14] But Vallien has moved away from these early figures towards abstract symbolism as his work has become more sculptural. At first in his cast pieces the figures were lifted straight from the bowl and became three-dimensional. Gradually the symbolism concentrated on bridges and

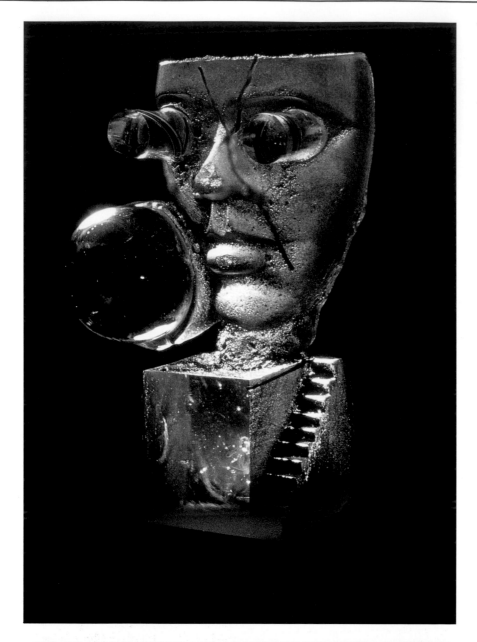

Bertil Vallien, 'Jerzy Kozinski
– a portrait of an author
describing the evil of man',
sand-cast, cut and polished
sculpture. H. 30.5 cm (12 in)

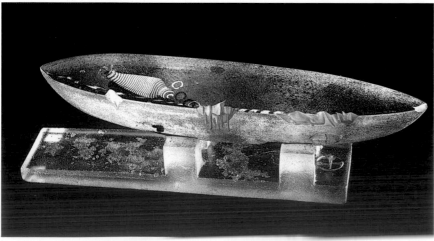

Bertil Vallien, ship, c. 1987,
sand-cast sculpture, offhand
details, cut and polished

houses. For Vallien the house, both in real and philosophical terms, represents a symbolic container for all life's forces; the bridge is a structure that
stretches towards hope, a link between one state of mind and the next. The
imagery in his work is to do with the cut and thrust of life's energy. More
recently all this rich symbolism has been contained in boat forms; the boats
seem like shipwrecks lying secretly on the sea-bed. In his descriptive note
for a ship made in 1984 for the second Coburg exhibition he wrote, 'The
ship is a symbol of the universe. You can neither be seen nor heard in a ship.
The ship is a symbol of life, birth, womanhood.'[15]

The method he uses to make sculpture is sand-casting, a skill which he
has refined and developed with all the artistry and talent in him. He is
attracted to this technique because it provides the possibility of being able
to create in a spontaneous way, letting the inspiration of the moment be a
part of the process. Before the sand-casting session there are preparatory
drawings to be made and careful planning to be done, and after a cooling
process lasting two days the sculptures are worked on with a variety of cold
processes, including sand-blasting, cutting and polishing.

INDUSTRIAL STUDIO GLASS

In Sweden the ties between art and industry remain strong, despite the
secessionist tendencies of the 1970s. Both at Kosta and at Orrefors there is
an impressive range of studio glass made by some of Sweden's top designers.
At Orrefors a studio workshop was established in 1980 devoted to the
research of new techniques and the development of artistic concepts.
Pieces are still produced in the Ariel technique – in which there is air-
trapped decoration in between layers of glass – which they are justifiably
proud of having invented, to designs by Eva Englund and Olle Alberius.

Eva Englund, three bowls,
1984, Graal technique.
(Collection von Bartha)

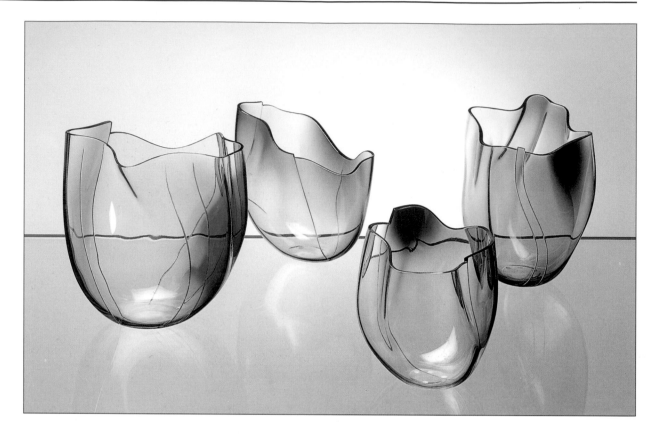

Gunnar Cyren, who has been a designer there since 1959, continues to pour out new ideas, and his most recent cut pieces are among the finest to have come out of Sweden. Lars Hellsten and Jan Johannson both design sculptural forms for production by the studio department. Kosta has of course managed to keep Bertil and Ulrica Vallien, but there are also younger designers working there, such as Kjell Engman, who are still attracted by the technical skills that the industry can put at their disposal. As in Czechoslovakia glass design is considered a worthwhile tradition, and this applies in all the Scandinavian countries.

Gunnar Cyren, Orrefors, Sweden, four blown and cut unique glass bowls, 1985–6. H. c. 15 cm (6 in). (Collection von Bartha)

FINLAND

The Finnish glass industry has had an excellent reputation in post-war years, largely due to the genius of two men, Tapio Wirkkala and Timo Sarpaneva, both of whom designed for Iittala. Tapio Wirkkala was the industrial designer par excellence, sensitive to the aesthetic and technical possibilities of whatever material he worked in. Some of his pieces, like the 'chanterelle' vase of the 1950s, are classics of modern design. Sarpaneva has designed in wood and ceramics as well as glass, but has devoted his energies mainly to glass in recent times, dividing his time between designing limited-edition series pieces and large unique sculptures. He is a romantic at heart. Of the 'Claritas' collection of vases designed in 1984, he said, 'I wanted to seal bands of eternity into the silence of the glass. I wanted to deposit this fast-fading present moment there in all its fragile beauty.'[16] This series was made up of sixty-six basic designs in black, white or clear cased glass, in

which the focal point was a trapped bubble of air or a series of trapped bubbles. Most recently he has been working on a series of massive 'Glass Age' sculptures in which he carves glass blocks, sometimes weighing several hundreds of kilos, resting on carved granite bases. There is a primeval quality about them.

Sarpaneva has tried hard to break away from the role of industrial designer in which he has been cast for so long, but the pull of an industrial setting is strong, particularly when it has become second nature during the course of nearly a whole lifetime. It is a pull felt by the younger generation of glass artists in Finland as well. Many of these are conscious of what has been happening in America and elsewhere, but in Finland the umbilical cord between art and industry has not yet been broken, perhaps because the ties established during the course of the twentieth century have been so

ABOVE LEFT: **Timo Sarpaneva**, 'Fecunditas', 1983, sculpture in clear glass. 37 × 17 × 7 cm (14½ × 6¾ × 2¾ in)

ABOVE: **Timo Sarpaneva**, Black Ittala lancet vase, 1957, blown glass. H. 21 cm (8¼ in)

strong and healthy that there is no need for a break. Oiva Toikka is one of the best-known artists working in Finland today and his wide-ranging work includes designs for industry as well as light-hearted decorative sculptural pieces, loosely related to pop art. But significantly Toikka sees himself above all as a designer, as do most others working in glass in Finland today.

DENMARK

In Denmark glass is produced in about twenty different places, with a concentration of four small glasshouses on the island of Bornholm and the rest spread throughout the country. 'Most of the art glass is in the "painterly" style, usually superimposed on traditional, functional shapes and seldom with completely realised sculptural qualities.'[17] The principal glassworks, Holmegaard, has a studio glass department where Michael Bang and Per Lutken have been designers for over twenty years. Functionalism continues to be the determining factor in Danish glass design, together with a cool sense of colour, as seen in the bowls of Darylle Hinz and Anja Kjaer, who have a workshop and gallery combined in Copenhagen. Hinz is a Californian, but his glass training has been in Scandinavia and his glass makes little reference to his American background.

Finn Lynggard is virtually the only Dane whose glass tends toward the sculptural, often made up of mould-blown components partly of architec-

ABOVE LEFT: **Oiva Toikka**, 'Helen's Bath', 1987, glass sculpture, cubes made by the paperweight technique, cut and glued. 50 x 31 x 31 cm (19¾ x 12¼ x 12¼ in)

ABOVE: **Finn Lynggard**, 'Archaic Scenery I', 1985, sand-cast, sand-blasted and polished sculpture. 44 x 25.5 x 9.5 cm (17¼ x 10 x 3¾ in)

Darylle Hinz and **Anja Kjaer**,
three vases, free-blown glass

tural inspiration, partly figurative, like the two pieces shown at the second Coburg Glass Prize exhibition in 1985. In one of them a rhinoceros is perched on a Greek column; in the other a different model of a rhinoceros stands on a series of architectural fragments in glass surmounted by arches, and there is a rainbow in the background. After years of planning, master-minded by Lynggard, a glass museum was opened in Ebeltoft, 'that would offer a panorama of glass art which the artists themselves would determine'.[18] It opened with five hundred objects given by three hundred artists from twenty-eight countries, and is a glass museum intended to 'belong to the glass artists themselves'.[19]

NORWAY

In Norway there is still little interest in artistic glass away from the industry. The best-known and most innovative Norwegian glass artist in post-war years has been Benny Motzfeld, who turned to glass in mid-career after having been a successful watercolourist. Her restless creative urge and a continual search for new materials and combinations led her to develop several new techniques. At first she created graphic effects by the inclusion of metal particles in the glass, and later she invented a process whereby glass-fibre fabric was fused onto the glass, making it possible to make collages in glass with some striking effects.

5. BRITAIN, HOLLAND, FRANCE, BELGIUM AND ITALY

BRITAIN

During the first half of the twentieth century British glass was somewhat staid. There was little excitement apart from the occasional innovative design and no studio glass tradition worth mentioning. It is all the more surprising, therefore, how many new glass artists have emerged in Britain over the last two decades. Perhaps lack of precedent has been a positive contributing factor to so much originality among a new generation of British glass artists. During the 1950s there was some very fine glass engraving, particularly from Laurence Whistler and John Hutton, both of whom are great originals in their own ways. Laurence Whistler's soft-wooded landscapes stippled onto glass are unmistakably English. He developed a technique in which he worked on both sides of the glass, thereby creating an illusion of

Laurence Whistler, 'The Overflowing Landscape', 1974, lead crystal bowl, stipple engraving. H. 23 cm (9 in), diam. 23 cm (9 in). (Photo: The Crafts Advisory Committee)

OPPOSITE: **David Taylor**, scent bottles, 1986, blown, cut and carved glass. H. 22–25 cm (8¾–9¾ in)

perspective. John Hutton, like Whistler, was also a technical innovator, who, rather than moving the glass about against a rotating wheel to engrave it, devised a method whereby the glass could be held still and the grindstones fitted to a flexible drive, allowing the engraver to work with a skill more closely related to drawing with a pencil. In this way Hutton could use his considerable drawing talents as an engraver on glass. In spirit both artists were ahead of their time, but nothing they did could have been a pointer to what would happen when a modern glass programme was initiated by Sam Herman at the Royal College of Art in the late 1960s.

Sam Herman had studied with Harvey Littleton before he came to Britain on a Fulbright scholarship in 1965. After a brief period at Edinburgh College of Art, he was awarded a Research Fellowship at the Royal College of Art in London and later became tutor in charge of the glass department of the School of Ceramics and Glass. Writing in *Crafts* magazine in 1976, Dillon Clarke, one of the first graduates from the glass department, referred to him as 'perhaps the doyen of studio glass artists in this country and the apostle who inspired many of us to take up our blowpipes'.[1] In those early days Sam Herman was quickly noticed because he introduced a freedom and fluidity never before seen in British glass. He had the nerve and irreverence of the hippie generation which, combined with a feeling for rich swirling colours and strong form, soon earned him his reputation as an artist with something unusual to say and, more important perhaps, an unusual medium to say it in. Herman has always worked principally in hot glass, sometimes with a premeditated approach using drawings and watercolours to help develop his ideas, but more often starting with no preconceived

ABOVE LEFT: **John Hutton**, vase, 1958–9, stipple engraving. H. 42.5 cm (16¾ in)

ABOVE: **Sam Herman**, vase, 1967, free-blown and applied glass. H. 18.5 cm (7¼ in)

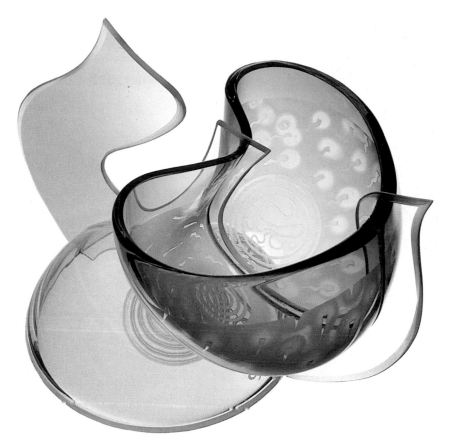

intentions. 'Once the initial choice of glass is made, instinct and experience lead onward. As the form alters, it is necessary to be alert to this so that the piece may be developed through the plastic changes that occur during creation. In effect it is to be hoped that the glass itself will initiate its own final form.'[2] Apart from a six-year interlude (1974–80) when he also introduced the wonders of contemporary glass to Australia, Herman has made his home in England, working, teaching and exhibiting. It is the graduates from his classes at the Royal College of Art who have been responsible for establishing a modern glass tradition in Great Britain.

GLASS EDUCATION IN BRITAIN

Sam Herman taught at the Royal College of Art from 1969 to 1974 and during that period had the greatest influence on glass students in Britain whether they were students of his or not. His free and easy, somewhat haphazard style did not suit everybody, but it did a great deal to introduce new life into British glass and generate enthusiasm and excitement where there had been none for a long time. This was true even when he had the effect of making people react against him, because what he was doing with glass seemed so extreme at the time that the reaction was always a positive one. The artist Ray Flavell commented, 'At the time I found Sam Herman's emphasis on free expression rather limiting without a thorough grasp of technique, so I went to Orrefors glass school to learn.'[3]

When Ray Flavell returned to England from Orrefors he taught at the West Surrey College of Art and Design in Farnham, where he had previously worked from 1966 until he went to Sweden; there he influenced, with fellow teachers Stephen Procter and Annette Meech, a whole generation of artists. His style, as one might expect from someone trained in Scandinavia, is much more controlled than Sam Herman's. A deep respect for the material and for glass-working techniques always shows in his work. He very often works in clear glass, and when he uses colour that too has a clarity about it. He is basically a vessel maker, though he has also used vessel forms as elements in a series of sculptures that have poise and charm. His method of decorating the surface is usually by sand-blasting. 'The colourless crystal bowls are treated with sand-blasting and explore a fantasy world of light and imagery that at first looks familiar but on close scrutiny is lacking a known identity.'[4] Apart from his artistic work he has also designed glass for Stevens and Williams and Royal Brierly Crystal.

West Surrey College and the Royal College of Art have the two longest-established glass programmes in Britain, but there are now several other art colleges with up-to-date undergraduate glass programmes. The other principal ones are at Leicester Polytechnic; at Stourbridge in the heart of the main glass-making area in England; and in Sunderland. In addition there are a number of others throughout Britain, making a total of about thirty in all – a large number for a comparatively small country. The postgraduate course at the Royal College of Art remains the only available one.

THE GLASSHOUSE AND GLASS CO-OPERATIVES

Sam Herman's lifestyle as much as his teaching was an influence in England, where the idea of living as an independent artist in glass was virtually unknown. Whilst at the Royal College of Art he was instrumental in setting up The Glasshouse, which has been in existence since 1969 and is still flourishing today. It was the first time a 'group of young glass students for once had not sat down and moaned about the poor prospects in established industry, but had decided to go it alone'.[5] The Glasshouse inspired others either to set up on their own or to form similar co-operatives, and as a result there is now a large and interesting group of artists working in Britain.

The Glasshouse and other glass co-operatives provide another new tradition in Britain. The Glasshouse is the longest-established co-operative, combining a workshop with a gallery in the heart of London. There has been a change of personalities there over the years and none of the founding members remains. At the time of writing The Glasshouse is made up of five artists – Annette Meech, Chris Williams, Fleur Tookey, David Taylor, and the most recent addition Annabel Newman. All of them are glass-blowers who blow their own shapes, which are then worked on according to the needs of each individual. Christopher Williams' vessel shapes are blown into moulds (often made of steel) and the surfaces worked on with cutting and sand-blasting when the glass is cold to reveal or modify the colour. In Fleur Tookey's bowls and plates, 'many layers of coloured glass powders and "chips" are "trailed" around the "bubble" before the object is fully expanded and shaped. A final coating of colour on the outside of the objects gives a background to the design.'[6] David Taylor, who trained initially as a jeweller at the Central School of Art and then studied glass in Sweden, joined The Glasshouse in 1972. He makes scent bottles of two types. In the simpler ones, blown elements of various colours are assembled to form rhythmic shapes. The others are technically more complicated and

OPPOSITE TOP LEFT: **Annette Meech**, The Glasshouse, 'Scratched Bowl', 1987–8, free-blown glass with diamond engraving on the inside. H. 36 cm (14¼ in), diam. 28 cm (11 in)

OPPOSITE BELOW LEFT: **Catherine Hough**, scent bottles, 1988, blown and cut glass. H. c. 12.5 cm (5 in)

Christopher Williams, The Glasshouse, 'Melon Bottle', 1988, mould-blown glass, sand-blasted and cut. H. 37 cm (14½ in)

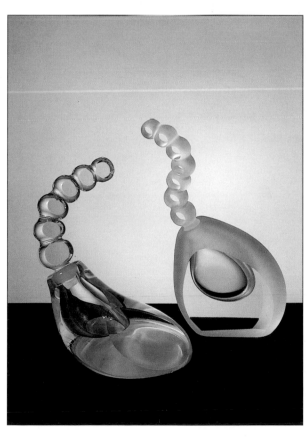

involve detailed carving in which his skills as a jeweller are employed. The surface finish on these pieces is achieved by acid-etching.

Three artists – Catherine Hough, Steven Newell and Simon Moore – who once used to be at The Glasshouse, have recently formed another partnership, called Glassworks (London) Ltd, which allows them to share running expenses. Catherine Hough also makes scent bottles but she

seldom uses colour, preferring to cut or slice a pattern onto the surface of the glass. Steven Newell, who was a founder member of The Glasshouse, is American by birth but has studied and worked principally in England. His large plates and bowls are decorated with dream-like fantasies in a style unmistakably his own, often involving animal or human figures etched or sand-blasted onto the surface. Simon Moore is the youngest of the three by a decade or more and the difference in age is underlined by the obvious influence of newer trends such as post-modernism and Memphis in his work. His pieces began by being more conventional than they are now that he has yielded to the temptations of current fashion and likes to mock functionalism. 'His work totally defies classification, a humorous mixture of English bonbons and Venetian Baroque.'[7]

Simon Moore, group of three vases, 1987, blown glass, with clear triangular prunts. H. 24–32 cm (9½–12½ in)

OPPOSITE: **Steven Newell**, '1988 Free Style Champions', 1988, bowl, inside cased, sand-blasted and polished. H. 23 cm (9 in), diam. 23 cm (9 in)

One of the other founding members of The Glasshouse, Peter Layton, established the London Glassblowing Workshop in 1970 at Rotherhithe in East London. Partners and associates have come and gone over the past two decades while he stays on working in hot glass, usually with a combed iridescent pattern and sometimes combining metals with glass by electroforming, which he sees as a logical extension of the oxidization process in iridescent glass. Another successful partnership has been that of David Kaplan and Anika Sandström at Lindean Mill in Scotland, where this husband and wife team have been developing their own style of Graal glass with figurative imagery on vases and bowls.

In 1977 a small group of British glass-makers formed their own association, British Artists in Glass (BAG), which by 1985 already had well over two hundred members. They have an annual conference and have also held several exhibitions, providing virtually the only opportunity on home ground of forming a general impression of what is happening in the country. Apart from the BAG activities there have been at least two important glass conferences, one of them in 1976 devoted to hot glass, and the other a decade later based on the theme of glass in architecture. The earlier

Peter Layton (with René Roubíček at Nový Bor Symposium), 'Pyramid', 1988, hot-cast glass, assembled. 250 x 160 x 160 cm (98 x 63 x 63 in). (Photo: Stano Slušný)

conference was important because it offered the first wide-scale opportunity to introduce American ideas in glass to Europe; to hear the ideas of some leading Czech artists, including Libenský (whose lecture received a standing ovation); and generally to exchange ideas at a time when the glass movement in Europe was still more or less in its infancy. 'No-one seemed to stop talking about glass for the entire five days.'[8]

THE FIRST BRITISH STUDIO GLASS ARTISTS

Many of the first glass artists to emerge in Britain are in their prime today. Only a handful can sustain themselves with artistic work alone, as the glass public is still small, and in order to survive an artist needs to become internationally known. A number therefore teach, a few also design for industry, and some have set up small production studios of their own. One of the first artists to become independent after leaving college was Pauline Solven. She has had her own glass studio at Ravenshill in Gloucestershire since 1975. As a student of Sam Herman in the late 1960s her glass tended to be imitative of what he was doing, but after a period in Sweden and time to evolve her own style, she has ended up finding the perfect formula for expressing her individual talents as a colourist sensitive to the way in which light can illuminate or change either a whole landscape or a detail of it. Over the years she has developed techniques of colour application and manages to achieve an extraordinary luminosity in her work with overlapping transparent colours. She controls every stage of the work herself as she also blows her own shapes, and the changes have happened as a result of an intimate relationship with glass over many years. Her globe forms often have a small lens ground onto the surface, an optional added attraction, as it were, which goes into action when the eye catches it, transforming and distorting the imagery and producing a kinetic effect.

It is a credit to British glass artists that very few fell into the trap of imitating American styles, even in the late 1960s and early 1970s. They very soon abandoned the initial urge to pinch and stretch the surface of the glass in

ABOVE LEFT: **David Kaplan** and **Anika Sandström**, Lindean Mill, 'Heads', 1986, Graal technique. H. 22 cm (8¾ in), diam. 20 cm (7¾ in)

ABOVE: **Pauline Solven**, rocking globe from the 'Sail d'Azur' series, 1983, blown, cut and sand-blasted glass. H. c. 12.5 cm (5 in)

Stephen Procter, 'Double
Rhythm', 1985, blown form with
sand-blasting and prismatic
cutting. H. 29.5 cm (11⅝ in),
base 89 x 45.5 cm (35 x 18 in)

favour of more sophisticated techniques and a more controlled aesthetic.
Stephen Procter, who began working with glass at the end of the 1960s as an
engraver, found himself captivated by the wider implications of what was
happening in glass around him. He has been living, working and teaching at
the West Surrey College in Farnham since 1981, and the attitudes
expressed by him are shared by many artists in Britain: 'It seems that nothing is created without a sense of order and I am constantly reminded of this.
Conflict dissipates energy whereas harmony focuses it. Thus harmony has
the greater potential. No matter what we are trying to achieve or create, the
task is to orchestrate elements into a unified rhythm, and this is what I
attempt to do.'[9] Procter refers to his work as a 'celebration of light';[10] his
meticulously planned clear-glass sculptures catch the light in their pocket
shapes. For him, 'Pure light holds the secret of colour.'[11]

A remarkable number of those caught up in the glass happenings of the
late 1960s in Britain have gone on to become glass artists of merit. Most of
them have spent a part of their career teaching and have felt an unspoken
responsibility as pioneers to establish new traditions in British glass. John
Cook initiated the glass course at Leicester Polytechnic in 1970, two years
after leaving the Royal College of Art; he was also one of the first of a new
generation of British glass artists to attract attention with his dream-like
fantasies in glass. To begin with, the vaguely surrealist imagery was formed
of hot glass, but later he showed a preference for sand-casting. Annette
Meech also has a connection with Leicester because that was where she first
became fascinated by glass when Sam Herman built a glass furnace there
and gave a two-hour blowing demonstration during her final year as a

ceramics student. She joined The Glasshouse early on in 1972, immediately after leaving the Royal College of Art, and has been there ever since, still managing to devote a lot of her time to teaching and lecturing at various institutions, most recently at West Surrey College. She has always worked in hot glass and is one of the few artists left over from the early 1970s who have continued to find new ways of expressing themselves without resorting to other techniques.

Keith Cummings has been a great influence at Stourbridge College where he has been teaching since 1968. His own glass education took him nowhere near Sam Herman or the Royal College of Art. After studying fine art with Victor Pasmore and Richard Hamilton at Durham University, he worked on architectural glass at Whitefriars Glass Co. Although not intended as such, it was a fitting background for a sculptor in glass. When he went to Stourbridge he can have had little thought of teaching the art rather than the craft of glass, let alone becoming an artist in glass himself; but he reacted with sensitivity and intelligence to what was happening and in the process became a good teacher whilst managing at the same time to find the artist in himself.

His book *Techniques of Glass Forming* has been a standard textbook since it first appeared in 1980. If kiln forming has become one of the most popular techniques amongst a younger generation of British glass artists, he has been largely responsible. Cummings uses a variety of kiln-forming techniques in his own sculptural work, which has been slow to emerge. A natural reticence prevented him from exhibiting until the beginning of the 1980s, though he has been involved with glass as a designer and teacher since the early 1960s. In his own work technical wizardry assumes a secondary role. The sculptures are usually formed of glass elements mounted in bronze, with complex cellular patterns inside the glass mass. The baroque feeling of these bronze mounts provides a romantic setting for the organic glass structures. Visually the effect is one of the most striking to be seen in British glass today.

The generation of British artists which emerged during the 1970s is distinguished by this combined lifestyle of creating and teaching. It was a period when interest was growing so fast that there was room for nearly everybody graduating from a glass programme to become involved in creating a new one elsewhere. There was an excitement about being involved

John Cook, 'Figure', c. 1980, sand-cast glass. H. c. 10 cm (4 in)

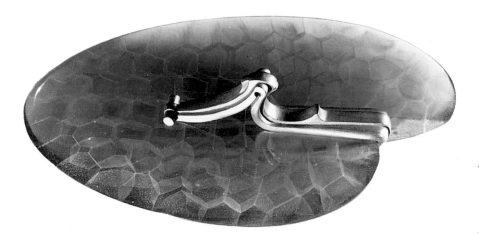

Keith Cummings, 'Sprung Leaf', 1987, pre-formed lost-wax cast glass, bronze mounted. H. 6 cm (2¼ in)

in glass both as teacher and artist that was completely of its time and cannot be recaptured. Clifford Rainey has managed to convey this excitement in both aspects of his life. His scope as an artist is wide-ranging, including a 10 m (33 ft) high sculpture in granite, glass and steel in Jeddah, a granite and cast iron sculpture for Queen's University in Belfast, a 40 m (131 ft) long glass wall for Lime Street Station in Liverpool, as well as a considerable amount of smaller sculptural work. He is a passionate traveller and his work is full of references to the things he has seen: Greek columns, Coca-Cola bottles, the human figure and St Sebastian intermingle to provide sculptural imagery charged with emotion. 'The column becomes "St Sebastian or Belfast after Pollaiuolo" broken like a rock rift – a sacred icon which then is replaced by an icon of contemporary international currency – the coke bottle. The drums of this "coke" column, pierced by rusting arrows, eventually fall and disintegrate and we are back to the fragment and the sands of time – glass as material and idea.'[12] Rainey, along with all the others who made glass and taught glass-making throughout the 1970s in Britain, has laid a strong foundation upon which future generations can build.

GLASS ENGRAVERS
It is difficult to give an overall picture of the British glass scene because of the strong individuality of each artist. This individuality (sometimes bordering on eccentricity) is partly the result of a tradition of minimum interference in British art schools. Even in an area as narrow as glass engraving, a number of British artists have attracted attention with their unusual approach to long-established traditions. Ron Pennell, for example, applies gem-engraving techniques of intaglio and cameo-cutting to glass. He has developed an army of tiny strange tools with which he concocts his

OPPOSITE: **Clifford Rainey**, 'Standing Figure', 1984, cast glass, metal base. H. 61 cm (24 in), base 61 x 51 cm (24 x 20 in)

Ron Pennell, 'A Walk to the Paradise Garden', 1984, engraved glass bowl. H. c. 10 cm (4 in)

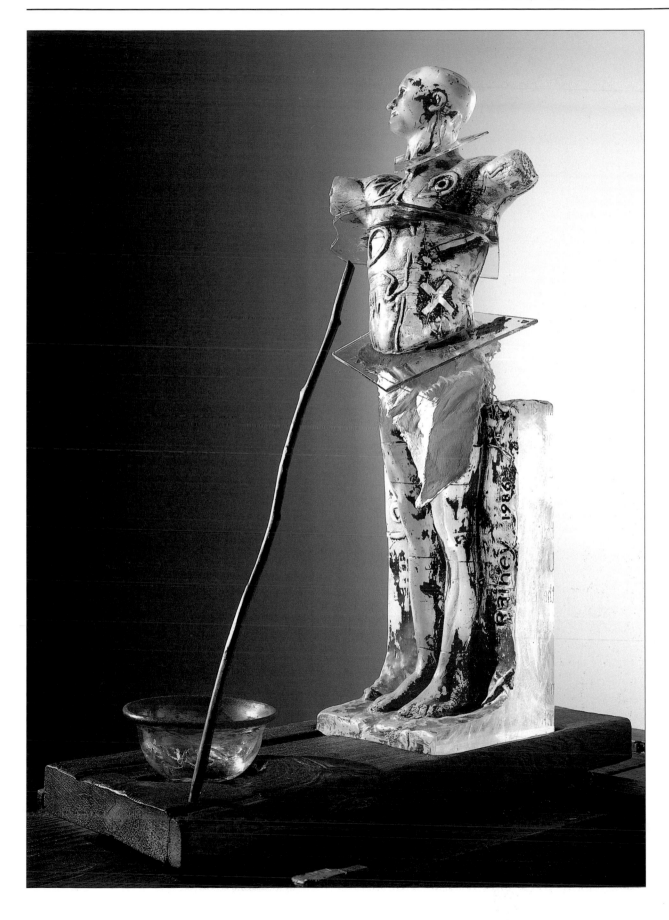

Peter Dreiser, 'The Price of Oil', 1983, vase with wheel engraving (glass by Berry Cullen). H. 20 cm (7¾ in). (Fitzwilliam Museum, Cambridge)

David Prytherch, 'Opposition', 1985, engraved and carved crystal bowl. H. 16.5 cm (6½ in)

narrative imagery, a menagerie of strange lovable humans and animals who act out their lives in his engravings:

> I have engraved one or two characters, such as Major Egmont Brodie-Williams (last seen lying beneath what I trust is a friendly tiger), who are wholly imaginary. Others, like Mr William Hodgkins, late postman of Hemsworth, really existed. Some have been seen at country markets and regarded with interest and affection before they were translated into the hardstone materials beloved in the past by caesars, kings and emperors.[13]

In contrast, Peter Dreiser uses more conventional engraving techniques, which he learnt in Germany before making England his home in 1955. In 1970 he set up his own engraving workshop in London, and since then has used the traditional techniques, of which he is a great master, to develop a free-flowing style. Among younger engravers David Prytherch has produced a number of impressive pieces. He works slowly, making carved and engraved pieces in a strong figurative style which reflects his own inner conflicts. The contours of his vessel forms are often determined by carved figures that extend beyond the rim, giving them a three-dimensional effect.

HOT-GLASS ARTISTS

A surprising number of British artists work in hot glass apart from those already mentioned. Arlon Bayliss, who is responsible for the hot-glass workshop at the college in Stourbridge, has an outgoing personality that goes with his virtuoso glass-blowing skills. For his degree show at the Royal College of Art in 1981 he produced elegant blown pieces which were part of a continuing series called 'Proteus', in which the blown forms were sliced in half and then transformed in a process of reassembly. Later his blowing skills were seen in a lively group of work called the 'Pod' series, which showed imagination, rhythm and humour, and demonstrated a way of

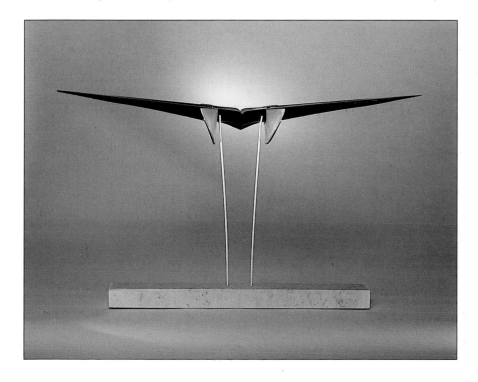

Arlon Bayliss, 'Proteus 54', 1988, blown glass, cut and polished, white marble base. H. 52.5 cm (20⅝ in), W. 86.5 cm (34 in)

Anna Dickinson, group of
bowls and a vase (detail), 1987,
blown glass, sand-blasted with
electro-plated metal rims.
H. c. 6–10 cm (2¼–4 in)

using traditional hot-glass skills in a modern sculptural idiom. Deborah
Fladgate, Charlie Meaker and Anthony Stern are all vessel makers who,
without being particularly innovative, make blown vessels of fine quality.
Anna Dickinson's very precise way of working has quickly won her a wide
reputation. She says, 'Most of my inspiration comes from tribal body jewellery, patterns in architecture and African ceramics. I like to combine several
materials in my work, usually metal. Once I have blown the piece I use the
electro-forming technique to build the metal onto the surface of the glass.
One piece may take several weeks to complete.'[14] Rachel Woodman, with
her partner Neil Wilkin, works in the *overfang* technique, which involves
two people blowing bubbles of different colours joined at one end and
folded over each other. The technique is an old one, into which Rachel
Woodman has breathed new life. She uses no surface decoration, preferring to rely on her feeling for form. 'She saw forms for what they are and
realised that they could stand alone, presenting subtle variations on the
themes of two surfaces and an edge, colour suspended in colour and the
play of light.'[15]

CASTING TECHNIQUES

Several British artists (many of them ex-students of Keith Cummings) have
made their mark using casting techniques. These include Tessa Clegg, with
her neat pleated bowls in soft pastel shades; Tatiana Best-Devereux, in a
series of sculptural 'engobe' forms which combine cast glass with ceramic
elements; David Reekie, with his eccentric sculptures of figures in desper-
ate situations; and Colin Reid, who has won international acclaim for

Rachel Woodman, bowl,
1985, free-blown, overlay
technique

BELOW: Tessa Clegg, blue
pleated bowl, 1983, *pâte de
verre*. H. 6.5 cm (2½ in), diam.
24 cm (9½ in)

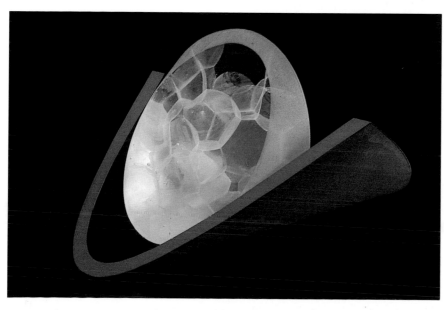

Tatiana Best-Devereux,
untitled glass and ceramic form,
1985, glass kiln-formed and cut.
H. 13.5 cm (5¼ in), L. 27.5 cm
(10¾ in)

his interlocking modular glass sculptures which combine natural surface texture and movement with precise geometric form.

Colin Reid has developed a complicated lost-wax casting process over a decade or more, progressing from vessel form to pure sculpture. At first the pieces were scent bottles, but gradually the container sections got smaller and smaller until they disappeared altogether. The sculptural work remained a composition of two split elements that could join to make a whole. 'I like things that fit together, and for two halves to make a complete form. To begin with, this made a vessel. Now it makes a complete shape.'[16] Recently he has been making arch forms and double arch forms, cruciform shapes, ovals and double ovals, and slowly his work is getting larger in scale.

David Reekie's strange lost-wax figures sit forlornly against glass walls, or crawl about on all fours in search of a way out of an impasse. More recently they are depicted with doom-laden expressions, peering out of windows. They are at once humorous and threatening. At first the only colour Reekie used was in the glass itself, but in his latest work he uses coloured enamels in a range of off-beat pastel shades.

Liz Lowe is an artist who uses a warm technique that is related to casting. Her work is usually small to miniature in scale – carefully thought out vessel forms decorated in a highly individual palette of muted colours with an unerring feel for pattern. 'Inspiration for my work comes through dreams, shapes are achieved by controlled melting of lead crystal blanks, and the surfaces treated with enamel lustres, sand-blasting and etching.'[17]

Casting in *pâte de verre* has also attracted a number of British artists, including Diana Hobson, Margaret Alston and Keith Brockelhurst. Margaret Alston's small vessel forms are simple shapes with sparse moulded decoration in soft colours. Keith Brockelhurst is known mainly for his

Liz Lowe, 'Saturday Pyjama Jar', 1988, mould-blown glass, lustre enamel and engraving, hand-painted. H. 18 cm (7 in)

BELOW: **Colin Reid**, double arch form, 1985, lost-wax cast glass, sand-blasted, cut and polished. H. 27 cm (10⅝ in), W. 47–65 cm (18½–25½ in)

David Reekie, 'Wall with Sitting Man', 1984, kiln-formed and cast glass. H. 30 cm (11¾ in)

BELOW: **Keith Brockelhurst**, 'Underworld Bowl', 1986, *pâte de verre*. H. *c*. 7 cm (2¾ in)

Diana Hobson, 'Progressive Series No. 5', 1986, *pâte de verre*. H. 15.5 cm (6⅛ in), W. 26 cm (10¼ in)

boxes and bowls in brightly contrasting colours with mask finials or feet. Diana Hobson discovered *pâte de verre* by chance at the hot-glass conference in 1976. At the time she was working with enamels and felt a desire to create whole forms in them, but only if they could be transparent. Since then she has created what can only be described as a new art form. In her work every technical innovation serves to give birth to a visual concept deep inside her. Whatever she produces is creative and its magic captivating. Although the *pâte de verre* she makes is paper thin, she gives it texture by incorporating all sorts of weird and wonderful found materials – bits of rusty metal, fragments of sea-shells, or glistening pebbles. Her work is about energy and tension, and despite its small scale it has great presence and strength of character. She was justly rewarded with a major prize at Coburg in 1985 and exhibits her work worldwide.

No account of British glass can be complete without some reference to the ultimate eccentricity of Danny Lane, who, after studying stained glass, set up his own studio in 1983 and branched out in a completely new direction. He produces furniture, often in collaboration with other glass- and metal-workers – chairs made of stacked sheet glass, tables with tops that look jagged and dangerous, but are in fact polished smooth. The chairs are quite comfortable and the tables practical despite an appearance that suggests they might be instruments of torture. Lane makes art which maximizes the emotive quality of the danger inherent in broken glass. His furniture, sculpture and architectural pieces are decorative, practical and provocative.

OPPOSITE: **Danny Lane**, 'Chair', 1988, stacked and cut sheet glass

HOLLAND

Dutch glass-makers were among the first in Europe to become aware of what was happening in America. Sybren Valkema has been a central figure in the development of the European glass movement for twenty-five years. In 1964 he and another important glass artist, Willem Heesen, attended the World Crafts Council conference in New York and two years after that Valkema constructed the first studio kiln on the Continent at the Rietveld Academy in Amsterdam where he taught glass and pottery. Both he and his son Durk Valkema work in glass and, apart from their artistic work, have

Sybren Valkema, with Gary Beecham at Harvey Littleton Studio, oval sculpture with dancing figurines under clear overlay, 1983. H. 39 cm (15⅜ in), W. 21 cm (8¼ in)

Willem Heesen, 'Teared Up Landscape', 1988, free-blown glass, yellow and white overlay. H. 35 cm (13¾ in)

been very much involved in the problems of studio kiln construction. They have been instrumental in building or supervising the installation of kilns for individual artists or universities all over the world. When he began building the studio kiln at the Rietveld Academy, Sybren Valkema had already been teaching there for seventeen years, and by the time he retired he had been responsible for glass at the academy for three decades. Bert van Loo, who was studying sculpture at the Rietveld Academy in the late 1960s and early 1970s, writes, 'In 1969 the Gerrit Rietveld Academy in Amsterdam started up a glass studio, started by Sybren Valkema. The students came from various disciplines such as sculpture, painting, ceramics and jewelry design; few of them intended ever to work in industry. This soon caused the industrial aspect, the invention of new forms for production, to take a back seat.'[18]

The Rietveld Academy still remains at the centre of glass education in Holland, attracting students from all over the world. Veronika Poschl, who was born in Austria, studied at the Rietveld Academy and has made her home in Amsterdam. Although principally a potter, she has used glass in her work with great sensitivity. The combination of materials is particularly successful in a series of precise elegant forms where the transition from glass to clay is beautifully managed. A number of the most talented young British glass artists (Tim Shaw, Tatiana Best-Devereux and Lisa Gherardi) have gone to the Academy after finishing their studies in England. It is now run by Richard Meitner and Mieke Groot, both of whom are

Veronika Poschl, untitled sculpture, 1983, glass and ceramic. H. c. 6 cm (2¼ in), L. 17 cm (6¾ in)

Rietveld Academy graduates. The very first museum exhibition of contemporary glass, showing the most recent developments in Europe and
America, was held at the Boymans van Beuningen Museum in Rotterdam
in November 1969.

THE LEERDAM GLASSWORKS

The grand old man of Dutch glass, Andreas Dirk Copier, was born in 1901
and is still involved in glass production today. It was he who established a
modern studio glass tradition at the glassworks in Leerdam in the 1920s,
maintained there until the present day. Copier has remained essentially a
glass designer, and though fully aware of the aims and aspirations of
younger generations of glass artists, has continued to work much in the
same tradition for over half a century, creating designs for series production
as well as unique pieces, and relying on the skill of master craftsmen to
interpret them. Until the influence of younger designers was felt in the
1950s the Leerdam glass look was completely determined by Copier.

The three most significant older Dutch glass artists – Sybren Valkema,
Floris Meydam and Willem Heesen – have all been involved with the Royal
Glassworks in Leerdam, and all of them also began their lives in glass studying at the glass school there. It is these three who have fashioned a new glass
tradition for Leerdam since the 1950s. Sybren Valkema's close involvement with the production team there made for a very different kind of
working relationship from that which Copier maintained. Valkema worked
from the inside rather than from the outside looking in, getting closer to the
glass than his predecessors had done, but it fell to his pupils actually to start
handling the glass themselves. Valkema progressed from vessel forms in the
1960s to glass sculpture the following decade. All his pieces are free-blown,
sometimes in clear glass, sometimes with colour casings or colour effects
achieved in other ways; he has always been interested in the optical illusion
created by both large and small inclusions of air.

Floris Meydam chose a much stricter geometric look for his free-blown
vessel shapes during the 1960s. He too became more interested in sculpture
during the 1970s, producing a series of cubes and cylinders with varying
internal optical effects achieved with colour or cutting. While he was at
Leerdam, Willem Heesen's work was closely related to what Meydam was
doing, partly due to the fact that both artists were working with the same
craftsmen. During the 1970s, in mid-career, Heesen had the courage to
leave Leerdam and set up his own workshop, De Oude Horn, in Acquoy.
As he said in an interview in 1985, 'I said to the industry I'll give you my
safety and you give me my freedom.'[19] It was a difficult new beginning.
Heesen has gradually acquired glass-blowing skills and feels free in his more
recent work to express the poetry of the landscape he lives in.

Two other artists who work with optical cutting, mainly using the cube as
their point of departure and working in a closely related style, are Durk
Valkema and his wife Anna Calgren, who have set up their own studio in
Amsterdam. Valkema's taste for optical effects must have developed during postgraduate studies first at Orrefors and then with Libenský, after leaving the Rietveld Academy in 1975. In Sweden he collaborated over a series
of sculptures with Ulla Forsell. Anna Calgren is of Swedish origin and
studied at the Orrefors glass school, then the Rietveld Academy.

Andreas Dirk Copier, vase,
blown glass with colour
inclusions. (Photo: Paul
Williams)

Floris Meydam, sculptural
form, c. 1980s, clear glass,
blown, red and white glass
inside. H. 15 cm (6 in),
diam. 28 cm (11 in)

Durk Valkema, cube
sculpture, 1983, optical glass.
15 x 15 x 15 cm (6 x 6 x 6 in)

BELOW: **Anna Calgren**,
'Golden Yellow and Turquoise',
1986, optical glass sculpture

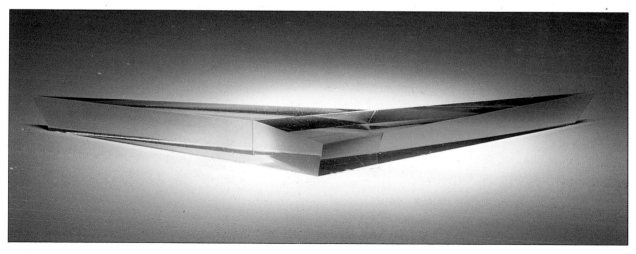

THE RIETVELD ACADEMY

In the 1980s graduates from the Rietveld Academy have come to express themselves much more freely, whether as sculptors or vessel makers. Bert van Loo's previously mentioned observations about the academy would apply to most glass artists of his generation. They now form the Establishment, as it were, and are responsible for handing on their ideas to a younger group who studied at the Rietveld Academy during the 1980s and are starting on a career. Richard Meitner's fertile imagination about what to do with glass has inspired a whole generation of pupils at the academy. He is American by birth and began his studies in glass at the University of California in Berkeley with Marvin Lipofsky before coming to Holland (where he has lived ever since) in 1972. An article in *Neues Glas* states:

> *Very often it seems that each successive exhibition of his work is that of a different artist entirely. His reason for choosing the material glass is that he sees in the enormous number of possibilities of the material, a chance to use it in a way consistent with his own changing moods and experiences. He attempts with his work to manipulate the viewer by deregulating his systematically acquired viewing habits. . . . The forms he uses most frequently are vase- or urn-related, this being a logical result of the blowing process by which he arrives at the basic forms for his work.[20]*

Meitner is fearless about working in materials other than glass, though glass always remains the central ingredient in his work and the other materials seem to serve more as props. He has experimented with wood, clay, metal and paint, respecting each of these materials and never debasing them in

ABOVE LEFT: **Richard Meitner**, untitled vase form, 1981, blown and enamelled glass

ABOVE: **Mieke Groot**, untitled piece, 1987, blown and enamelled glass. H. c. 40 cm (15¾ in)

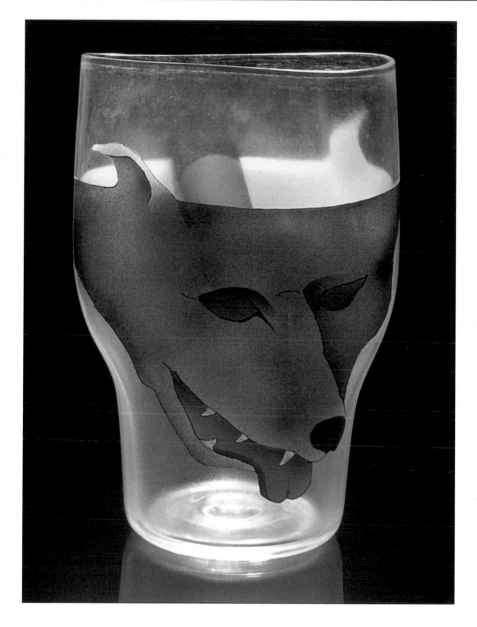

Richard Meitner, untitled vase
form, 1984, free-blown glass,
painted with enamels.
H. 34 cm (13⅜ in)

any way in their subsidiary role. At Coburg in 1985 he was awarded second
prize for an object entitled 'Tuna-fish' made of painted wood combined
with mould-blown, enamel-painted glass. It is beautiful and also full of wit
and humour, making reference to his own life and his fascination for Japanese culture. At the same time it deals with current fashion, making a
scurrilous reference to Memphis, whilst maintaining its own dignity and
individuality. Each piece contains a new idea, often a philosophical one,
which he wants to think about and formulate by translating it into art.

Mieke Groot has taught with Richard Meitner at the Rietveld Academy
from the beginning. Her mould-blown and enamel-painted vessel forms
are instantly seductive; recently she has changed her style, partly as a result
of the highly successful installation she did in 1986 for the sculpture exhibition in Leerdam entitled 'Weak bricks'. In this piece glass bricks block an
open window in a brick wall; an empty chair, tilted backwards, stands in
front of the wall, suggesting a body seated there staring at this visual pun.

Bert van Loo, 'Blind Faces', 1983, blown glass, slumped, fused, cut and laminated, with plywood back. 200 x 110 x 4 cm (78½ x 43½ x 1½ in)

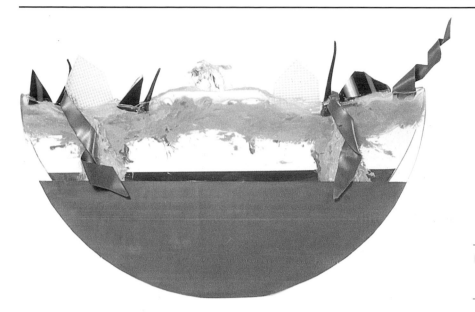

Bert van Loo, 'Horizon', 1985, mixed techniques. 55 × 35 × 17 cm (21½ × 13¾ × 6¾ in)

'BEELDEN IN GLAS', 1985

The 1985 symposium in Leerdam, 'Beelden in Glas', for which Bert van Loo must take chief credit, was a landmark. It marked the foundation of the Stichting Glas (Glass Foundation) and was organized 'with a view to promoting a dialogue between artists working largely in glass and artists from other disciplines'.[21] Bert van Loo has always remained an independent thinker, and whether he makes sculpture or organizes a symposium his mark is unmistakable. He thinks of himself as a sculptor first and foremost who happens to like expressing his sense of ironic allegory in glass. 'It is impossible to establish what is real. On the one hand I have the tendency to offer objective information, but on the other, I feel an urgency towards the subjective.'[22] 'Beelden in Glas' was an international symposium in which Dale Chihuly, Clifford Rainey, Richard Tuttle and Bruce Chao took part, as well as a number of the best Dutch glass artists. Among them was Bert Frijns, who has worked independently in Amsterdam since 1980. His work, which is mainly sculptural, is concerned with tension caused by bending

Bert Frijns, 'Soft Glass with Stone and Water', 1987, blown and slumped glass, stone and water. 49 × 49 × 27.5 cm (19¼ × 19¼ × 10¾ in)

glass in unexpected ways. For the Coburg exhibition in 1985 he produced an object made of two elements, one of which was a curved glass plate, the other a glass 'scroll' balanced on it and free to rock. This was intended as a play between immobility and motion. In another more recent work a giant bowl filled with water gives the appearance of having been slumped like a heavy sack over the iron bar on which it rests. The result is a highly sophisticated visual pun, in which a carefully thought out intellectual concept has been translated into visual terms. The simplicity of Frijns' sculptures belies the great technical skill required to make them.

Toots Zynsky, bowl, 1987, blown glass with *filet de verre* (threads of coloured glass, fused and slumped) rim. H. c. 12 cm (4¾ in)

Another American who has made Amsterdam her home is Toots Zynsky. In America she helped at the inauguration of Pilchuck School and worked in the hot-glass workshop there in 1971 and 1973. She studied at Rhode Island School of Design, and in the early 1980s helped with the founding of the New York Experimental Glass Workshop. An invitation to design a series of unique pieces for Paolo Venini brought her to Europe. It was her meeting with the Dutch designer and inventor Mathijs Teunissen van Manen that changed her way of working in glass. He invented two things for her: a bell furnace that can be assembled or dismantled in two hours, and a machine for making glass thread, inspired by fibre optics technology. In a highly ingenious process she lays these coloured strands, in up to twenty colours, on rice paper, 'swatch by swatch, even thread by thread. The ensemble is then placed on a double metal mould and will slump into it in the heating process in the kiln. She works on the glass while hot to shape the rim.'[23] Toots Zynsky has been referred to as an 'impenitent colourist';[24] she was inspired by the magnificent colours of tribal costumes during a period spent in Africa. What she has achieved with those colours and the skills she has developed for herself with unique technical equipment (which she was instrumental in instigating) is remarkable. The glass seems to bend completely at her will, undergoing a total metamorphosis in the process. These three-dimensional drawings in glass have an excitement about them which is mysteriously compelling yet completely self-evident.

OPPOSITE: **Toots Zynsky**, bowl from the 'Exotic Birds' series, 1987, *filet de verre* (threads of coloured glass, fused and slumped). H. c. 12 cm (4¾ in)

FRANCE

Despite a rich French glass heritage established during the first half of the twentieth century, first by Gallé and Daum at the turn of the century, and by a number of artists including Lalique and Marinot during the 1920s and 1930s, France was one of the last European countries to react to new ideas in glass. Even now, many of those who have made their reputation working in France (like Jutta Cuny, Yan Zoritchak, Matei Negreanu, Czeslaw Zuber and Monica Damian-Eyrignoux) are immigrants who were educated elsewhere. Daum is the only company that has maintained an interesting studio department, principally by commissioning artists to design sculpture cast in *pâte de verre*, notably Salvador Dali during the 1960s and more recently a number of Americans, including Dan Dailey.

Despite various abortive attempts it has proved difficult to establish an educational glass programme anywhere, and only very recently have things begun to change. In 1984 the Centre Internationale de Recherche sur le Verre, set up by the Ministry of Culture, was opened and later integrated with the École des Beaux Arts in Aix en Provence, and teaching courses have been established there under the supervision of Yan Zoritchak. The first glass symposium in France was at Sars Poteries in 1982, which coincided with the opening of a contemporary glass museum at the Sars Poteries Glass Centre. Before that artists worked in isolation, and except for those who had come from abroad there was very little that attracted attention in French glass on an artistic level. Claude Monod, one of the few independent glass artists in France during the 1960s, trained in glass-blowing during school vacations in his father's factory at Biot. His sisters Isabelle and Veronique also work in glass there. Alain Begou learnt glass skills while working at the Monod glassworks and then went on to open his own glass studio with his wife. Jean-Claude Novaro is another artist who set up his own studio after working at Biot for seventeen years, and Claude Morin, recently joined by his son Nicolas, has also had his own studio since 1970. All of these artists work in hot glass, making traditional vases, very often with metallic oxide decoration.

Jutta Cuny, 'Paysage Métaphysique', 1983–4, cast and sand-blasted glass sculpture. 22 x 65 cm (8¾ x 25½ in). (Musée des Arts Décoratifs, Paris)

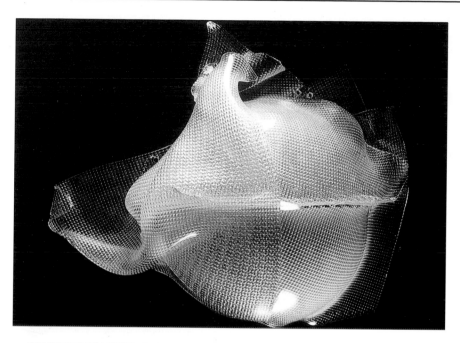

Veronique Monod, 'Wall Sculpture', 1980s, pressed glass, fused. H. 30 cm (11¾ in)

LEFT: **Claude Morin**, scent bottle, 1983, blown glass

BELOW: **Claude Monod**, 'Black Bowl', 1981, free-blown glass

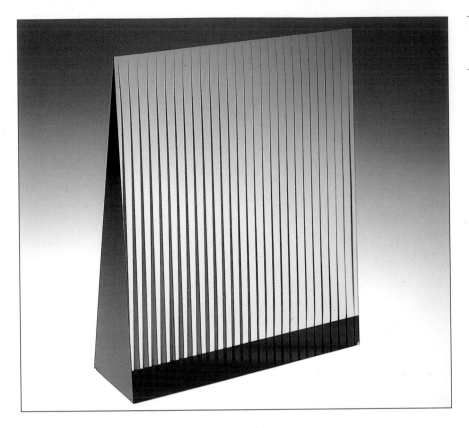

Yan Zoritchak, untitled form, laminated sheet glass, fused, cut and polished

Catherine Zoritchak, bowl, blown glass, cased, sand-blasted and etched

Matei Negreanu, fused glass sculpture. H. 35 cm (13¾ in)

Yan Zoritchak has lived in France since 1970 and came there after glass studies in Czechoslovakia, first at Železný Brod and then at the Academy of Applied Arts in Prague where he was a pupil of Libenský's during the 1960s. Like so many other Czech artists, his work, which is always highly skilled, concentrates on optical cut. The cold processes are usually carried out on a combination of coloured and clear glass blocks which have been fused together. As an artist Zoritchak is interested in making light dance in and around his multi-coloured forms, transforming the glass mass into kinetic sculpture. His wife, Catherine Zoritchak, became interested in glass through her husband and likes contrasting colours on large surfaces. She works on double- or triple-overlay glass, with engraving and sand-blasting, in her desire to 'reveal the inner life in multi-layered glass'.[25]

The majority of immigrant artists in France have come from Eastern Europe. Matei Negreanu was born in Rumania and came to France in 1981. He is a sculptor in glass whose totem columns and winged forms are made by cutting individual glass sheets which are then glued and cut with a diamond saw. Detail is added by engraving and sand-blasting. The spiralling whirlwind forms he creates seem to defy the laws of gravity. Czeslaw Zuber turned up in Paris in 1982 after leaving Poland because he found no way of pursuing his interests in glass there. He works on crystal blocks, using a diamond saw, sand-blasting and brightly coloured paints to make bizarre, grotesque animal or human figures with mask-like faces. His work has a primitive quality reminiscent of tribal art.

Recently a few French-born artists have begun showing their work. There was a short-lived attempt to form a glass co-operative by a group of artists calling themselves RIM (Raymond Martinez, Ingrid Maillot and Michel Mouriot), all of whom had previously been involved in the theatre in some way, 'and developed a series of highly original projects and concepts to combine the expressive qualities of theatre, architecture and sculpture'.[26] François Vigorie, who is self-taught, opened his own studio in Paris in 1981 and works on sculptural forms, using basic painting and sand-

François Vigorie, 'Interpenetration', 1984, optical glass, cut, polished, sand-blasted and engraved. 71 x 19 x 11 cm (28 x 7½ x 4¼ in)

Czeslaw Zuber, 'The Beast', 1988, glass cut with a hammer, polished, sand-blasted and painted. 29 x 15 x 11 cm (11½ x 6 x 4¼ in)

Antoine Leperlier, 'Vasque',
1982, *pâte de verre*. H. 22 cm
(8¾ in), L. 30 cm (11¾ in)

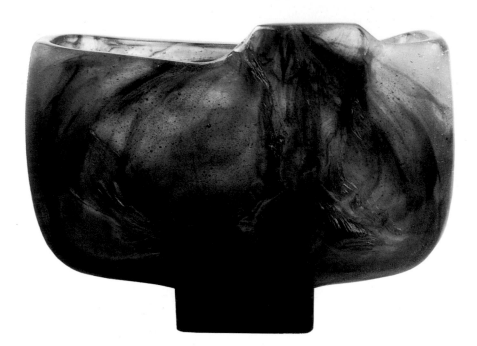

blasting techniques. Another artist, Jean-Pierre Umbdenstock, has been
making a name for himself since his return from a year's study with Lipofský
at the University of California. He likes to make large pieces, on which he
works with a team of three others. He greatly enjoys the processes involved
in glass-making and works with multiple layers of glass, making the colours
merge into each other and trying to create a sense of lightness that belies the
scale of his work and the heaviness of the material.

Perhaps the only evidence of any continuing glass tradition in France is in
the work of two brothers, Antoine and Etienne Leperlier, the grandsons of
François Decorchemont. In 1979 Antoine Leperlier, joined a year later by
his brother Etienne, became interested enough in the *pâte de verre* techniques of their famous grandfather to research them afresh and to rekindle
the furnace in his old studio at Conches. Working from old notebooks kept
by François Decorchemont, they matched their skills with his and have
each evolved a personal style in the process. In their early vessel forms the
influence of their grandfather is very apparent in the texture and character
of the glass and in the murky colours, all of which are reminiscent of his
later work. Antoine's style has since evolved to become more personal and
his vessel forms are now more three-dimensional, whilst Etienne's work
is more inspired by architectural form and has been strongly influenced by
the ideas of Howard Ben Tré. Erich Schamschula, another Czech immigrant, has also been fascinated by *pâte de verre* since the late 1950s. After
a number of technical setbacks he has been working exclusively in this
medium since 1980, and is 'constantly spurred on by the endless possibilities of this art form'.[27]

LEFT: **Jean-Pierre Umbdenstock**, 'Signe . . . particulier', 1987, blown glass, hot decorative techniques. H. 35 cm (13¾ in)

RIGHT: **Etienne Leperlier**, 'Sculpture 22', 1985, *pâte de verre*. H. 26 cm (10¼ in)

BELGIUM

In neighbouring Belgium the principal glass manufacturer, Val St Lambert, has maintained a studio glass tradition thanks mainly to Louis Leloup, who was chief designer there from 1948 to 1971, when he opened his own studio. During his long career at Val St Lambert he worked mainly in hot glass. Before joining the company he had worked in ceramics and gained a thorough knowledge of oxides, which he made use of during a period of collaboration with Sam Herman, who was invited to make a series of pieces at Val St Lambert just before Leloup left. In part it was this collaboration which inspired Leloup to work differently. In the work he has done on his own account since 1971 he has developed a marquetry technique in which 'patches' of hot colour and coloured glass threads are inlaid on the surface of hot glass and spread as the glass is blown into its ultimate shape. He has continued making vessel forms as well as venturing into sculpture.

Since 1972 Edward Leibowitz has also been working in Belgium after emigrating from Israel where he studied art in Haifa and Jerusalem. Apart from his work in stained glass, he has been working on a series of sculptural pieces which resemble model stage sets. The allegorical imagery in them is made up of household objects and furniture (mainly chairs and tables), and often there is an engraved 'backdrop'. His work displays an impressive range of glass techniques, including blowing, diamond-cutting, etching, engraving and sand-blasting.

Louis Leloup, 'Friendship', 1981, clear glass, free-blown, overlaid and engraved. H. 32 cm (12½ in)

Edward Leibowitz, untitled
sculpture, 1984, free-blown glass,
engraved, sand-blasted and
etched. 56 x 37 x 37 cm (22 x
14½ x 14½ in)

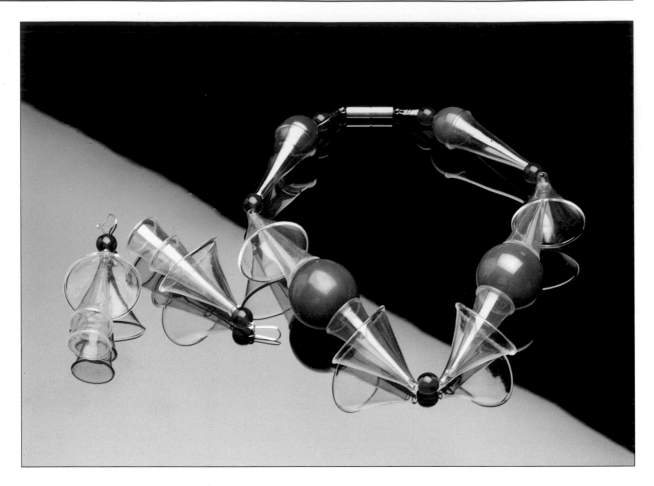

ITALY

Italy (or rather Venice), which from the sixteenth to the eighteenth centuries was the most important glass centre in the world, enjoyed a brief renaissance spanning the career of Paolo Venini, whose inspired patronage ended with his death in 1959. Venini had attracted a lively group of artists and designers (the best known of whom are Carlo Scarpa and Fulvio Bianconi) to collaborate with him at his glassworks in Murano and he established a tradition which his heirs have tried to continue since his death. His granddaughter Laura de Santillana worked as a designer there until the family lost control of the company in 1986. Some interesting Italian designers, notably Riccardo Liccata and Toni Zuccheri, worked for the Venini glassworks after the death of Paolo Venini. A number of Americans were also invited to work in Murano, either as designers or merely to experiment by availing themselves of the unusual skills of Venetian craftsmen. The American artist Thomas Stearns did some interesting designs for Venini during the early 1960s, and Dale Chihuly went there on a Fulbright scholarship in 1968. Chihuly says it was there that he learnt about teamwork: 'I saw by watching that really the way to work with glass was to work it with a team of people. That was a little contradictory to what had happened in this country.'[28]

Murano still has some of the best glass-blowers in the world working there, a few of whom have become independent artists or have used their

Laura de Santillana, designed for Venini, necklace and earrings, 1985, blown elements, assembled

OPPOSITE: **Livio Seguso**, two untitled pieces, 1987, lead crystal, cut and polished, with polished steel (left) and blown glass and stainless steel (right). H. 42.5 cm (16¾ in) and 45 cm (17¾ in)

skills in collaboration with other artists. Ligno Tagliapetra maintains the Venetian virtuoso glass-blowing tradition in his solo work and has also worked together with a number of Americans. Livio Seguso has worked as an independent artist in Venice since 1965 and his main preoccupation as a sculptor in glass is the role played by light, for once in blown rather than optically cut work. 'The light that bewitched Turner and the Impressionists, and still enchants every visitor to the city of Venice, is the same light that emanates from the work of Livio Seguso.'[29]

Paolo Martinuzzi, untitled sculpture, 1977, blown and scratch-engraved glass on a wooden base.
H. 21.5 cm (8½ in)

Paolo Martinuzzi is also a Venetian, a solitary figure who is not really concerned with modern developments in glass, but is very much an artist of his time. His haunting vessels are covered with a myriad of microscopically small, child-like, engraved figural graffiti; they rest on bases composed of dark wood, stone, rust-coloured metal and nails, which suggest debris washed up from the canals. In his figures the eyes dominate: 'Eyes that observe the observer while looking directly through him. He lets his figures talk for him and in this manner he reaches man in the inmost regions of his heart. Paolo Martinuzzi is a fanatic who impregnates every material with his archetypal image of man.'[30] For Martinuzzi engraving is an emotional experience, which he refers to as 'making the glass bleed'.

Since it was established in the late 1970s, the Memphis group led by Ettore Sottsass has had a worldwide effect on all aspects of design and interior decoration. The range of Memphis glass manufactured by Toso Vetri d'Arte in Murano must rank as some of the most innovative to have emerged during the 1980s. There is always radical change when architects become involved in design, and most of the designers at Memphis have been at some time involved in architecture. There is a distinctly post-modern feeling about the brightly coloured non-functional vessel forms designed for Memphis by Sottsass, Zanini and Matteo Thun. Of all of them Matteo Thun has been the most seriously involved with glass in the long term. Some brilliantly witty champagne glasses – one with a handle in the form of a double curve, another in the form of a double zig-zag – were like a breath of fresh air at the Coburg Glass Prize exhibition in 1985, an immediate invitation to open a bottle of champagne and celebrate. He now has his own architectural studio in Milan, where he creates designs for metal, glass, ceramics and furniture.

During the last two decades there have been radical changes in attitudes to design by the Italians, first in the work of Mendini, who founded the Hot-House design group, and then at Memphis. It has given a higher profile to industrial designers and allowed them to be much more radical in their approach. As yet it is too soon to judge what the wider implications will be, but Matteo Thun's crazy shapes, which combine fantasy with functionalism, have been making a noticeable impact both in terms of art and design, initiating a new sort of cross-fertilization that looks as if it is here to stay.

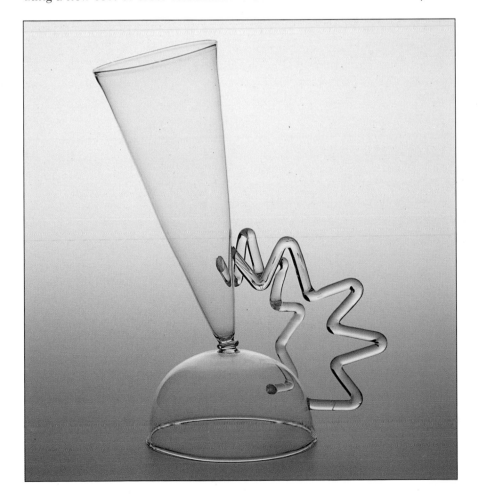

Matteo Thun, designed for Barovier, goblet from the 'Sherry Netherlands' series, 1987, blown glass

6. CANADA, AUSTRALIA, NEW ZEALAND AND JAPAN

CANADA

Despite their proximity to the United States, Canadian contemporary glass artists have not looked across the border for inspiration. If there have been American influences, they have been technological ones. Artistically speaking, the Canadians seem to find the greatest inspiration in the landscape and cultural heritage of their own country. It cannot be easy for any branch of Canadian art to avoid being overshadowed by its American counterpart, but in a very short space of time Canadian glass has developed a strong identity of its own, and in recent years particularly a group of young artists has been producing work in which the chief characteristic is a fresh and uninhibited approach to the material.

The Canadian glass movement is a decade younger than the American one, but it took very little time to become a strong cultural force. In 1968 the American ceramist Robert Held proposed the establishment of Canada's first programme of glass study at Sheridan College in Mississauga, Ontario. He suggested the course after a visit to Penland School (in America) in 1968 to conduct a workshop with Mark Peiser. Sheridan College's School of Crafts and Design accepted the proposal and by 1971 glass had become a major programme under the direction of Held. From 1974 to 1980 the distinguished American glass artist Karl Schantz joined the staff, adding to the repertory of techniques already taught there by introducing his cold working methods as well as the use of precious metals on glass, techniques of iridizing, cameo-cutting, lampwork and sand-casting. A number of Held's early pupils went on to establish glass programmes elsewhere in Canada: at Georgian College, Barrie, Ontario in 1971; at Alberta College of Art in 1974; and at the Université du Quebec à Trois-Rivières in 1974. Since 1980 Schantz has been at the Ontario College of Art, where, with the young Canadian glass artist Max Leser, the existing glass workshop was redesigned and expanded. The most recent development in glass education in Canada was the opening of Le Centre des Métiers du Verre du Quebec in Montreal under the direction of François Houde in 1987. This has been designed as the first educational centre devoted entirely to glass, and is well equipped to cater for a wide range of glass techniques.

OPPOSITE: **Karl Schantz**, 'Royal Thorn', 1981, sculptural goblet, laminated Vitrolite. H. 18 cm (7 in)

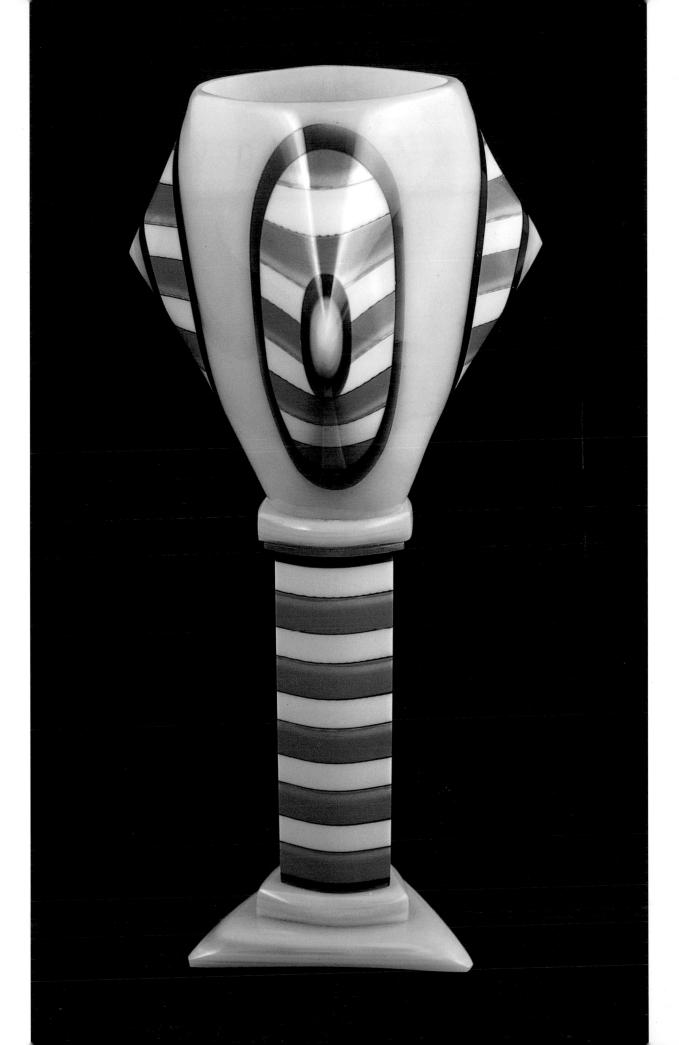

Edward Roman, 'Landscape Vase', blown glass with applied motif of a landscape

The Glass Art Association of Canada was incorporated in 1983; prior to that it had been known as Glass Art Canada, a more informal group of interested artists, collectors, academics and enthusiasts. The Glass Art Association of Canada has been responsible for organizing most of the conferences and symposia that have taken place in the country, the first of which was at Sheridan College in 1976. There have been a number since then, the most successful and dynamic of which was in 1984: 'The Glass Works '84 Conference (at Harbourfront, Toronto) signalled the explosion in this medium in Canada.'[1] The first large-scale exhibition devoted entirely to Canadian glass, entitled 'Art Glass of Canada', was held in 1987 at Indiana State Museum. There are also a number of good glass galleries, which have played a vital part in educating the Canadian public. Most of these are in Toronto and the oldest is The Glass Art Gallery, which was the first gallery space devoted exclusively to glass when it opened in 1979. In Quebec Galerie Verre d'Art has been showing glass since 1976. In addition, there are a number of private glass collectors, but in general museum interest has been slow to develop and there is a feeling that Canadian artists have to rely heavily on the interest of the American buying public for survival.

THE VESSEL MAKERS

Most Canadian artists working with glass have shown a preference for sculpture, but, as in other countries, the first to emerge were primarily vessel makers working in hot glass. Robert Held has been making vessels for two decades and at present runs his own company, Skookum Art Glass, which he started in Calgary in 1979. It is essentially a production company, making vases, perfume bottles and paperweights which, like much glass that was made during the 1960s, rely on iridescent effects similar to those found in Art Nouveau glass. Norman Faulkner is also inspired by Art Nouveau, using sand-blasting techniques to decorate his blown vessels and whimsical sculptural forms. Another artist, Edward Roman, produces landscape vases which have lampworked decoration between layers of glass. Kathryn Thompson's elegant blown forms are decorated with etched figures. More recently she has begun to incorporate copper, silver wire, and wire mesh in her work, to create figurative vignettes inside her blown shapes. Daniel Crichton, Sheridan College's present glass master, is considered Canada's foremost vessel maker. 'Dazzling dots, blobs and splashes of colour',[2] picked up on the marver while the glass is hot, decorate his vessel forms. Metallic lustres and sand-blasting further enhance his work. 'There is virtuosity in Crichton's glass, but its effect is ever soothing, never jarring.'[3]

Max Leser is best known for vessels of a different kind:

His perfume bottles are manufactured from a disc of structural glass (which has an aqua tint) produced to his specifications. The glass is a rare 25 mm thick and is more commonly used in CAT scanners and other hi-tech applications. Once the discs arrive in Toronto, they are sand-blasted under Leser's supervision. He has turned down a bid from Japan for the patent and production of the bottles because he would have had to relinquish quality control. When details are restrained to a bevelled edge and a dozen sand-blasted lines, exactly how and where they go is crucial.[4]

BELOW LEFT: **Daniel Crichton**, vase, 1985, blown with coloured inclusions. 28 x 13 cm (11 x 5⅛ in)

BELOW: **Max Leser**, untitled sculpture, 1987, cut and sand-blasted glass. H. 38 cm (15 in), diam. 25.5–30.5 cm (10–12 in)

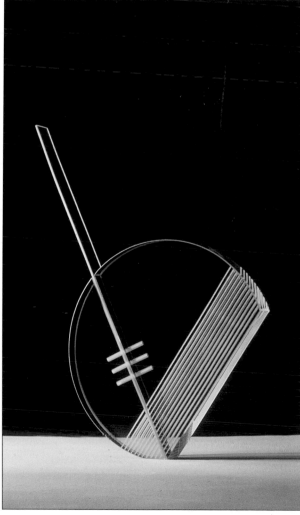

Leser's loyalties are divided between glass-making and flying, which would account for the clear-cut aerodynamic lines that give his work its character. Having abandoned earlier attempts at sculpture on the grounds that 'something that started out as self-expression began to feel like self-indulgence',[5] Max Leser now uses his training as a glass artist to design affordable artefacts in glass (a desk, a standing mirror and a coffee pot). It marks something of a reversal in current trends when somebody trained as an artist in glass chooses to concentrate his efforts on design.

GLASS SCULPTURE

Most Canadian sculptors in glass prefer to work in mixed media and only a few of them have limited themselves to a single technique. Among those who have, Karl Schantz makes colourful laminated sculptures using Vitrolite. They have been described as 'twilight fantasy buildings and structures scale-reduced to the possibility of the artist's studio'.[6] Andrew Kuntz, working in a similar technique, 'leaves an impression of relics or fragments of artefacts from the distant past'.[7] Elisabeth Marier slumps industrial panes of glass, making them look as pliable as folded fabric.

Among those who use casting or blowing skills, the work of Peter Keogh and Robin Fineberg is interesting. Peter Keogh works in a combination of glass and bronze, each separately cast by the lost-wax method and then fitted closely together. In his sculptures he experiments visually and conceptually with a dialogue between the two materials. Robin Fineberg,

ABOVE: **Robin Fineberg**, 'Rotating', 1987, blown glass and copper. 15 x 28 x 23 cm (6 x 11 x 9 in)

BELOW: **Peter Keogh**, 'Interiors', 1987, cast glass and bronze. 30.5 x 20 x 5 cm (12 x 7¾ x 2 in)

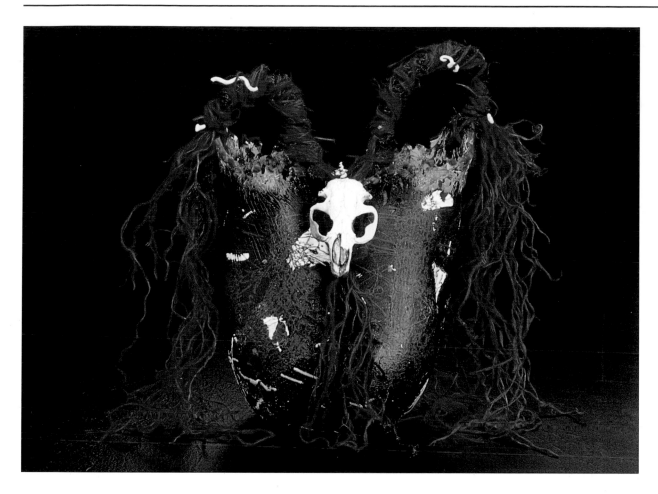

who shares a studio with Keogh, has similar artistic concerns, though her working methods are different and she is a vessel maker more than a sculptor. Her blown forms with sand-blasted decoration are enriched with decorative designs of electro-formed copper. Susan Edgerly is another artist who experiments with a dialogue between materials, seeing it as a way of expressing her concerns about the fragility of human nature; in her case, the combination is one of paper and glass. Laura Donefer's imaginative mix of materials knows no limits. Her brightly coloured ritualistic vessels, which she calls 'Witch Pots', make use of dried grasses, pieces of bone, applied shards and cane; the glass element is implied rather than seen in these pieces, which are intended to evoke a sense of dark powers and evil sorcery.

Two of the most expressive Canadian sculptors in glass are Irene Frolic and Kevin Lockau, both of whose work is charged with emotion. Irene Frolic has so far shown two completely contrasting aspects in her work. In 1986 she took part in an installation by an avant garde group of young Canadian artists known as the Dangerous Art Group, who set out to 'challenge the viewer's preoccupations about the beauty of glass by showing it as dangerous and able to wound'.[8] Her contribution consisted of 'grave-like beds of jagged glass and painfully distorted depictions of human figures made from glass and wire'.[9] Two years later she showed a 'spiritual preoccupation much removed from her earlier work'.[10] The work was also technically different, with a 'bravura example of casting . . . [a] stunning glass female figure',[11] standing 102 cm (40 in) high and dominating the show.

ABOVE: **Laura Donefer**, 'Double Skull Witch Pot', 1987, mixed media. 48 x 40.5 cm (19 x 16 in)

BELOW: **Irene Frolic**, 'Dialogue' (detail), 1988, cast glass and copper

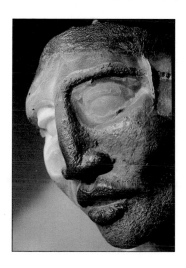

Kevin Lockau is one of the youngest Canadian artists, graduating from Ontario College of Art in 1986. He has spent time travelling in the wilds and feels close to nature: 'We are all tied to the land, the land is the biggest thing that makes Canadians Canadian.'[12] His style is a narrative one expressed in totem-like sculptures which are up to 2.5 m (8 ft) high. In a recent series of work entitled 'Wood Spirits', 'glass heads speak with mouths open wide. Long rusted metal arms writhe in space. Gender apparent, these "Wood Spirits" . . . remind us of Native Spirits, each with its specific personality and reason for existence.'[13] Another series is entitled 'Furs of Canada', which consists of 'five glass heads – three raven heads filled with fur, wounded and broken, and one dog head relating to the ravens'.[14]

Prepared glass of one sort or another is frequently used by Canadian artists. Astri Reusch uses prisms, panels and mirror glass, all of which are embellished using cold processes. She has a liking for 'objets trouvés', too. She has worked in flat glass and also makes sculptural pieces in which there are cast elements. Her work is often experimental: 'There are many visual devices that I exploit which are especially suitable to the medium of glass: overlays, interference patterns, fall-through, blocking, parallax, shifting image planes, etc. In glass these effects are a reality; in pictorial media (painting, drawing, etc.) they can only be anecdotal at best.'[15] She looks on her work as 'visual choreography', and likes to feel that she can involve the viewer by making him use all his mental processes when viewing. Alfred Engerer uses either fabricated glass plates or cast elements in his work, which is sometimes monumental in scale. The piece he made for the

Astri Reusch, 'Needlepoint', glass, cut and polished, patinated bronze. 35.5 x 35.5 x 23 cm (14 x 14 x 9 in)

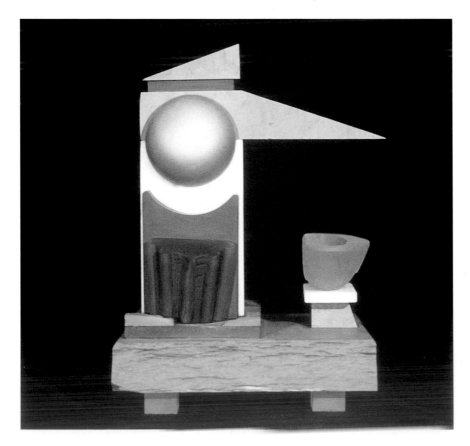

Alfred Engerer, untitled sculpture, 1987, cast and plate glass, sand-blasted, with sandstone and marble. 58.5 x 38 x 33 cm (23 x 15 x 13 in)

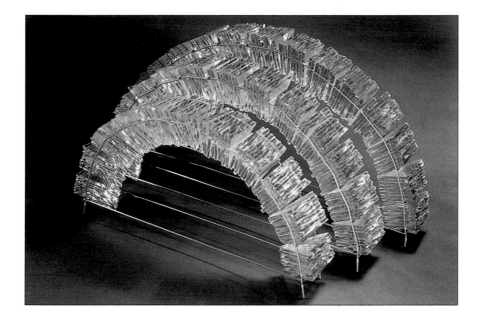

Lisette Limieux, 'Triade', 1987, plate glass, cut and assembled. 26 x 53 x 27.5 cm (10¼ x 20¾ x 10¾ in)

Peter Zips, 'Convergence No. 5', 1984, glass and cement. 50 x 40 cm (19¾ x 15¾ in)

'Dangerous Art' show was made of stacked glass plates, wood and steel. Lisette Limieux also works on a large scale, again using prepared elements – in her case, inexpensive window glass combined with other materials, which she arranges with logic and 'ordered manipulation of thought. Work such as J. S. Bach's "Art of the Fugue" exhibits a similar concept as to how a work of art can be based on the application of rigorous governing logic rather than on the element of chance or ongoing personal decision making.'[16]

Peter Zips was one of the first Canadian artists working in glass to combine it with other materials, though the prepared glass elements play the central role. His work has often been described as architectonic because he creates 'sites – places invested with meaning that capture the viewer's imagination . . . glass punctuated structures'.[17] He uses glass 'in a manner that is both true to its substance and to its metaphysical possibilities'.[18] In a short career to date, François Houde has shown a fertile imagination and considerable versatility as an artist. He has a rich fund of ideas and goes from series to series, working his way through one idea until he has explored it fully before going on to the next. He began in 1982 with a series called 'Broken Vessels', free-blown pieces which were broken and reassembled, incorporating wood, glue, wire, screws and dowels, in an attempt to give the vessels 'a new level of existence'.[19] The 'Pygmalion' series of 1983 'investigated sculptural concerns and thermal properties of glass. The series consisted of broken flat panes of glass slumped into a very shallow bowl shape and stacked.'[20] The following comments relate to the 'Ming' series, which is his most recent:

> The presentation of windows causes us to become aware of the glass, which we normally see through without noticing. By forcing us to see what we don't usually see, the work becomes a metaphor for our blindness. This is accomplished by cutting the edges of the glass in the shape of a horse. With the three separate frame sections, the result is a line drawing in space. The subject matter of the horse refers to the past and Houde's interest in historical traditions. On a further level the work is a reference to power, as traditionally symbolised by the horse.[21]

One of François Houde's concerns as an artist is to find hope in what he sees as a world without a future. Paradoxically his own work, together with that of a group of young Canadian glass artists in their prime, would seem to indicate that on an artistic level at any rate there is good reason to be optimistic.

Australia, New Zealand and Japan have each responded to American glass culture in their own way with interest and enthusiasm. Now that all three countries have a more established contemporary glass tradition, they have begun to exchange ideas with one another which should prove particularly interesting. There is no doubt that during the 1970s the main influences came from America, but in Japan it was a matter of incorporating new ideas into an already existing glass tradition. The decorative arts have always been highly esteemed in Japanese culture and have never been cast in a secondary role. Lacquerwork, metalwork, ceramics, and ivory carving are much respected and there is no need to build bridges between craft and art. Ordinary household objects are imbued in Japanese culture with a ceremonial importance reserved for religious artefacts in Western civilization. In contrast, there was no hand-made glass tradition to speak of in Australia and New Zealand, and it was not until the early 1970s that some Australian and New Zealand craftsmen began to blow glass again. Australia's lack of tradition is amply compensated for by the country's compelling natural beauty, which cannot fail to rouse the senses and stir them into action. The Australian artist's direct emotional response to his environment has always been one of the most noticeable features of Australian art, and has played an important role among a surprisingly large group of young glass artists working there today. Glass is even newer to New Zealanders than it is to Australians, but for a small country a lot of interest has been shown, particularly in the last few years.

OPPOSITE: **François Houde**, 'Ming XVII', 1987, sheet glass, sand-blasted, acid-etched, wood and metal. 89 x 153 x 171 cm (35 x 60 x 67½ in)

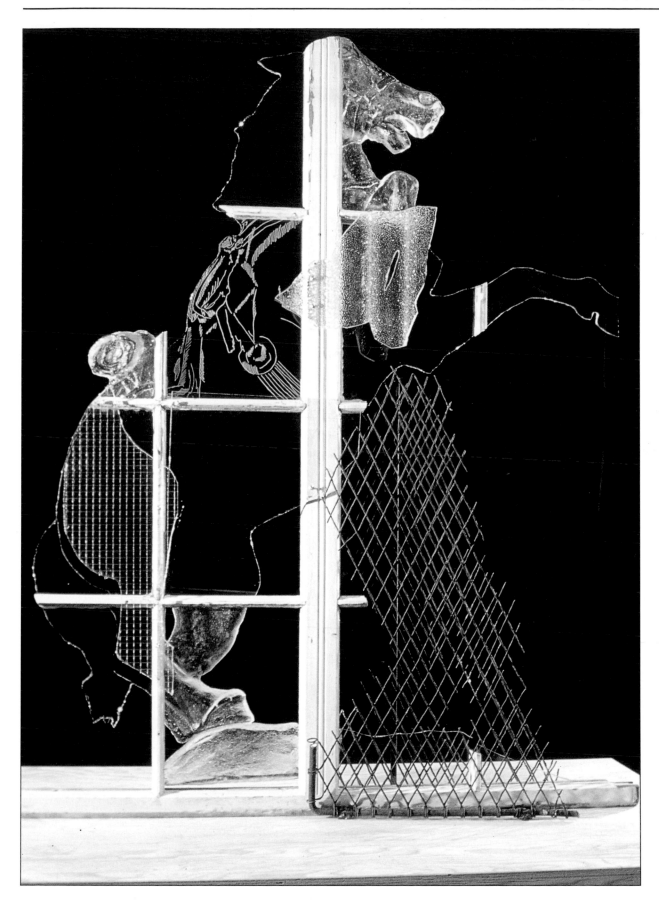

AUSTRALIA AND NEW ZEALAND

'The mid 1970s saw Australia and New Zealand visited by roving minstrels from the initial baby-boom. A few visited, many remained.'[22] The time was somehow right for introducing new ideas. Robert Bell, the curator of craft at the Art Gallery of Western Australia since 1978, has been instrumental in generating enthusiasm, and he wrote in the introduction of the catalogue for 'International Directions in Glass Art', the first major international glass show to be held in Australia, 'The revival of interest in all of the crafts began early in the 1960s and by the 1970s had become one of the most vital facets of the arts in Australia.'[23]

In 1974 Sam Herman introduced Australia to the misshapen bubble. He came to Australia on a visit and decided to stay on in Adelaide, where he established a glass workshop at the Jam Factory, a government-sponsored enterprise where craftsmen of all kinds could make and sell their work. This idea of converting a derelict factory into a series of artists' workshops has proved popular in Australia and a second, similar enterprise, called The Meat Market, was opened in Melbourne. Both of them are still thriving today. Sam Herman's workshop was an important influence; the Australians were excited by what seemed at the time to be wild ideas about glass forming and they responded enthusiastically with their own attempts at blowing glass. At about the same time the American artist Richard Marquis was invited by the Crafts Board to visit Australia, and during the course of his stay established glass workshops in Melbourne and Hobart. Although the population of Australia is small, there is great inter-state rivalry, so that an innovation in one state is seen as a challenge to the others, setting up a chain reaction. Bill Boysen, another ex-Harvey Littleton pupil who came over, set up a mobile tank furnace with which he could tour the country and give demonstrations, sponsored by the Crafts Board of the Australia Council.

Maureen Cahill, 'Colour Series', 1977, group of kiln-worked sculptures. Tall form: 8 x 8 cm (3⅛ x 3⅛ in)

Since then there have been a great many visiting lecturers and a number of Australians have also visited America and studied there, returning to Australia to work and teach with their new-found skills. Stephen Skillitzi, for instance, discovered glass-blowing whilst studying ceramics at the University of Massachusetts, and eventually took up a teaching position in ceramics at the South Australian College of Advanced Arts, where he introduced glass studies into the curriculum. Maureen Cahill, who had been a student at Stourbridge and at the Rietveld Academy, set up the first glass department in New South Wales at the Sydney College of Arts in 1978 and introduced Australia to kiln-forming techniques. In New Zealand there have also been several American visitors who have stayed to help establish glass education and a new glass tradition. In 1974 Tony Kupfer set up a studio at Inglewood, creating an apprenticeship programme, and two years later a New Zealander, Mel Simpson, returned from postgraduate studies at the University of California to set up a glass programme at Elam College of Art. But perhaps the most significant appointment of a foreigner has been that of Klaus Moje, who was invited to head the glass studio division at Canberra College of Art in 1983. 'His mosaic technique has created a distinct lineage among Canberra graduates.'[24] This observation is evidence of the enthusiastic response shown by young Australians to new ideas in art, particularly when one compares Moje's influence in Australia with his career in Germany, where he worked in comparative isolation and with only modest recognition.

At Canberra twelve students join the glass course each year, some to follow a four-year BA degree course, others for a two-year associate diploma, which is a postgraduate course. Durk Valkema from Holland came to construct a furnace there, and Klaus Moje has invited a number of other Australians and artists from abroad as guest lecturers. In 1988 the World Crafts Council glass symposium was held at the college. Moje's own reactions to Australia have been as dramatic as the influence that he has had, and there have been great changes in his work since he moved there. 'The sun hits you like a fist. The Canberra sunsets are spectacular. Deep dark colours are struck by sudden rays of light like a diamond. After thunderstorms you often see a double rainbow up so close you can walk into it.'[25]

The first opportunity that Australians had to look at a wide selection of contemporary glass came in 1975 when there was a touring exhibition showing the work of ten American artists. Since 1979 Wagga Wagga City Art Gallery has played a major part in focusing attention on glass, both with a series of biennial exhibitions and by building an extensive permanent glass collection. The major exhibition 'International Directions in Glass Art', held in 1982, was sponsored by Australia's oldest glass manufacturer, Australian Consolidated Industries, and the Crafts Board of the Australia Council. The task of choosing the glass for that exhibition fell to Michael Esson, a British immigrant who had trained at the Edinburgh College of Art and the Royal College of Art in London. Although intended to be a truly international exhibition, no Australian glass was included. This is somewhat surprising as by 1985 the third 'National Glass Biennial' had been organized at Wagga Wagga, for which work by fifty-six artists was considered for selection (thirty-one of whom were chosen) and most of these had already been working for some time. But the most important thing about

'International Directions in Glass Art' was that it set up a direct link with what was happening elsewhere. As Robert Bell said in his introduction to the catalogue, 'This "people-link" is a major part of the background of the contemporary glass movement in Australia.'[26]

CANBERRA COLLEGE OF ART

In Australia a number of artists have come and gone, leaving their knowledge behind them to be either digested and put to use, or discarded with time; but Klaus Moje at Canberra would appear to be laying down the most solid groundwork so far. He has been involved in glass for a long time, having begun his career working in his father's glassworks after earning his

Klaus Moje, 'No. 6 Sculpture', 1985, fused coloured glass, wall-mounted. 58 x 45 x 5 cm (22¾ x 17¾ x 2 in)

Klaus Moje, two untitled pieces, 1987, fused mosaic glass, ground. 16 x 16 x 18 cm (6¼ x 6¼ x 7 in) and 45 x 45 cm (17¾ x 17¾ in)

master's certificate in glass-cutting and etching in 1959. He never had any formal art training. When he met and married Isgard Moje-Wohlgemuth they started working together and opened a combined workshop and gallery in Hamburg. They began by selling their work at Christmas fairs, and their individual tasks were clearly defined in the simple painted glassware they made: Klaus handled the cutting and his wife was responsible for the painting with metal oxides dissolved in oil. It is only since 1975 that Klaus Moje has been working in the mosaic glass technique, which he discovered purely by chance. The discovery was the making of him as an artist, because he had at last found a technique which both satisfied his need to work with his hands and offered endless possibilities for the kaleidoscopic colour effects at which he excels. The story of his chance discovery pays tribute to his ingenuity as a craftsman. What he had in fact arrived at by cutting up coloured glass canes and fusing them together in a makeshift mould of plaster and grog was the ancient Roman technique of mosaic glass:

> He has taken an ancient Alexandrian or Roman luxury glass concept and updated both its form and technique. Moje cuts his coloured glass canes into ribbons or strips with a diamond saw, arranges their design as a flat sheet and fuses them together in a pottery kiln or firing furnace at a precisely controlled temperature. A second, low-temperature firing slumps the flat glass slowly into the mold. Final stages involve many tedious hours of grinding to smooth the rim and create a matt finish on the upper surface of his mosaic bowls. He leaves the bottom surface shiny for tactile contrast.[27]

As Moje's skills have developed so has his colour palette and the range of visual effects he creates. He can make his glass look as shiny as marble or as soft and pliable as silk. It is a technique with which he feels like challenging the whole world of art. He has gone from making vessels to experimenting with more sculptural forms, and his work, whilst being instantly recognizable, is always changing in the quest for new horizons. As a teacher he says modestly of himself, 'The only thing I can teach is independence of thought.'[28]

BLOWN GLASS AND GLASS ENGRAVING

It is still too early to say what effect Moje will have in the long run, but recent graduates from Canberra certainly display a degree of sophistication only very rarely seen before in Australian glass. Canberra provides the sort of all-round education a glass artist needs these days in order to compete on an international level. Before Moje's arrival in Australia most glass was either blown or engraved. A lot of it was reminiscent of what had happened in America in the 1960s and a little later in every other country which

Dennis O'Connor, 'Eroded Form I', 1982, free-blown and sand-blasted glass in three sections. 21 x 26.5 cm (8¼ x 10½ in)

responded to the idea of the independent artist blowing glass in his own studio. There were special problems for artists in Australia because of the difficulty of assimilating knowledge in a country which is at once so spread out and sparsely populated. When the first fully representative exhibition of glass from New Zealand and Australia was put together in Melbourne in 1984, and later travelled to Germany, Jenny Zimmer wrote in the catalogue introduction, 'Calls for participation in this exhibition revealed, for the first time, the broad extent of new glass activities in the country. The processes of selection brought individuals to our attention whose work was, hitherto, completely unknown.'[29] The exhibition showed the work of forty-five artists, the majority of whom had had less than five years' experience in making glass. At least half of the exhibition was devoted to flat glass, a discussion of which falls outside the scope of this book but which has been

Gerry King, 'Room for a
Nuclear Family', 1987, cast and
assembled glass. 47 x 29 cm
(18½ x 11½ in).
(Photo: M. Kluvanek)

one of the most important factors in the development of Australian glass.
The interest in possibilities for flat glass in architecture arose largely as a
result of a workshop in architectural glass design conducted in Australia by
Ludwig Schaffrath during 1981, and some of the best new Australian glass –
such as the work of Klaus Zimmer, John Greig, David Clegg or Wayne
Rayson – belongs to that tradition.

Among the hot-glass artists many blew vessel forms, experimenting with
what for them were completely new decorative techniques. Nick Mount,
Don Wreford, Dennis O'Connor, Peter Goss, Pauline Delaney and Nick
Wirdham are all glass-blowers who either learnt or developed their skills at
Chisholm Institute of Technology in Melbourne or at the Jam Factory in
Adelaide. They made what are essentially attractive studio glass flower
vases. The blown glass of Scott Cowcher and Gerry King stretches vessel

form towards sculpture; in a sentiment shared by many who work in this way Gerry King describes his own intentions by saying, 'My aim is not to make beautiful glass but rather to retain and exploit the innate beauty of the material whilst constructing pieces that have meanings beyond those of superficial appearances.'[30] One or two artists began to evolve a personal style early on, among them Maureen Cahill and Stephen Skillitzi. Maureen Cahill wants her students at the Sydney College of Arts to challenge the traditional notion of glass, as she does herself in her own colourful sculptural pieces. Stephen Skillitzi, now living and working in South Australia, has been one of the most widely exhibited artists nationally and is represented in all the major public collections throughout Australia. He has attracted attention by being irreverent in his approach to the material; his work is somewhat naive, but it derives strength from Skillitzi's uninhibited approach. His earlier pieces were blown-glass objects with a penchant for the unexpected; more recently he has made mixed-media assemblages with a message: 'The content of my work reflects situations in our world.'[31]

Among Australian glass engravers Tony Hanning has made a name for himself, mainly by engraving landscape imagery – native flora, fauna and insect life, derived from his large garden in Gippsland country – onto his vessel forms. Anne Dybka is a self-taught glass engraver who began life as a painter. She teaches part-time at Sydney College of Arts and in her own work concentrates on wildlife themes, the sea and the rain forest.

The two Australian artists whose work stands out from the rest are Warren Langley and Brian Hirst. Langley began working in glass after graduating from the University of Sydney in 1972, but glass-making only became a full-time passion for him in the late 1970s. After travelling the world for six years from 1972 to 1978, mainly with the objective of studying glass in England and America, he opened his own studio in Australia on his return. His way of working is to choose a theme and explore it with variations. He is inventive and always keen to investigate new possibilities, using new techniques to express new ideas. His first introduction to the kiln was through Maureen Cahill in Sydney, and casting has always been his main working method, though he often incorporates a number of different techniques in one piece, managing to do so with just the right amount of technical exhibitionism. As an artist Langley builds his imagery with a vocabulary of symbols – cows, sheep, the Southern Cross, arrows, crosses, the Australian flag – incorporating them into panels, sculptures and vessels in a vibrant range of colours. He is a keen observer, translating into abstract imagery a variety of concepts which occupy his mind and intrigue him. His works show 'where the mutually exclusive merge, where environmental ugliness becomes aesthetic value, where day becomes night and where a gestalt changes with the blink of an eye'.[32] He is particularly fascinated by the idea of man imposing himself on nature as seen, for example, when a road penetrates a mountain, or the concrete arc of a dam spans a river gorge: 'Unlike the arch environmentalist, I found a distinct beauty in this "collage" of man on nature.'[33] Langley is becoming increasingly involved with architectural commissions and is one of many Australian artists involved in the decoration of the new parliament building in Canberra.

Brian Hirst is still very young, but has already completed some interesting work, particularly a series of vessels inspired by Cycladic art. These are

Tony Hanning, 'Lost Symbols Certain Clouds', 1986, sand-blasted footed bowl. 12 x 22 cm (4¾ x 8¾ in)

Warren Langley, 'Druid
Suite', 1986, fused glass.
H. c. 58 cm (22¾ in)

Brian Hirst, 'Votive Bowl',
1987, blown glass.
H. c. 10 cm (4 in)

mould-blown pieces, finished in lustrous enamels, and hark back to a lost civilization. He is sensitive to the romance of archaeology, which has inspired him to use his feeling for antiquity in a modern idiom.

STUDIO GLASS IN NEW ZEALAND

It is almost too soon to conduct a survey of glass in New Zealand, but the enthusiasm is such that the future for glass there looks bright. 'The resurgence of the hot-glass studio is a recently stimulated phenomenon, full of energy and rich in promise . . . . Studio hot glass reached the shores of New Zealand in the mid 70s, a curious blend of honest tableware, West Coast USA funk, hippie flower-power, and an Americanised German aesthetic.'[34] As already mentioned, Tony Kupfer, an American by birth, must take credit for introducing New Zealanders to studio glass, and Mel Simpson for being the first native New Zealander to become a studio glass artist. Together with John Croucher, Peter Raos and Peter Viesnik, they form the first group of glass artists to emerge from New Zealand. Recently the work of two very young artists has been attracting attention. Ann Robinson works in *pâte de verre*, making bold vessel forms which are impressive for their simplicity, honesty and clarity of colour. Garry Nash is a versatile artist whose wide-ranging technical abilities enable him to work in both hot and cold processes. His blown vessel forms are worked on with acid-etching, sand-blasting and diamond cutting wheels. Striking large vessels combine freedom and formality, and he has an original way of using form as an extension to the poignancy of his very personal engraved imagery.

Part of the natural process of evolution in the contemporary glass movement is an obligatory period of initiation and discovery in each country. Only when a proper glass programme has been established can graduates set out on a career without wasting a decade on trial and error as the pioneers had to do. The first decade of glass in countries without much of a glass tradition has tended to look much the same whether it occurred during the 1960s or the 1970s. It is easy to forget that it took the Americans a good ten years to establish themselves as serious artists, and it has been no different in New Zealand or Australia.

OPPOSITE: **Gary Nash**, sculptural vase form, 1987, free-blown glass, fused and engraved. H. *c.* 50 cm (19¾ in)

Ann Robinson, 'Ice Bowl', 1987, *pâte de verre*. H. 33 cm (13 in)

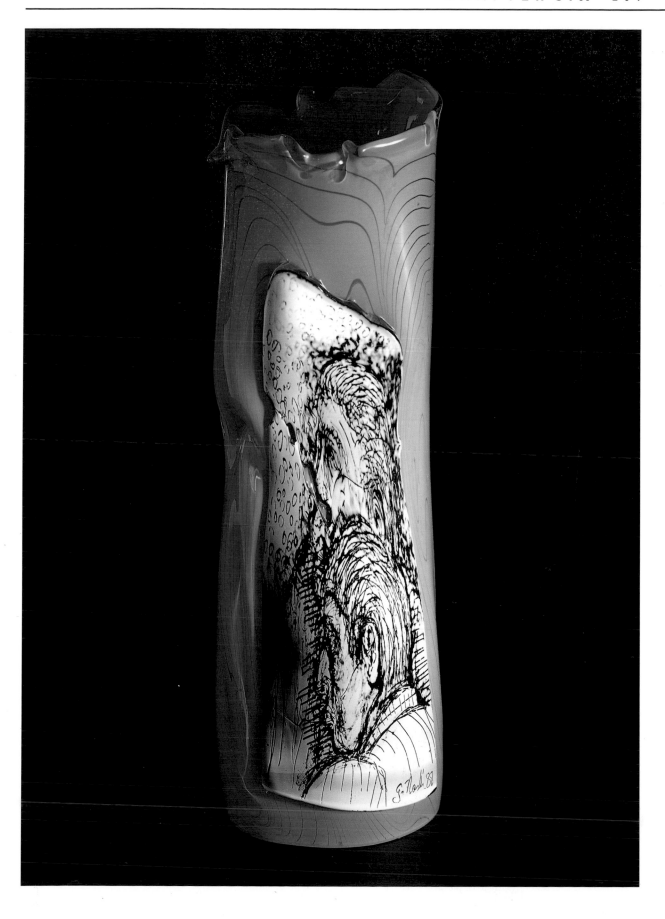

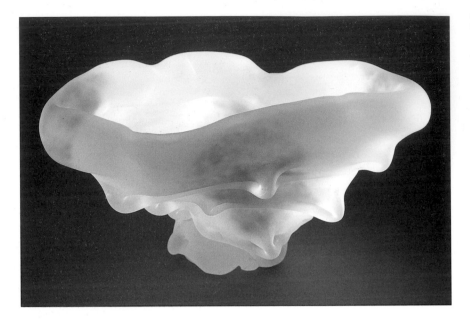

JAPAN

There are well over one hundred glass artists working in Japan, although only a few of them are known in the West. Of these, Kyohei Fujita, who manages to be both modern and deeply rooted in the Japanese decorative art tradition, is the only one to have a firmly established international reputation. There is an innate respect among Japanese artists for what has gone before, and though no modern artist wishes to be an imitator, it also goes against the grain to flout convention. For this reason there is a reluctance to lower craft standards; imperfection is simply not an acceptable artistic device in Japan. There is not, perhaps never will be, the same abandon among Japanese glass artists as there has been in other countries. And yet the art of glass is taken very seriously: there has been a great deal of museum interest, mainly by Hokkaido Museum of Art and the National Museums of Art in Tokyo and Kyoto, and a great many international glass exhibitions have been organized over the last decade. In 1978 the eighth World Crafts Council conference was held in Kyoto, providing many Japanese artists with their first opportunity to see what was happening on the international scene. Their own Glass Art-Crafts Association was founded in 1972 by Hisatoshi Iwata, whose family has been involved in glass for more than half a century.

There is very little twentieth-century glass tradition to speak of in Japan. Cheap household glass and window glass was manufactured with technology learnt from Europe, and the only glass designers at all interested in the idea of studio glass were Toshichi Iwata and Kozo Kagami. Apart from this there was no thought that glass might develop into an art form. Compared with porcelain, metal or lacquer, glass has played a minor to non-existent role in Japanese twentieth-century decorative art. Toshichi Iwata, his son Hisatoshi, and Kagami struggled on after the Second World War and it was mainly due to them that there was any foundation upon which to build for the future. Toshichi Iwata devoted the whole of his long life (1893–1980) to the bettering of glass design, trying to make glass a part of the Japanese tea

ceremony, to initiate the idea of glass screens, and generally to find more ways of incorporating glass into the Japanese way of life.

Even now only a handful of Japanese glass artists have their own studios, and most are employed as designers in the industry, making their own work alongside their other commitments. Gradually the standard of glass education has improved, and whilst most is still conceived primarily as training for industry, there are exceptions such as at the University of Tama and the Glass Art Institute in Tokyo. The institute was founded by Toshiio Yoshimiziu in 1981 and employs twenty-five teachers and six students. It admits up to fifty students and fifteen postgraduates per year.

Hisatoshi Iwata, untitled free-blown footed vase with applied decoration

There is no doubt that the chief protagonist in the fast-developing glass scene in Japan has been Kyohei Fujita. He was a pupil of Toshichi Iwata's and has in many ways managed to consolidate his master's life work by his acceptance as a top-ranking artist in his own country. Since 1973 he has been making the caskets for which he is best known, changing their shape and colour for his yearly shows like a fashion designer might do from one season to the next. He has an exceptional colour sense, rooted in Japanese culture, with which he has created a language of his own. 'They are not just colours, but also represent spirit, thoughts and human relations.'[35] The caskets or boxes of various shapes, sizes and colours are closely related to *casuri bako* (lacquered boxes), which form an important part of the tea ceremony. They are all mould-blown and the basic colour is inlaid with gold or silver foil (often a combination of the two), mostly with splashes of richly contrasting colour. The craftsmanship is superb and the finished pieces perfect objects which are visually thrilling and, unlike most glass, very tactile. It is the treatment of silver and gold foil that reminds one most of lacquerwork, as well as the splashes of white, when he uses them, which seem to imitate the effect of crushed egg-shell in lacquerwork. But the similarity bears no hint of plagiarism; it merely provides a relationship that makes perfect sense within the context of Japanese decorative art.

Fujita has gained acceptance in Japan because there is a place for what he does in the Japanese home. He explains: 'Most Japanese cannot understand non-utilitarian objects; their houses are small and lack the space to display such works.'[36] Fujita has in recent years widened his scope by working in Murano and at Orrefors. The pieces made in Murano – a range of vases and lamps – use *latticino* techniques, in a colour range very much his own, and show the same respect for Italian tradition that he has for that of his own country; he makes repeated reference to it both in the shapes that he chooses and the decorative detail, such as the pinched trailing of applied handles. The Orrefors pieces are done in the same spirit of co-operation, using clear crystal either on its own with decorative cutting or with blushes of subtle colour, reminiscent of the colour that punctuates Japanese masks.

ABOVE LEFT: **Kyohei Fujita**, 'Heian', decorative box with a cover, blue moulded glass with applied gold and silver decoration. 16 x 23 cm (6¼ x 9 in)

ABOVE: **Kyohei Fujita**, two-coloured bowl, free-blown glass. H. 14 cm (5½ in), diam. 24.5 cm (9⅝ in)

GLASS STYLES

A lot of Japanese glass is limpid, colourless, top-quality crystal, cut and polished, sometimes in vessel form and sometimes sculptural. Chikara

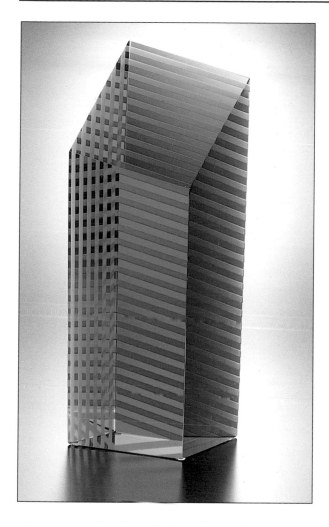

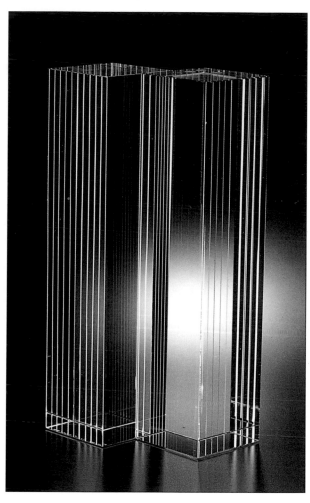

Hashimoto, Yutaka Otuka, Denji Takeuchi, Takahasi Yoshihiko, Takikawa Yoshihiko and Nobuyasu Sato all work mainly in clear crystal and each has evolved a sculptural style of his own; if there is a linking factor between them, it is in their clarity of thought. Each piece contains one simple idea which is executed to perfection. In Sato's 'Manhattan Skyline', for instance, five elements are skilfully cut to suggest such famous landmarks as Twin-Towers, the Rockefeller Building, the Chrysler Building and the Conran Building. Like most related Japanese sculpture it makes perfect sense with great simplicity. Akira Shirahata, Saburo Funakoshi and Yamada Teruo display similar skills in their carefully planned vessels, whereas Niyoko Ikuta uses a technique of cutting, polishing and stacking sheet glass to make rhythmic aerodynamic shapes that seem to defy gravity.

If there is one area that Japanese artists have chosen to develop more than any other it is *pâte de verre*. The widest range of *pâte de verre* yet to be seen together was at the first Japan *Pâte de Verre* Competition in 1984, organized by The Glass Loving People's Association and sponsored by the Tokyo Glass Art Institute. Work by forty different artists was chosen for the accompanying exhibition. Before this exhibition there was virtually no Japanese *pâte de verre*. The instigator of the competition and exhibition was Tsuneo Yoshimizu, the president of the association, who had already been researching the technique for ten years. In the introduction to the cata-

ABOVE LEFT: **Denji Takeuchi**, 'Composition No. 101', 1988, cast, cut, polished and sand-blasted glass. 28.5 x 11 x 6 cm (11¼ x 4¼ x 2¼ in)

ABOVE: **Nobuyasu Sato**, 'Twin', 1986, clear glass, cast, cut, polished and glued. 20 x 12.5 x 7 cm (7¾ x 5 x 2¾ in)

Masamichi Hashiguchi,
untitled *pâte de verre* vessel,
1988. H. 17.5 cm (6⅞ in), diam.
21 cm (8¼ in)

logue he wrote, 'This is practically the first *pâte de verre* competition in the world. I hope this competition and exhibition will motivate the development of a new genre of glass in Japan.'[37] With the technique at an experimental stage for most of the artists involved the results were mixed, but with a surprising number of good pieces. The most successful were compact vessel forms, among which was a pair of vases by Kinuko Ito – two cylinder forms composed of what resemble sheets of glass folded like fabric with a corner 'flap' projecting out to one side – entitled 'The Girls in Their Summer Dresses'. Mhoko Shimoda's simple tea-bowls, Yukiko Nakata's octagonal plate, Masamichi Hashiguchi's lidded jar, entitled 'The Shade Of Trees', Kazuyo Misaki's octagonal vase, Saiko Mizukami's 'Next Box', and Naomi Murasagi's 'Pitcher' are all translations of traditional Japanese shapes into the new language of *pâte de verre*. There are also a few brave attempts at sculpture, such as Ryoji Shibuya's 'From The Earth', a pair of pyramids supporting rectangular boulder shapes that are joined by four metal rods. Internal veiling effects in the translucent pale blue glass provide the intended 'other worldly' effect.

Apart from the styles already mentioned, the most popular seems to be a Memphis-inspired group of work, the earliest of which was a series of humorous blown pieces with applied decoration by Hisatoshi Iwata, dating from 1983 and 1984. These are fantasy vessels, decorated sometimes with Picasso-like faces or rococo ornament, but never snubbing function in the same way as work by the Memphis designers. The most successful pieces in

FAR LEFT: **Kinuko Ito**, untitled form, cast glass

LEFT: **Naoto Yokoyama**, 'Dance in a Flower Garden', blown glass with gold and silver work (by Kaoruko Yokoyama). H. 26 cm (10¼ in)

this vein have come in the recent past from Naoto Yokoyama, an 'avant-garde' designer who has designed glassware for twenty-five years, first for the Noritake China Company and later for Joetsu Crystal Company, before establishing his own design studio. He does not actually work the glass himself. He wants his glass to be used: 'I have the strong urge to make something that has never been seen before.'[38] He sees himself as a post-modernist who adapts freely from all styles and all times 'to meld them into something new, transcending style'.[39]

In addition to these distinct styles, experiments of all sorts are being carried out by Japanese glass-makers. There is a feeling that they are working hard, and with great success, at being accepted in the same way as their peers in other branches of the decorative arts. The pull of Japanese tradition is still the strongest force, though it is often harmoniously mingled with ideas from the West. Chikahiko Okada's slumped plate decorated with a single wintry tree, which was exhibited in the first important travelling exhibition of Japanese glass, 'Neues Glas aus Japan', shown in 1984 at the Badisches Landesmuseum in Karlsruhe, neatly combines both cultures. The work of some Japanese artists shows a close affinity with what has been happening in the American glass movement, though it is never without a very recognizable 'Japonisme'. One is particularly aware of this in Niyoko Ikuta's glass laminated onto concrete, or Makato Ito and Yukio Ueno's free-blown vessels. It is an exciting time in the history of Japanese glass, and one looks forward to seeing what new directions will be taken.

MUSEUM COLLECTIONS AND GALLERIES

SELECTED MUSEUM COLLECTIONS

AUSTRALIA
Art Gallery of Western Australia, Perth
Australian Council for the Arts, Sydney
Australian National Gallery, Canberra
City Art Gallery, Wagga Wagga
Museum of Applied Arts and Sciences, Sydney
National Gallery of Victoria, Melbourne
Queensland Art Gallery, Brisbane

AUSTRIA
Linzer Stadtmuseum Nordico, Linz
Österreichiches Museum für Angewandte Kunst, Vienna
Tiroler Landesmuseum Ferdinandeum, Innsbruck

BELGIUM
Musée du Verre, Charleroi
Musée du Verre, Liège
Museum of Decorative Art, Ghent

CZECHOSLOVAKIA
Muzeum Skla a Bižutérie, Jablonec nad Nisou
Severočeské Muzeum, Liberec
Uměleckoprůmyslové Muzeum, Prague

DENMARK
Det Danske Kunstindustrimuseum, Copenhagen
Glasmuseum, Ebeltoft
Holmegaard-Kastrup Glass Museum, Fensmark

FINLAND
Finnish Glass Museum, Riihmäki
Museum of Applied Arts, Helsinki

FRANCE
CIRVA, Marseilles
Musée des Arts Décoratifs, Centre du Verre, Paris
Musée du Verre, Sars-Poteries

GREAT BRITAIN
Broadfield House Glass Museum, Kingswinford,
  West Midlands

Holbourne Museum & Craft Study Centre,
  Holbourne, Bath
Pilkington Glass Museum, St Helens, Liverpool
Victoria & Albert Museum, London

JAPAN
Daimaru Museum, Osaka
Hokkaido Museum of Art, Sapporo
Museum of Fine Arts, Gifu
National Museum of Modern Art, Kyoto
Navio Museum, Osaka
Shimonoseki City Art Museum, Shimonoseki
Tokyo Metropolitan Teien Art Museum, Tokyo

NETHERLANDS
Groninger Museum, Groningen
Museum Boymans van Beuningen, Rotterdam
Stedelijk Museum, Amsterdam
Stichting Nationaal Glasmuseum, Leerdam

NORTHERN IRELAND
Ulster Museum, Belfast

SWEDEN
Glass Museum, Växjö
National Museum, Stockholm
Röhsska Konstslöjdmuseet, Göteborg

SWITZERLAND
Musée des Arts Décoratifs, Lausanne
Museum Bellerive, Zürich

UNITED STATES
American Craft Museum, New York
Bergström-Mahler Museum, Neenah, Wisconsin
Carnegie Institute, Museum of Art, Pittsburgh, Pennsylvania
Chicago Art Institute, Chicago, Illinois
Chrysler Museum, Institute of Glass, Norfolk, Virginia
Cincinnati Art Museum, Cincinnati, Ohio
Cleveland Institute of Art, Cleveland, Ohio
Cooper-Hewitt Museum, New York
Corning Museum of Glass, Corning, New York
Detroit Institute of Art, Detroit, Michigan
Everson Museum of Art, Syracuse, New York

High Museum of Art, Atlanta, Georgia
Huntington Galleries Museum, Huntington, West Virginia
Illinois State Museum, Springfield, Illinois
Johnson Wax Collection, Racine, Wisconsin
Leigh Yawkey Woodson Art Museum, Wausau, Wisconsin
Los Angeles County Museum, Los Angeles, California
Metropolitan Museum of Art, New York
Museum of Art of the Rhode Island School of Design,
    Providence, Rhode Island
Museum of Modern Art, New York
New Orleans Museum of Art, New Orleans, Louisiana
Philadelphia Museum of Art, Philadelphia, Pennsylvania
St Louis Art Museum, St Louis, Missouri
Seattle Art Museum, Seattle, Washington
Smithsonian Institution, Washington DC
Toledo Museum of Art, Toledo, Ohio
University of Wisconsin, Madison, Wisconsin

WEST GERMANY

Badisches Landesmuseum, Karlsruhe
Glasmuseum Frauenau, Frauenau
Glasmuseum Wertheim, Wertheim
Hessisches Landesmuseum, Darmstadt
Immenhausen Glasmuseum, Immenhausen
Kestner Museum, Hannover
Kunstgewerbe Museum, Berlin
Kunstmuseum, Düsseldorf
Kunstsammlungen der Veste Coburg, Coburg
Landesmuseum, Stuttgart
Museum für Kunst und Gewerbe, Hamburg
Museum für Kunsthandwerk, Frankfurt am Main

SELECTED GALLERIES

AUSTRIA

Glasgalerie Klute, Vienna
J. & L. Lobmeyr, Vienna

BELGIUM

Transparence Gallery, Brussels

CANADA

Galerie Verre d'Art, Montreal
The Glass Art Gallery, Toronto

FRANCE

Clara Scremini Gallery, Paris
Galerie d'Amon, Paris
Galerie Internationale du Verre, Biot
Galerie Suzel Berna, Antibes
Jean-Claude Novarro Gallery, Biot
Quartz, Paris

GREAT BRITAIN

Christie's, London
Coleridge, London
Contemporary Applied Arts, London
Crafts Council Gallery, London
Crafts Council Shop at Victoria & Albert Museum, London
The Glasshouse, London
Jeannette Hayhurst, London
Oxford Gallery, Oxford
Peter Dingley Gallery, Stratford-upon-Avon

JAPAN

Amano Gallery, Osaka
Misawa Interior Gallery, Osaka
Wacoal Ginze Space, Tokyo

NETHERLANDS

Braggiotti Gallery, Rotterdam
Galerie Kuhler, Amsterdam
Galerie Rob van den Doel, The Hague
Glasgalerie Arti-Choque, Velp

SWITZERLAND

Galerie Heidi Schneider, Horgen
Galerie Trois, Geneva
Sanske Galerie, Zürich

UNITED STATES

Betsy Rosenfeld Gallery, Inc., Chicago, Illinois
Christie's, New York
Compositions Gallery, San Francisco, California
Eileen Kremen Gallery, Fullerton, California
Foster White Gallery, Seattle, Washington
Habatat Galleries, Lathrup Village, Michigan
Heller Gallery, SoHo, New York
Holsten Galleries, Palm Beach, Florida
Judy Youens Gallery, Houston, Texas
Kurland Summers Gallery, Los Angeles, California
Maureen Littleton Gallery, Washington DC
Northwest Art Glass, Seattle, Washington
Snyderman Gallery, Philadelphia, Pennsylvania
Stein Glass Gallery, Portland, Oregon
Studio Glass Gallery of Britain, Montclair, New Jersey
Traver Sutton Gallery, Seattle, Washington
Vespermann Glass Gallery and Studio, Atlanta, Georgia

WEST GERMANY

CCAA Glasgalerie, Cologne
Essener Glasgalerie, Essen
First Glas Galerie Friederike Sauter, Munich
Galerie Bergmann, Coburg
Galerie Glashart, Hannover
Galerie Gottschalk-Betz, Frankfurt am Main
Galerie L, Hamburg
Galerie Monica Trüjen, Bremen
Kunsthaus am Museum Carola von Ham, Cologne
La Galleria, Frankfurt am Main

NOTES

CHAPTER 1

1 Paul Hollister, 'Studio Glass Movement', *New American Glass: Focus West Virginia II*, 1986.
2 Thomas Buechner, preface to *World Glass Now*, Corning Museum of Glass, 1979.
3 Dagmar Sinz, 'A Talk with Dale Chihuly', *Neues Glas*, 1/87.
4 Jack Cowart & Karen Chambers, *Chihuly: A Decade of Glass*, Bellevue Art Museum, 1984.
5 Harvey Littleton, *Glass Blowing – A Search for Form*, 1971.
6 Peter Layton, 'The Glass Menagerie', *Crafts*, March/April 1983.
7 Harvey Littleton, *Glass Blowing – A Search for Form*, 1971.
8 Miroslav Klinger, interview with Erwin Eisch at the second Glass Symposium at Nový Bor, *Glass Review*, 3/86.
9 David Huchthausen, introduction to *Americans in Glass*, Leigh Yawkey Woodson Art Museum, 1984.
'10 *Ibid.*
11 Stanislav Libenský, *New Glass Review 8*, Corning Museum of Glass, 1987.
12 Dan Klein, 'Diana Hobson', *New Work*, No. 31, Fall 1987.
13 Walter Darby Bannard, 'Craft Art and Envy – Glass Art Society Conference', *New Work*, No. 27, Fall 1986.
14 K. Günter Nicola, 'Bert van Loo', *Neues Glas*, 4/82.
15 Suzanne Muchnic, *Glass Art Society Journal*, 1985–6.
16 David Huchthausen, introduction to *Americans in Glass*, Leigh Yawkey Woodson Art Museum, 1985.
17 Paul Hollister, 'American Studio Glass in the Next Decade', *Neues Glas*, 1/87.
18 Harvey Littleton, *Glass Blowing Λ Search for Form*, 1971.
19 Introduction to *Studio Glass in North America 1962-1982*, The Glass Art Gallery, Toronto.
20 Joel Philip Myers, 'Studio Glass Movement', *New American Glass: Focus West Virginia I*, 1976.
21 Paul Hollister, 'American Studio Glass in the Next Decade', *Neues Glas*, 1/87.
22 Thomas Buechner, introduction to *Glass 1959*, Corning Museum of Glass.
23 Paul Hollister, 'Studio Glass Movement', *New American Glass: Focus West Virginia II*, 1986.
24 *Ibid.*
25 Panel discussion, *Glass Art Society Journal*, 1982–3.

CHAPTER 2

1 Douglas Heller, preface to *The Steuben Project*, 1988.
2 *Ibid.*
3 *Ibid.*
4 Paul Hollister, 'USA Studio Glass Before 1962', *Neues Glas*, 4/85.
5 *Ibid.*
6 Joan Falconer Byrd, 'Harvey Littleton and Studio Glass', *Harvey Littleton: A Retrospective Exhibition*, High Museum of Art, Atlanta, 1984.
7 P.D., 'Harvey Littleton: A Retrospective', *Neues Glas*, 1/85.
8 Harvey Littleton, *Glass Blowing – A Search for Form*, 1971.
9 P.D., 'Harvey Littleton: A Retrospective', *Neues Glas*, 1/85.
10 *Ibid.*
11 Thomas Bosworth, 'Handbuilt at Pilchuck', *Craft Horizons*, April 1979.
12 *Ibid.*
13 *Ibid.*
14 Maureen O'Brien, 'N.Y.E.G.W. in Montclair', *New Work*, Summer/Fall 1982.
15 Foreword, compiled and edited by Ferdinand Hampson, to *Glass: State of the Art*, 1984.
16 Henry Geldzahler, foreword to *Chihuly: Color, Glass and Form*, 1986.
17 Jack Cowart & Karen Chambers, *Chihuly: A Decade of Glass*, Bellevue Art Museum, 1984.
18 Valerie Arber, 'Warm Glass', *Glass Art Society Journal*, 1983–4.
19 Paul Stankard, 'Lampworking', *Glass Art Society Journal*, 1983–4.
20 Paul Hollister, 'Mark Peiser: Exploration of Inner Space', *Neues Glas*, 3/84.
21 Richard Yelle, 'Sydney Cash', *New Work*, June/July 1980.
22 *Ibid.*
23 Karen S. Chambers, 'Howard Ben Tré', *New Work*, Summer/Fall 1983.
24 *Cast Glass Sculpture*, California State University, Fullerton, 1986.
25 *Americans in Glass*, Leigh Yawkey Woodson Art Museum, 1984.
26 Paul Hollister, 'Light Affecting Form in Space: William Carlson's Glasswork', *Neues Glas*, 2/82.
27 *Americans in Glass*, Leigh Yawkey Woodson Art Museum, 1984.
28 Paul Hollister, 'Tom Patti', *Neues Glas*, 2/83.
29 *Americans in Glass*, Leigh Yawkey Woodson Art Museum, 1984.
30 Paul Hollister, 'The Mace Kirkpatrick Collaboration', *Neues Glas*, 1/84.
31 Rick Bernstein, 'Concetta Mason', *Neues Glas*, 3/86.
32 Paul Hollister, 'Michael Aschenbrenner's Messages in Glass', *Neues Glas*, 4/84.
33 *Americans in Glass*, Leigh Yawkey Woodson Art Museum, 1984.
34 *Americans in Glass*, Leigh Yawkey Woodson Art Museum, 1976.
35 *Americans in Glass*, Leigh Yawkey Woodson Art Museum, 1984.
36 *Americans in Glass*, Leigh Yawkey Woodson Art Museum, 1976.
37 David Huchthausen, consultant's statement, *Americans in Glass*, Leigh Yawkey Woodson Art Museum, 1981.

CHAPTER 3

1 Alena Adlerová, 'Years of Change in Czechoslovakian Glass 1957–1962', *Neues Glas*, 1/88.
2 'A Talk with Stanislav Libenský', *Glass Art Society Journal*, 1981.
3 *Ibid.*
4 Alena Adlerová, 'Stanislav Libenský's Early Work', *Glass Review*, 6/86.
5 Stanislav Libenský, *A Review of Glass Education in Czechoslovakia*, 1983.
6 Alena Adlerová, 'The Glass Sculpture Exhibition – House of Art in Brno', *Glass Review*, 12/83.
7 Introduction to *Prostor 1* (catalogue), 1982.
8 Alena Adlerová, 'Prostor 3', *Neues Glas*, 4/86.
9 Jiři Harcuba, *Czechoslovak Glass: Seven Masters*, American Craft Museum, 1983.
10 *Ibid.*
11 Miroslav Klivar, 'Vaclav Cigler', *Glass Review, 9/82.*
12 *Ibid.*

13 Alena Adlerová, 'Modern Glass', *Glass Review*, 8/83.
14 Elly Sherman, 'Jiří Šuhájek', *New Work*, Winter 1986.
15 Jan Kriz, 'Václav Machač', *Glass Review*, 2/85.
16 Kristian Sudar, 'Jaromir Rybák', *Neues Glas*, 4/85.
17 Marie Mžykova, 'Pavel Trnka', *Glass Review*, 3/85.
18 Kenneth R. Trapp, 'Medium and Message', *Contemporary American and European Glass from the Saxe Collection*, Oakland Museum, California, 1986.
19 František Vízner, artist's statement, *Glass Art Society Journal*, 1983-4.
20 Robert Loeffler, MD, 'Contemporary Hungarian Glass Sculpture', *New Work*, Fall 1986.
21 *Ibid.*
22 *Ibid.*
23 A congratulatory letter from Kurt Wallstab, 'Albin Schaedel: 80 Years', *Neues Glas*, 3/85.

CHAPTER 4

1 Thomas Buechner, 'The Coburger Glaspreis 1977', *Craft Horizons*, December 1977.
2 Helmut Ricke, *New Glass in Germany*, Kunstmuseum, Düsseldorf, 1983.
3 Klaus Moje, 'Willi Pistor', *Neues Glas*, 1/82.
4 Helmut Ricke, *New Glass in Germany*, Kunstmuseum, Düsseldorf, 1983.
5 *Glass Art Society Journal*, 1982-3.
6 John Lucas, 'Erwin Eisch and his Revolutionary Glass', *Glass Review*, 3/69.
7 K. Günter Nicola, 'Theodor G. Sellner', *Neues Glas*, 1/87.
8 'Four Swedish Glass Artists', *Glass Art Society Journal*, 1982-3.
9 *Ibid.*
10 *Ibid.*
11 Sylvie Gerard, 'Ann Wärff', *La Revue de la Céramique et du Verre*, No. 17, 1984.
12 Verena Tafel, 'New Works by Ann Wärff', *Neues Glas*, 4/86.
13 Karen S. Chambers, 'Bertil and Ulrica Vallien: Designs for Art and Living', *New Work*, Winter/Spring 1985.
14 *Ibid.*
15 *Ibid.*
16 Kaj Kalin, *Sarpaneva*, Otava Publishing Company, Helsinki, 1985.
17 Jorgen Shou Christensen, 'A Conversation About Glass in Denmark', *Neues Glas*, 2/82.
18 M. Trüjen, 'Opening of the First Museum for Contemporary Glass Art in Ebeltoft', *Neues Glas*, 3/86.
19 *Ibid.*

CHAPTER 5

1 *Crafts*, November/December 1976.
2 *Sam Herman Glass* (brochure), 1980.
3 Contemporary glass discussed by Ray Flavell in relation to 'New Glass', the international exhibition at Corning Museum of Glass, New York, *Crafts*, March/April 1979.
4 *British Studio Glass*, a Sunderland Arts Centre touring exhibition, 1983-4.
5 Wendy Evans, 'The Glasshouse', *Crafts*, March/April 1976.
6 *Contemporary British Glass*, 15 April-

15 May 1988, Infokraf, Kuala Lumpur.
7 Emmeline Bauer, 'Simon Moore', *La Revue de la Céramique et du Verre*, September/October 1987.
8 Kim Evans, 'Hot Glass Conference', *Crafts*, November/December 1976.
9 Stephen Procter, *Thoughts About Light*, catalogue to an exhibition organized by Glas-Galerie Luzern, 28 June-31 August 1986.
10 *Ibid.*
11 *Ibid.*
12 Liam Kelly, *Clifford Rainey: Sculpture and Drawings, 1967-1987.*
13 Ron Pennell, 'Gem Engraving', *Crafts*, March/April 1974.
14 *British Studio Glass*, a Sunderland Arts Centre touring exhibition, 1983-4.
15 Rosemary Hill, 'Double Act: Rachel Woodman and Neil Wilkin', *Crafts*, July/August 1985.
16 Dan Klein, 'Abstractions in Glass', *Craft Arts*, October/December 1986.
17 *British Studio Glass*, a Sunderland Arts Centre touring exhibition, 1983-4.
18 *Glass Sculpture*, Stichting Glas, 1986.
19 Karen S. Chambers, 'A Conversation with Willem Heesen', *New Work*, Winter/Spring 1985.
20 Cees Strauss, 'Richard Meitner', *Neues Glas*, 2/85.
21 Bert van Loo, 'Recent Developments in Glass', *Beelden in Glas*, 1986.
22 Bert van Loo, 'Reflecting Image', *Glass Art Society Journal*, 1985-6.
23 Sylvie Gerard, 'Toots Zynsky', *La Revue de la Céramique et du Verre*, September/October 1987.
24 Aloine Jaulin, *Toots Zynsky: Oeuvres*, Clara Scremini, Paris, 1987.
25 Sylvie Gerard, 'Catherine Zoritchak', *La Revue de la Céramique et du Verre*, No. 21, 1985.
26 Yvonne Brunhammer, 'The French Glass Scene', *La Revue de la Céramique et du Verre*, 3/85.
27 *Verriers Français Contemporains: Art et Industrie*, Musée des Arts Décoratifs, 1982.
28 Karen S. Chambers, 'Mission Impossible', *New Work*, Winter/Spring 1983.
29 Livio Seguso, Heller Gallery catalogue, 1986.
30 Murra Zabel, 'Paolo Martinuzzi', *Neues Glas*, 3/86.

CHAPTER 6

1 'Glass Art's New Horizons: Some Highlights', *Ontario Craft*, Fall 1986.
2 K. Corey Keeble, 'Daniel Crichton: Freeblown Glass', *Ontario Craft*, Winter 1983.
3 *Ibid.*
4 Gloria Hickey, 'Profiles in Design - Max Leser', *Azure*, June 1988.
5 *Ibid.*
6 Robert Jekyll, statement on Karl Schantz, Toronto, 1985.
7 *Art Glass of Canada*, Indiana State Museum, 1987.
8 Juror's statement, *Art Glass of Canada*, Indiana State Museum, 1987.
9 Rosalyn J. Morrison, 'Vigil: The New Work of Irene Frolic', *New Work*, Summer 1988.
10 *Ibid.*
11 *Ibid.*
12 Rosalyn J. Morrison, 'Kevin Lockau',

New Work, Winter 1988.
13 *Ibid.*
14 *Ibid.*
15 Astri Reusch, artist's statement.
16 Allan Pringle, *Lisette Limieux: Recent Works*, Galerie Elena Lee Verre d'Art, 1986.
17 Gloria Hickey, 'Peter Zips', *New Work*, Summer 1986.
18 *Ibid.*
19 *Beyond the Object*, catalogue to an exhibition organized by the Saskatchewan Craft Council, 1987-8.
20 *Ibid.*
21 *Ibid.*
22 Marilynne Bell, 'Studio Glass Profile', *Craft Arts 11*, 1988.
23 Robert Bell, introduction to *International Directions in Glass Art*, Art Gallery of Western Australia, 1982.
24 Marilynne Bell, 'Studio Glass Profile', *Craft Arts 11*, 1988.
25 Paul Hollister, 'Klaus Moje', *American Craft*, December 1984/January 1985.
26 Robert Bell, introduction to *International Directions in Glass Art*, Art Gallery of Western Australia, 1982.
27 Paul Hollister, 'Klaus Moje', *American Craft*, December 1984/January 1985.
28 *Ibid.*
29 *Glass from Australia and New Zealand*, Hessisches Landesmuseum, Darmstadt, 5 December 1984-3 February 1985.
30 *Ibid.*
31 *Ibid.*
32 Lyndal Wilson, 'Glass from Australia: Warren Langley', *Neues Glas*, 2/85.
33 Peter Emmett, 'Aspects of Contemporary Australian Glass', *Neues Glas*, 1/83.
34 Paul Johnson, 'Recent New Zealand Glass', *Glass from Australia and New Zealand*.
35 Atsushi Takeda, 'Kyohei Fujita', *Neues Glas*, 2/87.
36 Jakelin Troy, 'Kyohei Fujita', *Craft Arts 8*, February/April 1987.
37 Catalogue to the first Japan Pâte de Verre Competition, organized by The Glass Loving People's Association and sponsored by the Tokyo Glass Art Institute, 1-16 November 1984, The Glass Gallery Kudan, Tokyo.
38 Janet Koplos, 'Made and Designed in Japan', *Crafts*, No. 90, January/February 1988.
39 *Ibid.*

SELECTED BIBLIOGRAPHY

BOOKS AND MAGAZINE ARTICLES

Adlerová, Alena, *Contemporary Bohemian Glass* (Odeon, Prague, 1979)

Beard, Geoffrey, *International Modern Glass* (Barrie & Jenkins, London, 1976)

Bloch-Dermant, Janine, *Le verre en France: Les Années 80* (Les Éditions de l'Amateur, Paris, 1988)

Buechner, T. S. and Warmus, W., 'Czechoslovakian Diary: 1980, 23 Glassmakers', *Journal of Glass Studies 23* (The Corning Museum of Glass, Corning, New York, 1981)

Flavell, Ray and Smale, Claude, *Studio Glassmaking* (Van Nostrand Reinhold Co., New York, 1974)

Grover, Ray and Lee, *Contemporary Art Glass* (Crown Publishers Inc., New York, 1975)

Hampson, Ferdinand, *Glass, State of the Art 1984* (Elliot Johnston Publishers, Huntington Woods, Michigan, 1984)
Insight: Collector's Guide to Contemporary American Glass (Habatat Galleries, New York, 1985)

Klein, Dan and Lloyd, Ward, *The History of Glass* (Orbis, London, 1984)

Littleton, Harvey, *Glass Blowing – A Search for Form* (Van Nostrand Reinhold Co., New York, 1971)

Loeffler, Robert, 'Contemporary Hungarian Glass Sculpture', *New Work*, No. 27, Autumn 1986, pp. 8–11

Lynggard, Finn, *Glas Handbogen* (Copenhagen, 1975)

National Museum of Modern Art, Kyoto (ed.), *Contemporary Studio Glass: An International Collection* (Weatherhill, New York, 1980; Tankosha, Tokyo/Kyoto, 1981)

Newman, Harold, *An Illustrated Dictionary of Glass* (Thames & Hudson, London, 1977)

Polak, Ada, *Modern Glass* (Faber & Faber, London, 1962)

Raban, J., *Modern Bohemian Glass* (Artia, Prague, 1963)

Ricke, Helmut, *Neues Glas in Deutschland* (Kunst und Handwerk Verlaganstalt, Düsseldorf, 1983)

Sellner, Christianne, *Geschichte des Studioglases* (Bergbau-und Industriemuseum Ostbayern, Theuern, Band 3, 1984)

Stenett-Willson, Ronald, *Modern Glass* (Van Nostrand Reinhold Co., New York, 1975)

EXHIBITION CATALOGUES

Coburg, Kunstsammlungen der Veste Coburg, *Coburger Glaspreis 1977 für Moderne Glasgestaltung in Europa*, 1977
Zweiter Coburger Glaspreis für Moderne Glasgestaltung in Europa 1985, 1985

Corning, New York, The Corning Museum of Glass, *Glass 1959: A Special Exhibition of The International Contemporary Glass*, 1959
New Glass: A Worldwide Survey, 1981
Czechoslovakian Glass 1350–1980, 1981

Darmstadt, Hessisches Landesmuseum, *Glass from Australia and New Zealand*, 1985

Dearborn, University of Michigan, *Contemporary Glass from the Sosin Collection*, 1987

Düsseldorf, Kunstmuseum, *Leerdam Unica – 50 Jahre Modernes Niederlandisches Glas*, 1977

Ebeltoft, Glasmuseum, *Young Glass '87*, 1987

Frankfurt am Main, Museum für Kunsthandwerk, *Modernes Glas aus Amerika, Europa und Japan*, 1976

Frauenau, Glasmuseum Frauenau, *10 Jahre Glasmuseum Frauenau/25 Jahre Studioglas-Bewegung*, 1985

Fullerton, California, Visual Arts Center, California State University, *Cast Glass Sculpture*, 1986

Huntington, West Virginia, Huntington Galleries Museum, *New American Glass: Focus West Virginia I*, 1976
New American Glass: Focus West Virginia II, 1986

Karlsruhe, Badisches Landesmuseum, *Neues Glas aus Japan*, 1985

Kassel, Orangerie, *Glaskunst 81, Internationale Ausstellung zur Studioglasbewegung der Gegenwart*, 1981

Lausanne, Galerie Bellefontaine SA, *European Studio Glass '82*, 1982–3

Lausanne, Musée des Arts Décoratifs, *Expressions en Verre* (text by Rosemarie Lippuner), 1986

Leerdam, Stichting Glas (Glass Foundation), *Beelden in Glas/Glass Sculpture* (ed. K. Broos), 1986

Leipzig, Museum des Kunsthandwerks, *Glaskunst in der DDR*, 1977

Liège, Générale de Banque, *Contemporary Western European Sculptures in Crystal and Glass (1983–1986)* (text by Joseph Philippe), 1986

Liège, Musée du Verre, *Verrerie Européenne 1958–1963*, 1963

London, Dan Klein Limited, *Masters of Czech Glass 1945–1965*, 1983

Nový Bor, Crystalex Nový Bor, *Interglas Symposium Ceskoslovensko* (text by Antonin Langhammer), 1985

Oakland, California, The Oakland Museum, *Contemporary American and European Glass from the Saxe Collection* (text by Kenneth R. Trapp and William Warmus), 1986

Paris, Musée des Arts Décoratifs, *Verriers Français Contemporains: Art et Industrie*, 1982

Perth, Art Gallery of Western Australia, *International Directions in Glass Art*, 1982

Riihmäki, Finnish Glass Museum, *The Modern Spirit – Glass from Finland*, 1985

Sapporo, Hokkaido Museum of Art, *World Glass Now '82*, 1982
World Glass Now '85, 1985
World Glass Now '88, 1988

Stockholm, Smalands Museum, Växjö/Kulturhuset, *Nordiskt Glas 78*, 1978

Sunderland, Sunderland Arts Centre, *British Studio Glass*, 1983

Tilburg, Centrum Voor Kunst en Vormgeving, *Vormen in Glas*, 1988

Tokyo, Japan Glass Artcrafts Association, Odakyu Department Store Grand Gallery, *Glass '78 in Japan*, 1978
Glass '81 in Japan, 1981

Glass '84 in Japan, 1984
Glass '87 in Japan, 1987

Toledo, Toledo Museum of Art, *American Glass Now*, 1972

Tucson, Arizona, Tucson Museum of Art, *Sculptural Glass*, 1983

Wausau, Wisconsin, Leigh Yawkey Woodson Art Museum,
Americans in Glass: 1978
Americans in Glass: 1981
Americans in Glass: 1984
Americans in Glass: 1986

Zürich, Museum Bellerive, *Glas Heute: Kunst oder Handwerk?*, 1972

JOURNALS

American Craft (American Craft Council, New York)

Craft Arts (Craft Art Pty. Ltd, Australia)

Crafts, The Magazine of the Decorative and Applied Arts (The Crafts Council, London)

Glass Art Society Journals

Glass Review (Rapid, Czechoslovakia)

La Revue de la Céramique et du Verre (Vendin-le-Viell, France)

Neues Glas (Verlagsanstalt Handwerk GmbH, Düsseldorf)

New Glass Review (The Corning Museum of Glass, Corning, New York)

New Work (New York Experimental Glass Workshop, Inc., New York)

INDEX

Numbers in **bold** refer to illustrations

Adams, Hank Murta, 79, **79**
Adamson, Rob, 40
Adensamová, Blanka, 100
Adlerová, Alena, 7, 87, 92, 100
Adolfsson, Wilke, 130, 134
Alberius, Olle, 139
Aldridge, Peter, 30, **31**
Alston, Margaret, 162
American Craft Museum, New York, 39, 42
'American Glass Now' exhibitions, 27
'Americans in Glass' exhibitions, 27, 39, 80
Anderson, Doug, 61, **61**, 62
Arber, Valerie, 54, **55**
Argy-Rousseau, Gabriel, 61
'Art Glass of Canada' exhibition, 192
Artzt, Lubomir, 103
Aschenbrenner, Michael, 76, **76**
Aufiero, Tina Marie, 62, **62**
Australia, 19, 20, 21, 27, 29, 130, 147, 198, 200–8
Austria, 130

Bahr, Walter, 124
Baldwin, Philip, 130, **131**
Bancila, Dan, 112, **112**
Bang, Michael, 142
Bannard, Darby, 16
Bayliss, Arlon, **159**, 159–60
Baz-Dölle, Walter, 116, **117**
Bechmann, Hartmut, 116
'Beelden in Glas' symposium, 173–4
Begou, Alain, 176
Belgium, 184
Bell, Larry, 70
Bell, Robert, 200, 202
Ben Tré, Howard, 28, **29**, 58, 60, 61, 66, **67**, 69, **74**, 75, 182
Berg, Karl, 128, **128**
Bergqvist, Gustaf, 132
Bernstein, Rick, 34, **35**
Bernstein, William, 51, **51**
Best-Devereux, Tatiana, 160, **161**, 167
Bianconi, Fulvio, 186
Bimberg, Dirk, 136
Blomdahl, Sonia, **50**, 51
Bohus, Zoltan, 114, **114**, 115
Borowski, Stanislaw, 124, **125**
Bosworth, Thomas, 37
Boylen, Michael, 45

Boymans van Beuningen Museum, 25, 168
Boysen, Bill, 200
Brandt, Asa, 132, **133**, 134
Bratislava Academy of Creative Arts, 91, 103, 106
Britain, 21, 25, 28, 118, 144–64
British Artists in Glass (BAG), 152
Brockelhurst, Keith, 162, **163**, 164
Brockmann, Ruth, 58, **59**
Brussels Expo 58: 86, 87, 88
Brychtová, Jaroslava, **20**, **25**, 87, 88, 90, **90**
Buba, Ovidio, 112
Buczko, György, 115
Buechner, Tom, 118

Cahill, Maureen, **200**, 201, 206
Calgren, Anna, 168, **169**
Canada, 190–8
Canberra College of Art, 29, 201, 202–4
Carder, Frederick, 30
Carlson, Donald, 45
Carlson, William, 44, **44**, 62, **63**, 65
Carpenter, Jamie, 48
Cash, Sydney, 56, **56**, 58
casting, 13, 28, 34, 40, 43, 44, 45, 58, 60–1, 65, 75, 88, 90, 126, 160–4, 194, 195, 206
Chao, Bruce, 173
Chardiet, José, 43
Chihuly, Dale, **10**, 11, 19, 28, 37, 44, 45, 46, **46**–7, 48, 75, 83, 173, 186
Cigler, Václav, 28, 91, 98, **98**, 103, 105
Clarke, Dillon, 146
Clegg, David, 205
Clegg, Tessa, 160, **161**
Cline, Mary van, 43, **43**, 60, **61**
Coburg Glass Prize exhibitions, 21, 25, 27, 112, 116, 118, 122, 134, 139, 143, 164, 171, 174, 189
Cohn, Michael, **70**, 70–1
cold processes, 13, 27, 43, 66–71, 115, 134, 139, 179, 190, 196
Cook, John, 154, **155**
Copier, Andreas Dirk, 168, **168**
Corning Museum of Glass, 18, 21, 26–7, 39, 62
Cowcher, Scott, 205–6
Cowles, Charles, 42
Cribbs, Keke, **68**, 69
Crichton, Daniel, 193, **193**
Cros, Henri, 61
Croucher, John, 208

Cummings, Keith, 155, **155**, 160
Cuny, Jutta, 176, **176**
Cyren, Gunnar, 140, **140**
Czechoslovakia, 7, 20, 21, 24, 25–6, 27, 28–9, 46, 84–111, 114, 118, 153, 179

Dailey, Dan, 7, 28, 34, 44, 71, **72**, 73, 83, 176
Dali, Salvador, 176
Damian-Eyrignoux, Monica, 176
Dancea, Silviu, 112, **113**
Decorchemont, François, 182
Delaney, Pauline, 205
Denmark, 22, 142–3
Despret, Georges, 61
Dickinson, Anna, 160, **160**
Donefer, Laura, 7, 195, **195**
Dowler, David, 30
Dreisbach, Fritz, 38
Dreiser, Peter, **158**, 159
Dudchenko, Boris, 45
Dybka, Anne, 206

East Germany, 28, 54, 112, 116
Eckhardt, Edris, 32, 33
Edelmann, Udo, 124
Edgerly, Susan, 195
Edwards, Stephen Dee, 48, **49**, 58, 60, **60**
Eisch, Erwin, **9**, 11, **11**, 13, 22, 25, 46, 118, 121, 121–3, **122**, 126, 128, 130
Eisch, Gretl, 122
enamelling, 32, 43, 54, 66, 95, 97, 100, 124, 162, 164, 171, 208
Engerer, Alfred, **196**, 196–7
Englund, Eva, 139, **139**
Engman, Kjell, 140
engraving, 30, 40, 66, 70, 89, 93, 95, 100, 103, 106, 122, 123, 124–8, 134, 144, 146, 154, 156–9, 179, 184, 188, 204, 206, 208
Esson, Michael, 201
etching, 87, 89, 108, 109, 111, 130, 137, 150, 184, 208
Exnar, Jan, **110**, 111

Faulkner, Norman, 192
Fineberg, Robin, **194**, 194–5
Finland, 140–2
Fladgate, Deborah, 160
Flavell, Ray, **147**, 147–8
Fleming, Thomas, **78**, 79
Forsell, Ulla, 132, 134, 188

France, 28, 176–82
Frauenau, 22, 25, 46, 122, 128
Frijns, Bert, **173**, 173–4
Fritz, Robert, 34
Frolic, Irene, 195, **195**
Fujita, Kyohei, 29, 210, 212, **212**
Funakoshi, Saburo, 213
fusing, 32, 40, 43, 44, 54, 58, 62

Gacs, Gyorgy, 114
Gate, Simon, 132
Gherardi, Lisa, 14, **14**, 167
Glancy, Michael, 28, 73, **73**
glass-blowing, 11, 13, 18, 28, 33–4, 40, 44,
    45–51, 52, 75, 89, 94, 95, 100, 112, 120,
    124, 137, 148, 159–60, 176, 184, 186–7,
    193, 194, 195, 204, 205–6, 214; see also
    hot glass; lampwork
glass co-operatives, 25, 39–40, 148–53, 180
glass-cutting, 27, 40, 45, 65, 66, 69, 70–1,
    89, 90, 100, 114, 139, 148; see also
    engraving; optical cutting
glass education, 28, 34–8, 84, 87–91, 118,
    120–1, 147–8, 176, 211
The Glass Eye, Seattle, 40
'Glass National' exhibitions, 22, 39
'Glass 1959, A Special Exhibition of
    International Contemporary Glass'
    (Corning Museum), 18, 21
The Glasshouse, London, 25, 148–52, 155
Goss, Peter, 205
Grebeničková, Stanislava, 111
Greig, John, 205
Greiner-Mai, Albert, 116, **117**
Groot, Mieke, 167–8, **170**, 171
Grover, Ray and Lee, 22
Guggisberg, Monica, 130, **131**

Habatat Galleries, Michigan, 22, 41–2
Hackl, Kuno, 124
Hald, Edward, 132
Halem, Henry, 38, 69, **69**, 81
Handl, Milan, 111, **111**
Hanning, Tony, 206, **206**
Harcuba, Jiři, 93, **93**, 124
Harmon, James, **50**, 51
Harvey, Lee, 13
Hashiguchi, Masamichi, 214, **214**
Hashimoto, Chikara, 212–13
Hauberg, John, 37, 38
Haystack Mountain School, 19
Heaton, Maurice, 32, **32**, 33
Heesen, Willem, 166, **167**, 168
Held, Robert, 190, 192
Heller Gallery, New York, 7, 22, 41–2
Hellsten, Lars, 140
Herman, Sam, **24**, 25, 118, **146**, 146–7,
    148, 153, 154, 155, 184, 200
Higgins, Michael and Frances, 32, 33, **33**
Hilton, Eric, 30
Hinz, Darylle, 142, **143**
Hirst, Brian, 29, 206, **207**, 208
Hlava, Pavel, 46, 95, **95**
Hobson, Diana, 16, **17**, 162, 164, **164**
Hoeller, Franz Xaver, 128, **129**
Holland, 28, 29, 166–74
Hollister, Paul, 18, 22, 65
Hora, Lubomír, 124
Horejc, Jaroslav, 84
hot glass, 11, 13, 20, 26, 28, 34, 42, 43, 52,
    99, 100, 101, 105, 115, 124, 130, 134,
    146, 152, 154, 155, 156, 159–60, 174,
    184, 192, 205, 208; see also glass-blowing
'Hot Glass Symposium', 25, 152–3, 164
Houde, François, 190, 198, **199**
Hough, Catherine, **149**, 149–50

Huchthausen, David, 62, **62**, 83
Hungary, 28, 114
Huntsdorfer, Helmut Werner, 130
Huth, Ursula, 124, **125**
Hutter, Sidney, **64**, 65–6
Hutton, John, 146, **146**
Hydman-Vallien, Ulrica, 134, **136**, 137, 140

Ikuta, Niyoko, 213, 215
Ink, Jack, 130, **131**
'International Directions in Glass Art'
    (Australia, 1982), 200, 201–2
Ion Andreescu Academy of Applied Art,
    Bucharest, 112, 114
Ipsen, Kent, 38, 45
Italy, 186–9
Ito, Kinuko, 214, **215**
Ito, Makato, 215
Iwata, Hisatoshi, 210, **211**, 214
Iwata, Toshichi, **210**, 210–11, 212

Jam Factory, Adelaide, 200, 205
Japan, 19, 20, 27, 29, 130, 198, 210–15
Jervis, Margie, 39, 66, **66**
Johannson, Jan, 140

Kagami, Kozo, 210
Kallenberger, Kreg, 45, **45**, 70
Kaplan, David, 152, **153**
Kaplický, Josef, 84, 88, 90, 91, 92, 93
Karel, Marian, 106, **106**, 111
Kehlmann, Robert, 69, **69**, 81
Kehr, Gunther, 120, 124
Keogh, Peter, 194, **194**, 195
King, Gerry, **205**, 205–6
Kirkpatrick, Joey, 38, 39, 48, **49**
Kizinska, Ingeborga Gladala, 112
Kizinski, Ireneusz, 112
Kjaer, Anja, 142, **143**
Klepsch, Kristian, 126, **126**
Klering, Matthias, 124
Klumpařová, Vladimira, 111
Knye, Günter, 116, **117**
Koch, Hubert, 116, **117**
Koepping, Karl, 116
Köhler, Helmut, 126, **126**
Kopecký, Vladimir, **85**, 97, **97**
Kosta Boda (Sweden), 134, 137, 139, 140
Krasnican, Susie, 39, 66, **66**
Krebs, Ernst, 126, **127**
Kruft, Gerd, 124
Kuhn, Jon, 44, **44**
Kulasiewicz, Frank, 45
Kuntz, Andrew, 194
Kupfer, Tony, 201, 208
Kurland Summers Gallery, Los Angeles, 7,
    42

Labino, Dominick, 18, 19, 26, **26**, 34, 118
Lalique, René, 18, 176
Lalonde, Richard, 58, **59**
laminating, 13, 26, 32, 62, 65–6, 75, 114,
    115, 194
lampworking technique, 28, 43, 45, 54, 56,
    89, 97–8, 116, 120, 123–4, 190
Lane, Danny, 164, **165**
Langley, Warren, 29, 206, **207**
Layton, Peter, 152, **152**
Le Quier, William, 43, **43**
Leafgreen, Harvey, 18
Leerdam glassworks, 168, 173
Leibowitz, Edward, 184, **185**
Leicester Polytechnic, 148, 154
Leigh Yawkey Woodson Art Museum, 27,
    39, 80
Leloup, Louis, 184, **184**

Leperlier, Antoine, 182, **182**
Leperlier, Etienne, 1, 182, **183**
Leser, Max, 7, 190, **193**, 193–4
Levin, Robert, 51
Lewis, John, 45
Libenský, Stanislav, 13, **20**, 24, **25**, 28, 29,
    87–8, **89**, 90, **90**, 92, 95–6, 98, 100, 105,
    153, 168, 179
Liccata, Ricardo, 186
Lierke, Rosemarie, 124
Limieux, Lisette, 197, **197**
Lipofsky, Marvin, **12**, 25, 34, 37, **37**, 44, 45,
    46, 83, 170, 182
Lišková, Věra, **97**, 97–8
Littleton, Harvey, **8**, 11, 18, 19, **19**, 22, 25,
    28, 34, **36**, 36–7, 39, 40, 42, 45, 46, 83,
    118, 122, 123, 146, 200
Littleton, Maureen, 42
Lockau, Kevin, 195, 196
London Glassblowing Workshop, 152
Loo, Bert van, 16, 167, 170, **172**, 173, 173
Lowe, Liz, 162, **162**
Lucas, John, 123
Lugossy, Maria, 114–15, **115**
Lutken, Per, 22, **23**, 142
Lynggard, Finn, **142**, 142–3

Mace, Flora, 38, 39, 48, **49**, 75
MacGlauchlin, Tom, 38
Machač, Václav, **100**, 101
MacNeil, Linda, 44, 71, **71**
Maillot, Ingrid, 180
Marier, Elisabeth, 194
Marinot, Maurice, 18, 176
Marioni, Paul, 38, **38**
Marquis, Richard, 34, **35**, 200
Martinez, Raymond, 180
Martinuzzi, Gian Paolo, 130, 188, **188**
Mason, Concetta, 75, **75**
Meaker, Charlie, 160
The Meat Market, Melbourne, 200
Meech, Annette, 148, **149**, 154–5
Meitner, Richard, 29, 167–8, 170–1, **170**,
    171
Memphis group, 188–9, 214
Meszaros, Maria, 115
Meydam, Floris, 168, **169**
Misaki, Kazuyo, 214
Mizukami, Saiko, 214
Modell, Reiner, 124
Moje, Klaus, 29, 120, 130, 201, 202–4,
    202–3
Moje-Wohlgemuth, Isgard, 130, **131**, 203
Molnar, Pavel, 120, 124
Monod, Claude, 176, **177**
Monod, Isabelle, 176
Monod, Veronique, 176, **177**
Moore, Simon, 149, 150, **150**
Morin, Claude, 176, **177**
Morris, William, 38, 48, **48**
Motzfeld, Benny, 22, 143
Mount, Nick, 205
Mouriot, Michel, 180
Muchnic, Suzanne, 16
Munich Academy of Fine Arts, 121, 122,
    126, 128
Murano glass, 186–7, 189, 212
Murasagi, Naomi, 214
Museum Bellerive, Zürich, 25, 130
Müller, Jay, **50**, 51, 69
Myers, Joel Philip, 18, **19**, 38, 51, 52–4,
    52–3, 69

Nakata, Yukiko, 214
Nash, Gary, 208, **209**
Negreanu, Matei, 176, **179**, 179–80

Nelson, Stephen, 60
'Neues Glas aus Japan' exhibition, 215
'New American Glass: Focus West Virginia' exhibition, 22, 39
New York Experimental Glass Workshop, 21, 40, 174
New Zealand, 29, 198, 200, 201, 204, 208
Newall, Steven, 149, 150, **151**
Newman, Annabel, 148
Niederer, Roberto, 130, **131**
North America (United States), 8–16, 18–19, 21–2, 26–8, 30–83, 118, 190, 198
Norway, 22, 143
Novák, Břetislav, 106, **107**, 108
Novaro, Jean-Claude, 176
Nový Bor, 20, 84, 87, 88, 91, 92

O'Connor, Dennis, **204**, 205
Okada, Chikahiko, 215
Ontario College of Art, 190, 196
optical cutting/glass, 13, 45, 69, 70, 90, 91, 92, 98, 100, 103–9, 121, 126, 128, 168, 179
Orrefors, 132, 139–40, 147, 168, 212
Otuka, Yutaka, 213

painting on glass, 40, 66, 87, 90, 97, 100, 103, 109–11, 123, 130, 137
paperweights, 28, 54–5, 192
Parriott, Charles, 38, 40, **41**
pâte de verre, 16, 43, 61–2, 162, 164, 176, 182, 208, 213–14
Patti, Thomas, 26, 51, 65, **65**, 75
Peiser, Mark, 45, 55, **55**, 190
Pennell, Ron, 124, 156, **156**, 159
Perkins, Flo, 48, **49**
Pilchuck School, 19, 22, 37–8, 48, 51, 75, 174
Pistor, Willi, 120, 128, **128**
Plíva, Oldrich, 106, **106**
Poland, 112
polishing, 45, 65, 66, 69, 114, 128, 139
Popescu, Adriana, 112
Poschl, Veronika, 167, **167**
Posner, Richard, 60
Prague Academy of Applied Arts, 24, 84, 87, 88, 92, 93, 100, 106, 111, 179
Prague Museum of Applied Arts, 91, 92
Precht, Volkhardt, 116
Procter, Stephen, 148, 154, **154**
Prostor exhibitions, 92, 105
Prytherch, David, **158**, 159

Quagliata, Narcissus, **82**, 82–3

Rainey, Clifford, **2**, 156, **157**, 173
Raos, Peter, 208
Rayson, Wayne, 205
Reekie, David, 160, 162, **163**
Reid, Colin, 160, 162, **162**
Reusch, Astri, 196, **196**
Rietveld Academy, Amsterdam, 166, 167–8, 170–1, 201
Robinson, Ann, 208, **208**
Roman, Edward, **192**, 192–3
Rosenfeld, Betsy, 42
Roubíček, René, 46, **86**, 86–7, **94**, 94–5, 98
Roubíčková, Miluše, **94**, 94
Royal College of Art, London, 20, 25, 118, 132, 146, 147, 148, 152–3, 154, 155, 159, 164
Rozsypal, Ivo, **110**, 111
Ruffner, Ginny, 56, **56**
Rumania, 112
Rybák, Jaromir, 103, **103**, 104, 105

Sabóková, Gisela, 111, **111**
Sadowski, Stefan, 112
sand-blasting, 13, 43, 66–9, 97, 100, 108, 109, 111, 115, 124, 130, 134, 137, 139, 148, 150, 179, 180, 184, 192, 193, 195, 208
sand-casting, 14, 58, 137, 139, 154, 190
Sandström, Anika, 152, **153**
Santarossa, Renato, 128, **129**
Santillana, Laura de, 186, **186**
Sarpaneva, Timo, 140, 141, **141**
Sato, Nobuyasu, 213, **213**
Scandinavia, 22, 28, 118, 132–43
Scanga, Italo, **81**, 81–2
Scarpa, Carlo, 186
Schaedel, Albin, 116
Schaffrath, Ludwig, 205
Schamschula, Erich, 182
Schantz, Karl, 190, **191**, 194
Schechinger, Gerhard, 124, **125**
Schindhelm, Otto, 116
Schulman, Norman, 18
Schulze, Freia, 126, **127**, 128
Schwarz, David, **68**, 69
Schwarz, Walter, 116
Seguso, Livio, 187, **187**
Seide, Paul, 75, **75**
Sellner, Theodor, 124, **125**
Semenescu, Valeriu, 112, **113**
Shaffer, Mary, **12**, 56, **57**, 58
Shapiro, Susan, 39, 60
Shaw, Tim, 167
Sheridan College (Canada), 190, 192, 193
Shibuy, Ryoji, 214
Shimoda, Mhoko, 214
Shirahata, Akira, 213
Simpson, Josh, 44
Simpson, Mel, 201, 208
Skillitzi, Stephen, 201, 206
slumping, 13, 27, 34, 40, 43, 54, 56–8
Šolcová, Ivana, 111
Solven, Pauline, 132, 153, **153**
Sottsass, Ettore, 188, 189
stained glass, 6, 32, 40, 88, 111, 121, 164, 184
Stankard, Paul, 28, **54**, 54–5
Statom, Thermon, **80**, 80–1
Stearns, Thomas, 186
Stern, Anthony, 160
Steuben glassworks, Corning, 30, 39, 70
Stiensmuehlen, Susan, 76, **77**
Štipl, Karel, 93
Stöckle-Krumbein, Karin, 126, **127**
Stourbridge College, 128, 148, 155, 159, 201
Stuttgart Academy of Fine Arts, 121, 124, 126
Suda, Kristian, 92
Šuhájek, Jiří, 100–1, **101**
Sweden, 22, 29, 118, 124, 130, 132–40, 148, 168
Switzerland, 130
Sydney College of Arts, 201, 206

Tagliapetra, Ligno, 187
Takeuchi, Denji, 213, **213**
Taylor, David, **145**, 148–9
Taylor, Michael, **45**, 65
Tejml, František, 97
Teruo, Yamada, 213
Teunissen van Manen, Mathijs, 174
Thompson, Kathryn, 193
Thun, Matteo, 189, **189**
Tichý, Dalibor, **100**, 101, 103
Tiffany, Louis Comfort, 30, 84
Trnka, Otto, 107, 111

Toledo Museum of Art, 6, 18–19, 22, 36, 38, 39
Tomečko, Pavel, 103
Tookey, Fleur, 148
Trinkley, Karla, **61**, 61–2
Trnka, Pavel, 91, 105, **105**
Tuttle, Richard, 173

Ueno, Yukio, 215
Ullberg, Eva, 134
Umbdenstock, Jean-Pierre, 182, **183**
United States; see North America

Vachtová, Dana, 99, **99**
Val St Lambert (Belgium), 184
Valkema, Durk, 166–7, 168, **169**, 201
Valkema, Sybren, **166**, 166–7, 168
Vallien, Bertil, 22, **23**, 29, 137, **138**, 139, 140
Vaňura, Karel, **26**, 96, 97
Vašiček, Aleš, 109
Velíšek, Martin, 111
Venini, Paolo, 174, 186
Viesnik, Peter, 208
Vigorie, François, 180, **180**
Vízner, František, 91, **108**, 108–9
Von Eiff, Wilhelm, 126

Wagga Wagga City Art Gallery, 7, 201
Wallstab, Kurt, 120, **120**, 123–4
Walter, Almeric, 61
Wärff, Goran, 134
warm techniques, 13, 27, 52–66, 162
Watkins, James, 66, **67**, 69, 81
Weinberg, Steven, 45, **45**, 58, 60, 70
Welzel, Josef, 128
West Germany, 20, 22, 28, 118–30, 203
West Surrey College of Art and Design, Farnham, 147–8, 154, 155
Whistler, Laurence, 144, **144**
Wilkin, Neil, 160
Williams, Christopher, 148, **149**
Wingard, Anders, 134
Wirdham, Nick, 205
Wirkkala, Tapio, 140–1
Wisconsin University, 8, 18, 19, 34, 36, 37, 38, 46
Wohlgemuth, Roderich, 124
Wolff, Ann (Mrs Goran Wärff), 14, **15**, 29, **119**, 130, 134, **135**, 136–7
Woodman, Rachel, 160, **161**
World Crafts Council, 19, 22, 46, 166, 201, 210
Wreford, Don, 205
Wudy, Alois, 124
Wünsch, Karel, 95

Yokoyama, Naoto, 215, **215**
Yoshihiko, Takahasi, 213
Yoshihiko, Takikawa, 213
Yoshimiziu, Toshiio, 211
Yoshimizu, Tsuneo, 213–14

Žačko, Askold, **102**, 103
Zámečníková, Dana, 109, **109**, 111
Zanini, 189
Železný Brod, 84, 87, 88, 89–90, 91, 179
Žertová, Jiřina, 99, **99**
Zimmer, Kenny, 204
Zimmer, Klaus, 205
Zips, Peter, 197, **197**
Zoritchak, Catherine, **178**, 179
Zoritchak, Yan, 176, **178**, 179
Zuber, Czeslaw, 176, 180, **181**
Zuccheri, Toni, 186
Zynsky, Toots, 171, 174, 175